SCIENCE
FUSiON

fusion [FYOO • zhuhn] a combination of two or more things that releases energy

This **Interactive Student Edition** belongs to

_____

Teacher/Room

_____

Consulting Authors

Michael A. DiSpezio

Global Educator
North Falmouth, Massachusetts

Michael DiSpezio is a renaissance educator who moved from the research laboratory of a Nobel Prize winner to the K–12 science classroom. He has authored or co-authored numerous textbooks and written more than 25 trade books. For nearly a decade he worked with the JASON Project, under the auspices of the National Geographic Society, where he designed curriculum, wrote lessons, and hosted dozens of studio and location broadcasts. Over the past two decades, he has developed supplementary material for organizations and shows that include PBS *Scientific American Frontiers, Discover* magazine, and the Discovery Channel. He has extended his reach outside the United States and into topics of crucial importance today. To all his projects, he brings his extensive background in science and his expertise in classroom teaching at the elementary, middle, and high school levels.

Marjorie Frank

Science Writer and Content-Area Reading Specialist
Brooklyn, New York

An educator and linguist by training, a writer and poet by nature, Marjorie Frank has authored and designed a generation of instructional materials in all subject areas, including past HMH Science programs. Her other credits include authoring science issues of an award-winning children's magazine; writing game-based digital assessments in math, reading, and language arts; and serving as instructional designer and co-author of pioneering school-to-work software for Classroom Inc., a nonprofit organization dedicated to improving reading and math skills for middle and high school learners. She wrote lyrics and music for *SCIENCE SONGS,* which was an American Library Association nominee for notable recording. In addition, she has served on the adjunct faculty of Hunter, Manhattan, and Brooklyn Colleges, teaching courses in science methods, literacy, and writing.

Acknowledgments for Covers

Front cover: *Solar tree, Italy* (bg) © Hemis/Alamy Stock Photo

Copyright © 2017 by Houghton Mifflin Harcourt Publishing Company

Printed in the U.S.A.

ISBN 978-0-544-77852-8

11 0877   24 23 22

4500848295   B C D E F G

Michael R. Heithaus

Dean, College of Arts, Sciences & Education
Florida International University
North Miami, Florida

Mike Heithaus joined the Florida International University Biology Department in 2003. He is a professor in the Department of Biological Sciences and has served as Director of the Marine Sciences Program and Executive Director of the School of Environment and Society. His research focuses on predator-prey interactions and the ecological roles of large marine species including sharks, sea turtles, and marine mammals. His long-term studies include the Shark Bay Ecosystem Project in Western Australia. He also served as a Research Fellow with National Geographic, using remote imaging in his research and hosting a *Crittercam* television series on the National Geographic Channel.

Donna M. Ogle

Professor of Reading and Language
National-Louis University
Chicago, Illinois

Creator of the well-known KWL strategy, Donna Ogle has directed many staff development projects translating theory and research into school practice in middle and secondary schools throughout the United States. She is a past president of the International Reading Association and has served as a consultant on literacy projects worldwide. Her extensive international experience includes coordinating the Reading and Writing for Critical Thinking Project in Eastern Europe, developing an integrated curriculum for a USAID Afghan Education Project, and speaking and consulting on projects in several Latin American countries and in Asia. Her books include *Coming Together as Readers; Reading Comprehension: Strategies for Independent Learners; All Children Read;* and *Literacy for a Democratic Society.*

Program Reviewers

Content Reviewers

Paul D. Asimow, PhD
Professor of Geology and Geochemistry
Division of Geological and Planetary Sciences
California Institute of Technology
Pasadena, CA

Laura K. Baumgartner, PhD
Postdoctoral Researcher
Molecular, Cellular, and Developmental Biology
University of Colorado
Boulder, CO

Eileen Cashman, PhD
Professor
Department of Environmental Resources Engineering
Humboldt State University
Arcata, CA

Hilary Clement Olson, PhD
Research Scientist Associate V
Institute for Geophysics, Jackson School of Geosciences
The University of Texas at Austin
Austin, TX

Joe W. Crim, PhD
Professor Emeritus
Department of Cellular Biology
The University of Georgia
Athens, GA

Elizabeth A. De Stasio, PhD
Raymond H. Herzog Professor of Science
Professor of Biology
Department of Biology
Lawrence University
Appleton, WI

Dan Franck, PhD
Botany Education Consultant
Chatham, NY

Julia R. Greer, PhD
Assistant Professor of Materials Science and Mechanics
Division of Engineering and Applied Science
California Institute of Technology
Pasadena, CA

John E. Hoover, PhD
Professor
Department of Biology
Millersville University
Millersville, PA

William H. Ingham, PhD
Professor (Emeritus)
Department of Physics and Astronomy
James Madison University
Harrisonburg, VA

Charles W. Johnson, PhD
Chairman, Division of Natural Sciences, Mathematics, and Physical Education
Associate Professor of Physics
South Georgia College
Douglas, GA

Program Reviewers (continued)

Tatiana A. Krivosheev, PhD
Associate Professor of Physics
Department of Natural Sciences
Clayton State University
Morrow, GA

Joseph A. McClure, PhD
Associate Professor Emeritus
Department of Physics
Georgetown University
Washington, DC

Mark Moldwin, PhD
Professor of Space Sciences
Atmospheric, Oceanic, and
Space Sciences
University of Michigan
Ann Arbor, MI

Russell Patrick, PhD
Professor of Physics
Department of Biology,
Chemistry, and Physics
Southern Polytechnic State
University
Marietta, GA

Patricia M. Pauley, PhD
*Meteorologist, Data Assimilation
Group*
Naval Research Laboratory
Monterey, CA

Stephen F. Pavkovic, PhD
Professor Emeritus
Department of Chemistry
Loyola University of Chicago
Chicago, IL

L. Jeanne Perry, PhD
Director (Retired)
Protein Expression Technology
Center
Institute for Genomics and
Proteomics
University of California, Los
Angeles
Los Angeles, CA

Kenneth H. Rubin, PhD
Professor
Department of Geology and
Geophysics
University of Hawaii
Honolulu, HI

Brandon E. Schwab, PhD
Associate Professor
Department of Geology
Humboldt State University
Arcata, CA

Marllin L. Simon, Ph.D.
Associate Professor
Department of Physics
Auburn University
Auburn, AL

Larry Stookey, PE
Upper Iowa University
Wausau, WI

Kim Withers, PhD
Associate Research Scientist
Center for Coastal Studies
Texas A&M University-Corpus
Christi
Corpus Christi, TX

Matthew A. Wood, PhD
Professor
Department of Physics & Space
Sciences
Florida Institute of Technology
Melbourne, FL

Adam D. Woods, PhD
Associate Professor
Department of Geological
Sciences
California State University,
Fullerton
Fullerton, CA

Natalie Zayas, MS, EdD
Lecturer
Division of Science and
Environmental Policy
California State University,
Monterey Bay
Seaside, CA

Teacher Reviewers

Ann Barrette, MST
Whitman Middle School
Wauwatosa, WI

Barbara Brege
Crestwood Middle School
Kentwood, MI

**Katherine Eaton Campbell,
M Ed**
Chicago Public Schools-Area 2
Office
Chicago, IL

**Karen Cavalluzzi, M Ed,
NBCT**
Sunny Vale Middle School
Blue Springs, MO

Katie Demorest, MA Ed Tech
Marshall Middle School
Marshall, MI

Jennifer Eddy, M Ed
Lindale Middle School
Linthicum, MD

Tully Fenner
George Fox Middle School
Pasadena, MD

Dave Grabski, MS Ed
PJ Jacobs Junior High School
Stevens Point, WI

Amelia C. Holm, M Ed
McKinley Middle School
Kenosha, WI

Ben Hondorp
Creekside Middle School
Zeeland, MI

George E. Hunkele, M Ed
Harborside Middle School
Milford, CT

Jude Kesl
Science Teaching Specialist 6–8
Milwaukee Public Schools
Milwaukee, WI

Joe Kubasta, M Ed
Rockwood Valley Middle School
St. Louis, MO

Mary Larsen
Science Instructional Coach
Helena Public Schools
Helena, MT

Angie Larson
Bernard Campbell Middle School
Lee's Summit, MO

Christy Leier
Horizon Middle School
Moorhead, MN

Helen Mihm, NBCT
Crofton Middle School
Crofton, MD

Jeff Moravec, Sr., MS Ed
Teaching Specialist
Milwaukee Public Schools
Milwaukee, WI

**Nancy Kawecki Nega, MST,
NBCT, PAESMT**
Churchville Middle School
Elmhurst, IL

Mark E. Poggensee, MS Ed
Elkhorn Middle School
Elkhorn, WI

Sherry Rich
Bernard Campbell Middle School
Lee's Summit, MO

Mike Szydlowski, M Ed
Science Coordinator
Columbia Public Schools
Columbia, MO

Nichole Trzasko, M Ed
Clarkston Junior High School
Clarkston, MI

Heather Wares, M Ed
Traverse City West Middle School
Traverse City, MI

Contents
in Brief

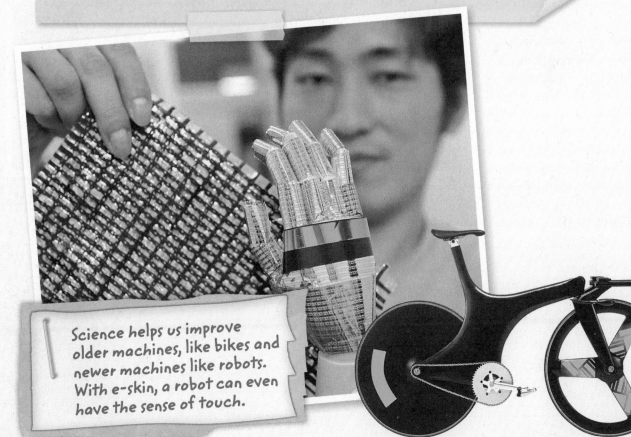

Science helps us improve older machines, like bikes and newer machines like robots. With e-skin, a robot can even have the sense of touch.

Contents

Assignments:

_____

_____

_____

_____

_____

_____

_____

_____

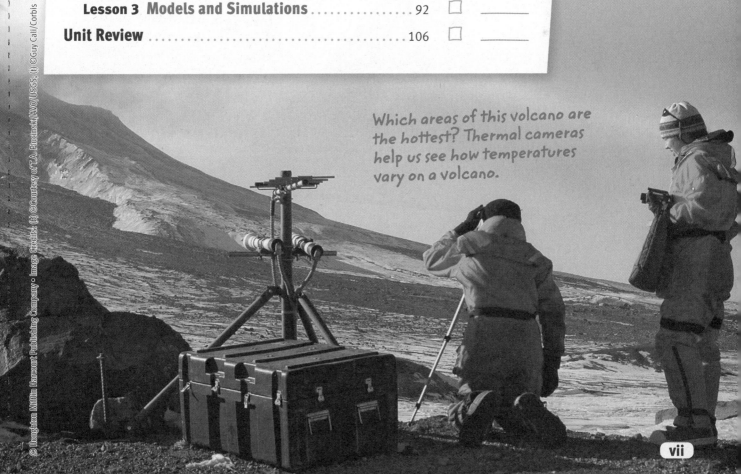

Building models helps us picture things that are hard to see, like this DNA double-helix shape.

Which areas of this volcano are the hottest? Thermal cameras help us see how temperatures vary on a volcano.

Contents (continued)

Have you ever designed something? Then you have taken your first step in the engineering process, just like those who engineered this ultralight plane.

© Houghton Mifflin Harcourt Publishing Company • Image Credits: ©Yoshikazu Tsuno/AFP/Getty Images

Assignments:

_____

_____

_____

_____

_____

_____

_____

_____

_____

_____

_____

_____

_____

_____

_____

_____

_____

_____

_____

_____

_____

Power up with Science Fusion!

Your program fuses...

e-Learning and Virtual Labs

Labs and Activities

Write-In Student Edition

...to generate energy for today's science learner — *you*.

Labs and Activities

ScienceFusion includes lots of exciting hands-on inquiry labs and activities, each one designed to bring science skills and concepts to life and get you involved.

By asking questions, testing your ideas, organizing and analyzing data, drawing conclusions, and sharing what you learn...

You are the scientist!

e-Learning and Virtual Labs

Digital lessons and virtual labs provide e-learning options for every lesson of Science Fusion.

On your own or with a group, explore science concepts in a digital world.

360° of Inquiry

The Nature of Science

Big Idea

Scientists use careful observations and clear reasoning to understand processes and patterns in nature.

People used to think that because Earth was flat, you would fall off the edge if you got too close.

What do you think?

Careful observations and experiments provide us with new information that may change or confirm what we know about the world we live in. What is one way in which science has changed your view of the world?

Today, we know that Earth is a sphere.

Unit 1
The Nature of Science

Things Change

People used to have strange ideas about the world in which they lived. How science has changed some of those ideas is shown here.

1687

People used to think that the sun and planets revolved around Earth. In 1687, Newton described gravity and how it affects objects. His work explained why all of the planets, including Earth, must revolve around the much larger sun. Newton's work finally convinced people that the sun and not Earth was at the center of the solar system.

Sir Isaac Newton

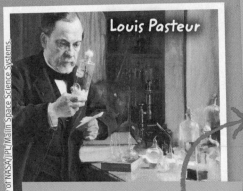

Louis Pasteur

EURASIA
NORTH AMERICA
PANGAEA
SOUTH AMERICA
AFRICA
Equator
INDIA
AUSTRALIA
ANTARCTICA

Modern continents used to be a part of Pangaea.

Water ice on Mars

1950s

In 1915, people didn't believe Alfred Wegener when he proposed that the continents were moving slowly. It wasn't until the 1950s that advances in technology provided four different lines of evidence, which proved that continents do move. Wegener was right.

1861

People used to think that living things could come from nonliving things such as flies and beetles from rotting meat. This idea was called *spontaneous generation*. It was Pasteur's experiments that finally disproved this idea.

2008

People used to think that there were Martians on Mars. However, probes and landers have replaced ideas of little green men with real information about the planet. In 2008, we discovered water ice there.

Create Your Own Timeline

1 Think About It

Choose a favorite science topic and write it down below.

_____

2 Conduct Research

Here are some questions to ask as you research your topic:

A What famous people contributed to the development of your topic and when?

_____

_____

_____

B What images can you use to illustrate the changes that occurred to your topic over time?

_____

_____

_____

3 Make A Plan

Sketch out how you would like to organize your information in the space below, including date, people involved, pictures, and brief passages showing the changes in your topic.

Take It Home

Describe what you have learned to adults at home. Then, have them help you create a poster of how your topic has changed over time. See *ScienceSaurus*® for more information about history of science time line.

What Is Science?

ESSENTIAL QUESTION

What are the characteristics of science?

By the end of this lesson, you should be able to distinguish what characterizes science and scientific explanations, and differentiate between science and pseudoscience.

Any chef will tell you, cooking is a lot like science. Today, there are a growing number of chefs using scientific knowledge to take traditional foods and recipes in new directions. Here, the chef is using super-cold liquid nitrogen to give a new meaning to the term "Hard-boiled egg."

Engage Your Brain

1 Predict Check T or F to show whether you think each statement is true or false.

T	F	
☐	☐	Science is the study of the natural world.
☐	☐	Scientific explanations should be logical and testable.
☐	☐	The methods of science can be used in other fields.
☐	☐	Scientific explanations do not change.
☐	☐	Creativity does not play a role in science.

2 Compose In this lamp, heating of the liquid at the bottom causes the wax globs in it to rise and fall in interesting patterns. What is a scientific question you could ask about this lamp? What is a non-scientific question you could ask about this lamp?

_____

_____

_____

_____

_____

 Active Reading

3 Synthesize You can often define an unknown word if you know the meaning of its word parts. Use the word parts and sentence below to make an educated guess about the meaning of the word *pseudoscience*.

Word part	Meaning
pseudo-	false; pretending to be
science	the systematic study of the natural world

Example Sentence
Their belief that space aliens visited the Earth in ancient times is based on <u>pseudoscience</u> and faulty logic.

pseudoscience: _____

_____

_____

Vocabulary Terms
- science
- empirical evidence
- pseudoscience

4 Apply As you learn the definition of each vocabulary term in this lesson, create your own definition or sketch to help you remember the meaning of the term.

Character Witness

What characterizes science?

Many people think of science as simply a collection of facts. **Science** is the systematic study of natural events and conditions. Scientific subjects can be anything in the living or nonliving world. In general, all scientific subjects can be broken down into three areas—life science, Earth science, and physical science.

Life science, or biology, is the study of living things. Life scientists may study anything from how plants produce food to how animals interact in the wild. Earth science, or geology, is the study of the surface and interior of Earth. An Earth scientist may study how rocks form or what past events produced the volcano you see in the photo. Physical science includes the subjects of physics and chemistry. Physicists and chemists study nonliving matter and energy. They may study the forces that hold matter together or the ways electromagnetic waves travel through space.

Of course, the three areas contain much more than this. Indeed, the subjects of science can seem practically limitless. As you will see, however, they all share some common characteristics and methods.

Community Consensus

One aspect that really sets the study of science apart from other pursuits is its need for openness and review. Whatever information one scientist collects, others must be able to see and comment upon.

The need for openness is important, because scientific ideas must be testable and reproducible. This means that if one scientist arrives at an explanation based on something he or she observed, that scientist must make the data available to other scientists. This allows others the chance to comment upon the results. For example, a scientist may claim that her evidence shows the volcano will erupt in five days. If the scientist declines to describe what that evidence is or how she collected it, why should anyone else think the claim is accurate?

© Houghton Mifflin Harcourt Publishing Company • Image Credits: (bkgd) ©Courtesy of T.A. Plucinski/AVO/USGS; (t) ©Vincent Realmuto, JPL-Caltech/Photo Researchers, Inc.

Active Reading

5 Identify As you read, underline three areas of science.

Visualize It!

6 Predict What kinds of evidence might the scientists in the photo be collecting about the volcano?

_____

_____

7 Explain How might the study of volcanoes affect the people who live near them?

_____

_____

_____

Use of Empirical Evidence

If scientific evidence must be open to all, it needs to be the kind of evidence all can observe. It must be something measurable and not just one person's opinion or guess. Evidence in science must be evidence that can be gained by the senses or empirical evidence. **Empirical evidence** includes observations and measurements. It includes all the data that people gather and test to support and evaluate scientific explanations.

For example, a scientist studying a volcano would visit the volcano to get empirical evidence. The scientist might use specialized tools to make observations and take measurements. Many tools help scientists collect more accurate evidence. Tools often make collecting data safer. For example, few scientists would want to go to the top of the volcano and look down into it. Mounting a thermal camera on an airplane allows scientists to get an aerial shot of the volcano's mouth. Not only does the shot show the detail they want, but also it's a lot safer.

Mount St. Helens volcano as seen with thermal photography.

Scientists use special thermal cameras to take photographs that show the temperature regions of volcanoes.

"Give me an explanation…"

What is a scientific explanation?

Empirical evidence is the basis for scientific explanations. A scientific explanation provides a description of how a process in nature occurs. Scientific explanations are based on observations and data. Beliefs or opinions that are not based on explanations that can be tested are not scientific.

Scientists may begin developing an explanation by gathering all the empirical evidence they have. This could be the observations and measurements they have made or those from other scientists. Then they think logically about how all of this evidence fits together. The explanation they propose must fit all the available evidence.

Often, other scientists will then further evaluate the explanation by testing it for themselves. The additional observations and tests may provide data that further support the explanation. If the results do not support the explanation, the explanation is rejected or modified and retested.

Consider a scientific explanation for how metal rusts. Rust is a compound of oxygen and a metal, usually iron. Oxygen makes up one-fifth of the air we breathe. Therefore, rust may form when oxygen in the air combines with metal. We observe that most rusted metals have also been exposed to large amounts of water. We also observe that the rate of rusting increases if the water contains salt, as it does near oceans. A scientist would propose that water causes metal to rust and that salt increases the rate of rusting. How might you test this statement?

Active Reading

8 Apply As you read, underline the characteristics of a scientific explanation.

How is a scientific explanation evaluated?

So, how would you evaluate the explanation of why some metals rust? Look at the explanation below and start to consider what you know.

First, look at your empirical evidence. Think of all the evidence you could gather to support the statement. A few examples are there for you. Think carefully about what you notice when you look at rusty metal.

Second, consider if the explanation is logical. Does it contradict anything you know or other evidence you have seen?

Third, think of other tests you could do to support your ideas. Could you think of a test that might contradict the explanation?

Last, evaluate the explanation. Do you think it has stood up to the tests? Do you think the tests have addressed what they were supposed to?

> **The Scientific Explanation:**
> Many metals that rust contain iron that reacts with water and oxygen.

The Evidence

9 Identify What evidence do you have about when some metal objects rust?

- I've seen rust on bridges, cars, and other metal objects exposed to the outdoors
- I left several garden tools outside that rusted

The Logic

Second, consider if the explanation is consistent with other evidence you have seen. Think about whether all metals rust in the same way.

 Inquiry

10 Infer Describe how well your explanation fits all of the evidence you have, with all that you know.

- Some metals, like aluminum, don't rust
- Older metals rust more than newer ones

The Tests

Next, think of other tests you could do that would support the explanation.

11 Predict How might you test the conditions under which different metals rust?

- Expose different metals to the same conditions and see if they rust
- Could put metals in regular water and saltwater and note the rate of rusting

The Conclusion

Only after gathering evidence, thinking logically, and doing additional testing do you evaluate the scientific explanation.

12 Evaluate Does this empirical evidence support your explanation? Explain your answer.

Common Habits

What is involved in scientific work?

Even though science and the people who study it are very diverse, scientists have several characteristics in common. Scientists are curious, creative, and careful observers. They are also logical, skeptical, and objective.

You do not have to be a scientist to have these characteristics. When you use these habits of mind, you are thinking like a scientist!

 **Active Reading**

13 Apply Which of the characteristics above do you use most often?

_____

_____

_____

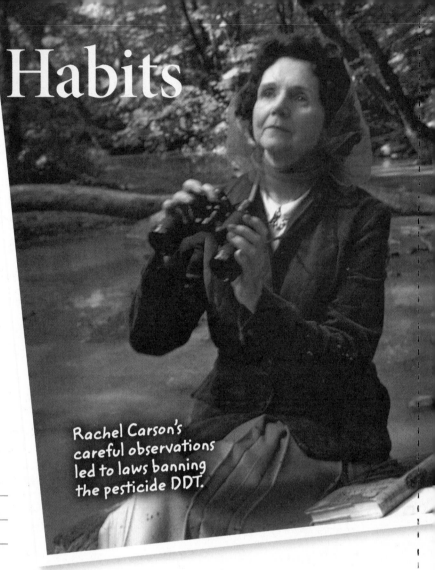

Rachel Carson's careful observations led to laws banning the pesticide DDT.

Careful Observation

Scientists observe with their senses as well as with scientific tools. All observations contribute to the understanding of a subject.

For example, ecologist Rachel Carson spent her entire life observing the natural world around her. She studied the oceans and wrote books and articles about them. She spent years researching and documenting the effects of pesticides, like DDT, on the environment. Her book, _Silent Spring_, drew the world's attention to the problem.

Curiosity

Scientists are curious about the world around them and about the things they observe. Most scientific discoveries are the result of someone asking why or how something happens.

For example, Rachel Carson was curious about all of nature. This curiosity drove her to identify the connections in it. It allowed her to understand how one part affects another.

14 List Name two things you are curious about.

_____

_____

Creativity

Being creative means to be original. Creative people think for themselves and always try to see other ways things might be.

In science, creativity is used when scientists apply their imaginations to come up with new solutions. For example, prairie fires can start suddenly and cause destruction. Instead of trying to prevent them, some scientists often start them under controlled conditions to minimize the damage.

15 Identify Name an activity you do in which you are creative.

© Houghton Mifflin Harcourt Publishing Company • Image Credits: ©Alfred Eisenstaedt//Time Life Pictures/Getty Images

© Houghton Mifflin Harcourt Publishing Company • Image Credits: (tl) ©Alfred Eisenstaedt//Time Life Pictures/Getty Images; (tr) ©Picture Contact/Alamy

19 Apply Research shows that interaction with animals can benefit humans. In the discussion of dolphin therapy to the right, fill in the blanks with the appropriate characteristics scientists are showing.

Scientists saw how well people responded to animals and imagined _____ that these interactions might be helpful in some types of therapy.

Scientists were _____ about whether dolphins could be used as therapy animals.

Early studies showed that dolphin therapy has helped to improve certain conditions in humans. But scientists must be _____. They must not draw conclusions too quickly.

They need to conduct more tests and make _____ to determine the effects of dolphin therapy.

When they have more data, they will assess it _____ before drawing a conclusion.

They will consider all the evidence _____ before making decisions about the advantages and disadvantages of dolphin therapy.

Logic

Thinking logically involves reasoning through information and making conclusions supported by the evidence. Logical thinking is an important tool for the scientist.

For example, toothpaste helps to prevent tooth decay. Some mouthwash also helps to prevent tooth decay. It is logical to think that if the two products are used together they might work even better. This logical conclusion should then be tested.

16 Infer What is another career that relies on logic?

_____

_____

Skepticism

Being skeptical means that you don't accept everything you hear or read immediately. You ask questions before deciding whether you will accept information as factual. Scientists are skeptical of drawing conclusions too quickly. Instead, they repeat observations and experiments, and they review and try to replicate the work of others.

17 Conclude Why should you be skeptical of some advertisements?

_____

_____

Objectivity

Being objective requires that you set aside your personal feelings, moods, and beliefs while you evaluate something. Science requires unbiased observations, experiments, and evaluations. Scientists want their tests to support their ideas. Scientists must be careful not to let this hope influence what they see.

18 Explain Describe a time when it was difficult to be objective.

_____

_____

_____

"Space Aliens built the Pyramids"

How is pseudoscience similar to and different from science?

People have marveled at the pyramids for thousands of years. Even today, scientists still question how ancient people could have built such awesome structures. Some have given a possible explanation for this—the pyramids were built by an advanced race of beings from outer space. Because it is unclear how ancient people could have built the pyramids, supporters of this idea think it provides one possible answer.

Some people will claim to have scientific evidence to support an explanation when in fact they do not. **Pseudoscience** is a belief or practice that is based on incorrectly applied scientific methods. Pseudoscience can seem like real science, but pseudoscientific ideas are based on faulty logic and are supported by claims that can't be tested.

Similarities

Pseudoscience is like science in that it often involves topics related to the natural world. People who believe in pseudoscience have explanations that can sound logical. Like science, pseudoscience uses technical language or scientific-sounding terms. Both science and pseudoscience claim to be based on empirical evidence.

Differences

The biggest difference between science and pseudoscience is that pseudoscience does not use accepted scientific methods. The evidence that supports pseudoscience may be very vague or lack any measurements. Some pseudoscientific claims lack the ability to be tested at all. Other pseudoscientific beliefs are supported only by personal experiences. Unlike scientists, pseudoscientists might claim that results not proven false must be true. This is faulty logic. Scientists must offer evidence for their conclusions. Pseudoscience asks skeptics to prove it false. In the case of the pyramids, pseudoscientists claim the pyramids' complexity is proof of their alien origin. To disprove the claim, you must prove aliens did not visit Earth 5,000 years ago. This is almost impossible to do.

Active Reading **20 Identify** Name two traits of pseudoscience.

_____

_____

Science vs. Pseudoscience

Science	Pseudoscience
Based on logic	Not based on logic or logic is exaggerated
Has testable explanations	Explanations generally not testable
Relies on empirical evidence	Empirical evidence is not available; personal opinions often are used as empirical evidence
Results can be reproduced by others	Results cannot be reproduced by others
Explanations that are not proven false continue to be tested	Explanations that are not proven false are assumed to be true
Explanations are modified by new evidence	Explanations do not change with new evidence

22 Analyze Someone tells you they've heard of a powder that, if worn in a pouch around the neck, will cure a cold. This person claims that the powder has cured everyone with a cold who has worn it. How do you explain to this person that, despite the positive results, this is a pseudoscientific claim?

_____

_____

_____

_____

21 Explain Would it be possible for something to initially be regarded as pseudoscience and then later be supported by science? Explain your answer.

_____

_____

_____

_____

Even today, researchers don't know how ancient people hauled the large stones needed to build the pyramids. Does this prove that aliens did it?

Think Outside the Book

23 Evaluate A popular hoax on the Internet warned of the dangers of the chemical dihydrogen monoxide. The supposed opponents claimed the chemical could cause death if inhaled and severe burns if touched. Do some research to find out what this chemical is. How are the claims made about it like the claims made by pseudoscientists?

Visual Summary

To complete this summary, fill in the blanks with the correct word or phrase. Then use the key below to check your answers. You can use this page to review the main concepts of the lesson.

What Is Science?

Science is the systematic study of natural events and conditions.

24 Explanations in science must be testable and have _____ of other scientists.

25 The _____ collected in scientific investigations is often in the form of measurements.

Scientists may study very different things, but they share many common traits.

26 Scientists use empirical evidence, logical thinking, and tests to _____ a scientific explanation.

27 Scientists are _____ about the subjects they study.

Science and pseudoscience both deal with the natural world, but pseudoscience only deceptively appears to be science.

28 Many claims of pseudoscience are not refutable because they can't be _____

Answers: 24 consensus; 25 empirical evidence; 26 evaluate; 27 curious; 28 tested

29 **Hypothesize** How might the characteristics of a scientist be displayed in a person of your age?

Lesson Review

Vocabulary

Fill in the blank with the term that best completes the following sentences.

1 _____ is the systematic study of the natural world.

2 _____ is often mistakenly regarded as being based on science.

3 _____ _____ is the name for the observations and data on which a scientific explanation can be based.

Key Concepts

4 Describe What are two things that characterize the practice of science?

_____

_____

5 Sequence What are the three steps scientists take to evaluate a scientific explanation?

_____

_____

_____

6 Describe What are six traits of a good scientific observer?

_____

_____

_____

_____

_____

7 Justify Why is it good for scientists to be skeptical?

_____

_____

Critical Thinking

Use the table below to answer the following questions.

Characteristic	Science	Pseudoscience
Concerns the natural world		
Explanations can sound logical		
Results can always be tested by others		
Explanations can be proven false		
Allows personal opinions to be used as evidence		

8 Assess Place an "x" in the appropriate box if the characteristic could describe science, pseudoscience, or both. What might this tell you about the relationship between science and pseudoscience?

_____

_____

_____

_____

9 Judge Good scientists use their imagination. What do you think is the difference between being imaginative in doing science and doing pseudoscience?

_____

_____

_____

My Notes

Scientific Investigations

ESSENTIAL QUESTION

How do scientists discover things?

By the end of this lesson, you should be able to summarize the processes and characteristics of different kinds of scientific investigations.

This scientist is studying DNA, the molecule of life!

Lesson Labs

Quick Labs
- Designing a Procedure
- The Importance of Replication

Field Lab
- Investigating Soil Microorganisms

Engage Your Brain

1 Discriminate Circle the word or phrase that best completes the following sentences.

A *hypothesis / dependent variable* is a possible explanation of a scientific problem.

Scientists conduct controlled experiments because this method enables them to test the effects of a single *variable / theory*.

Graphing of results is most often done as part of *writing hypotheses / analyzing data*.

A scientist who makes observations *in the field / in laboratories* is able to collect data about wildlife in their natural environments.

2 Explain Draw a picture of what you think a scientific investigation might look like. Write a caption to go with your picture.

Active Reading

3 Synthesize Many English words have their roots in other languages. Use the Latin words below to make an educated guess about the meaning of the words *experiment* and *observation*.

Latin word	Meaning
experiri	to try
observare	to watch

Example sentence
Shaun's favorite <u>experiment</u> involved pouring vinegar onto baking soda.

experiment:

_____

_____

Example sentence
Telescopes are used to make <u>observations</u>.

observation:

_____

_____

Vocabulary Terms
- experiment
- observation
- hypothesis
- independent variable
- dependent variable
- data

4 Apply As you learn the definition of each vocabulary term in this lesson, write a sentence that includes the term to help you remember it.

Testing, Testing, 1, 2, 3

What are some parts that make up scientific investigations?

An **experiment** is an organized procedure to study something under controlled conditions. Scientists often investigate the natural world through experiments. But scientists must learn about many things through observation. **Observation** is the process of obtaining information by using the senses. The term can also refer to the information obtained by using the senses. Scientific investigations may also involve the use of models, which are representations of an object or system.

Elements of Investigations

Hypothesis

A **hypothesis** (hy•PAHTH•eh•sys) is a testable idea or explanation that leads to scientific investigation. A scientist may think of a hypothesis after making observations or after reading findings from other scientists' investigations.

Hypotheses must be carefully constructed so they can be tested in a practical and meaningful way. For example, suppose you find a bone fossil, and you form the hypothesis that it came from a dinosaur that lived 200 million years ago. You might test your hypothesis by comparing the fossil to other fossils that have been found and by analyzing the fossil to determine its age.

If an investigation does not support a hypothesis, it is still useful. The information from the investigation can help scientists form a better hypothesis. Scientists may go through many cycles of testing and analysis before they arrive at a hypothesis that is supported.

Active Reading **5 Explain** Why should hypotheses be testable?

_____

_____

_____

This young plant is growing in a hostile environment.

Visualize It!

6 Infer Write a hypothesis offering a possible explanation of what will happen to the plant above.

_____

_____

_____

Independent and Dependent Variables

A variable is any factor that can change in a scientific investigation. An **independent variable** is the factor that is deliberately manipulated. A **dependent variable** changes as a result of manipulation of one or more independent variables.

Imagine that you want to test the hypothesis that increasing the heat under a pot of water will cause the water to boil faster. You fill three pots with the same amount of water, then heat them until the water boils. The independent variable is the amount of heat. The dependent variable is the time it takes for the water to boil. You measure this variable for all three pots to determine whether your hypothesis is supported.

If possible, a controlled experiment should have just one independent variable. Scientists try to keep other variables constant, or unchanged, so they do not affect the results. For example, in the experiment described above, each pot should be made of the same material because some materials change temperature more easily than others.

Observations and Data

Data are information gathered by observation or experimentation that can be used in calculating or reasoning. This information may be anything that a scientist perceives through the senses or detects through instruments.

In an investigation, everything a scientist observes must be recorded. The setup and procedures need to be recorded. By carefully recording this information, scientists make sure they will not forget anything.

Scientists analyze data to determine the relationship between the independent and dependent variables in an investigation. Then they draw conclusions about whether the data support the investigation's hypothesis.

7 Apply Suppose you want to test the hypothesis that plants grow taller when they receive more sunlight. Identify an independent variable and a dependent variable for this investigation.

_____

_____

_____

_____

_____

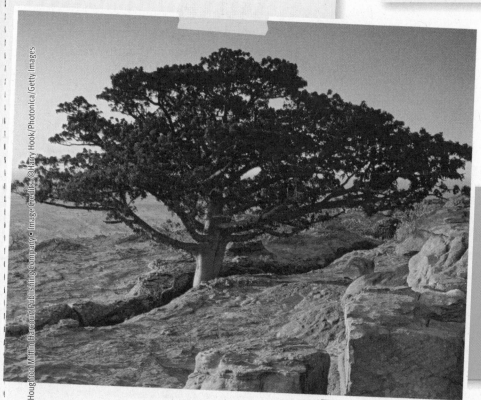

You may have thought that the plant at the left will die. But as this photograph shows, plants can get enough nutrients to thrive under similar conditions.

Many Methods

What are some scientific methods?

Conducting experiments and other scientific investigations is not like following a cookbook recipe. Scientists do not always use the same steps in every investigation or use steps in the same order. They may even repeat some of the steps. The following graphic shows one path that a scientist might follow while conducting an experiment.

 **Visualize It!**

8 Diagram Using a highlighter, trace the path a scientist might follow if the data from an experiment did not support the hypothesis.

Defining a Problem

After making observations or reading scientific reports, a scientist might be curious about some unexplained aspect of a topic. A scientific problem is a specific question that a scientist wants to answer. The problem must be well-defined, or precisely stated, so that it can be investigated.

Planning an Investigation

A scientific investigation must be carefully planned so that it tests a hypothesis in a meaningful way. Scientists need to decide whether an investigation should be done in the field or in a laboratory. They must also determine what equipment and technology are required and how materials for the investigation will be obtained.

Forming a Hypothesis and Making Predictions

When scientists form a hypothesis, they are making an educated guess about a problem. A hypothesis must be tested to see if it is true. Before testing a hypothesis, scientists usually make predictions about what will happen in an investigation.

Identifying Variables

The independent variable of an experiment is identified in the hypothesis. But scientists need to decide how the independent variable will change. They also must identify other variables that will be controlled. In addition, scientists must determine how they will measure the results of the experiment. The dependent variable often can be measured in more than one way. For example, if the dependent variable is fish health, scientists could measure size, weight, or number of offspring.

Collecting and Organizing Data

The data collected in an investigation must be recorded and properly organized so that they can be analyzed. Data such as measurements and numbers are often organized into tables, spreadsheets, or graphs.

Interpreting Data and Analyzing Information

After they finish collecting data, scientists must analyze this information. Their analysis will help them draw conclusions about the results. Scientists may have different interpretations of the same data because they analyze it using different methods.

Drawing and Defending Conclusions

Scientists conclude whether the results of their investigation support the hypothesis. If the hypothesis is not supported, scientists may think about the problem some more and try to come up with a new hypothesis to test. Or they may repeat an experiment to see if any mistakes were made. When they publish the results of their investigation, scientists must be prepared to defend their conclusions if they are challenged by other scientists.

Life Lessons

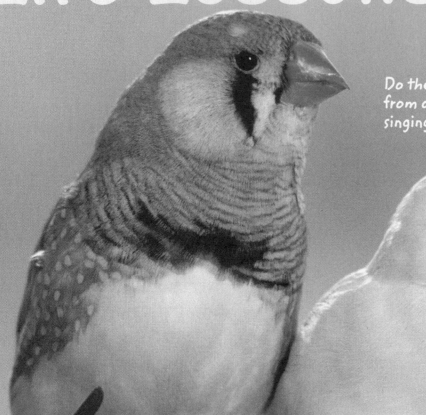

Do these birds learn their songs from older birds? Or is their singing genetic?

How are scientific methods used?

Scientific methods are used in physical, life, and earth sciences. Which methods are used depends on the type of investigation that is to be conducted.

Different Situations Require Different Methods

Scientists choose the setting for an investigation very carefully. Some problems are suited for field investigations. For example, many life scientists work in the field in order to study living things in their natural habitat. Many geologists begin in the field, collecting rocks and samples. But, those same geologists might then study their samples in a laboratory, where conditions can be controlled.

Sometimes scientists study things that are very large, very small, or that occur over a very long period of time. In these cases, scientists can use models in their investigations. A scientific model is a representation of an object or a process that allows scientists to study something in detail. Scientists can conduct experiments and make observations using models.

Think Outside the Book | Inquiry

9 Describe Do research to learn about a new hypothesis that has replaced an older explanation of something in the natural world. Describe the process that led to this change in thinking.

When finches were first isolated, they didn't sing like wild finches. But later generations of isolated finches sang just like wild birds.

10 Identify As you read, underline the scientific methods used in the study.

Scientific Methods Are Used in Life Science

Life scientists use scientific methods to study how traits are passed from parents to offspring.

One team of scientists recently studied birds called zebra finches. Zebra finches learn songs by imitating the singing of older relatives. But the scientists thought that genes might play a role in how the birds learn their songs.

To test this hypothesis, they isolated a group of young zebra finches from older birds. When these young birds grew up, they sang differently than wild finches did. Then, the scientists placed another group of young males in with the isolated finches. The younger finches imitated the songs of the older ones, but the songs were slightly different. As the scientists continued to add new groups of young finches in with the isolated ones, each new group started to sing more like wild finches. The scientists concluded that genes influence the way zebra finches learn how to sing.

According to legend, Galileo dropped two balls from the Leaning Tower of Pisa to demonstrate that objects of different masses fall at the same rate.

What are some characteristics of good scientific investigations?

Scientists may use different ways to test the same hypothesis. But good scientific investigations share some important characteristics. Scientific observations should be well-documented and have supporting evidence. In an experiment, the variables should be controlled as much as possible.

Experiments should be repeated multiple times by the original investigator. Scientific investigations should also be able to be replicated by scientists not involved with the original work. If the investigation is valid, the same results will be found.

Before publishing a study, scientific journals ask other scientists to review an article. This is called peer review. Scientists must provide answers to the questions raised by their peers.

Visualize It!

11 Infer When scientists replicate experiments, they will often do so under different conditions than the original investigations. Why might this be helpful? Why do you think the astronaut replicated Galileo's investigation on the moon?

_____

_____

_____

_____

_____

_____

_____

_____

© Houghton Mifflin Harcourt Publishing Company • Image Credits: (bkgd) ©Science Source/Photo Res

How can you evaluate the quality of scientific information?

Scientific information is available on the Internet, on television, and in magazines. Some sources are more trustworthy than others. The most reliable scientific information is published in scientific journals. However, these articles are often difficult to understand. Sometimes, summaries of these articles are published for the public.

Many scientists write books for the general public. These publications are trustworthy if the scientist is writing about their field of study. Reliable books may also be written by people who aren't scientists but who are knowledgeable about a particular field.

Usually, the most reliable Internet sources are government or academic webpages. Commercial webpages are often unreliable because they are trying to sell something.

12 Apply Find two sources of information about the same scientific investigation. Then, fill out the chart below to explain why you think each source is trustworthy or untrustworthy.

What is this investigation about? _____

_____

Source	Trustworthy? Why or why not?

Over 300 years later, scientists were still replicating Galileo's investigation. In 1971, astronaut David Scott traveled to the moon, which has no air. When he dropped a hammer and a feather, they hit the ground at the same time.

Think Outside the Book

13 Design Suppose that you are conducting a field experiment with plants. You are testing the hypothesis that plants grow faster when mulch covers the soil. Plan how you would conduct the experiment. Then plan how you would repeat it.

Visual Summary

To complete this summary, fill in the blanks with the correct word or phrase. Then, use the key below to check your answers. You can use this page to review the main concepts of the lesson.

Scientific investigations include experiments, fieldwork, surveys, and models.

14 A type of investigation that allows scientists to control variables is a(n) _____

15 Scientific experiments test relationships between _____ and _____ variables.

16 A scientific hypothesis must be _____

There is no single correct way to conduct a scientific investigation.
Some methods include making and testing hypotheses, collecting data, analyzing data, and drawing conclusions.

17 A(n) _____ is either supported or unsupported by the results of an investigation.

18 The results of an investigation are the _____

Reliable scientific information comes from investigations with reproducible results.
Sources of reliable scientific information include scientific journals and government web sites.

19 An investigation that has been done by more than one scientist with similar findings has been _____

20 The most reliable scientific information is published in _____

Answers: 14 experiment; 15 independent, dependent; 16 testable 17 hypothesis; 18 data; 19 replicated; 20 scientific journals

21 Apply Choose an organism that you can observe in its environment. Write a hypothesis that you could test about this organism.

Lesson Review

Vocabulary

Fill in the blank with the term that best completes the following sentences.

1 A scientific _____ is a proposed explanation that can be tested.

2 A(n) _____ is the factor that is deliberately changed in an experiment.

3 The information gathered in an investigation is called _____

4 A(n) _____ should have only one independent variable.

5 _____ can be made in the field or in the laboratory.

Key Concepts

6 Infer What kinds of scientific investigations involve making observations?

_____

_____

7 Apply In an experiment, which variable changes in response to the manipulation of another variable?

_____

8 Explain When might a scientist use a model?

_____

_____

_____

9 Compare How are repetition and replication alike and different?

_____

_____

_____

_____

Critical Thinking

Use the table below to answer the following questions.

Plant	Amount of Water Given	Amount of Fertilizer Given	Height
1	10 mL	none	6 cm
2	20 mL	5 g	8 cm
3	30 mL	10 g	7 cm
4	40 mL	15 g	12 cm

10 Evaluate The table above shows the data collected during an experiment about plant height. Based on the data collected, is this a controlled experiment? Why or why not?

_____

_____

_____

_____

_____

_____

11 Describe How would you experiment to find out how much water this plant type needs for optimal growth?

_____

_____

_____

_____

12 Recommend Write a checklist with at least three entries for how you can evaluate whether scientific information is reliable.

_____

_____

_____

_____

My Notes

Dijanna Figueroa

MARINE BIOLOGIST

Dijanna Figueroa has wanted to be a marine biologist for as long as she can remember. Like many scientists, she now wears a lab coat and safety glasses most days. She spends up to 12 hours a day in the lab. There, she studies the metabolisms of creatures that live in extreme environments. These creatures live more than two kilometers below the ocean's surface, in a habitat that sunlight never reaches. The water pressure is so great that it would crush a human being. Creatures living in these conditions must therefore produce foods in ways that were unknown until only recently. In order to get specimens of these animals for her lab, Dr. Figueroa had to go down to where they live.

Dr. Figueroa's job has taken her onto the big screen, too. She appeared in the IMAX film *Aliens of the Deep*, with other scientists. The film shows footage of expeditions down to the deep-sea ocean vents. These vents may be one of the harshest environments on the planet. The scientists traveled in *Alvin*, a deep-sea submarine.

Dr. Figueroa works to get young people interested in real-life science through fun and exciting hands-on activities. She currently works as the science coordinator for a private school in California.

Dr. Figueroa in *Alvin*—2,400 m deep!

Language Arts Connection

Think of a science-related job that you would like to know more about. Research the job and write a plan for a documentary film that teaches what you have learned about the job.

JOB BOARD

Museum Educational Interpreter

What You'll Do: Tell students and groups visiting a museum about what they are looking at. You might create educational programs, give tours, and answer questions.

Where You Might Work: Likely places are a science museum or a museum of technology.

Education: Educational interpreters usually need a bachelor's degree in science, and may need extra training in museums or in teaching.

Other Job Requirements: You need to enjoy working with people, be good at public speaking, and be able to answer questions clearly.

Pyrotechnician

What You'll Do: Work with explosives to create explosions and fireworks for special effects. Blow things up in the safest way possible, using a lot of safety measures to keep things from getting out of hand.

Where You Might Work: A company that designs special effects or that creates and performs fireworks shows is a possibility. A pyrotechnician spends time in the workshop and on-site, so you may find yourself on a film set blowing up cars, or on a hillside setting off fireworks.

Education: You need a high-school diploma with additional training in pyrotechnics and safety.

Other Job Requirements: Strong math skills, ability to concentrate, and careful attention to detail are required.

© Houghton Mifflin Harcourt Publishing Company • Image Credits: (bkgd) ©Science Source/Photo Researchers, Inc.; (br) ©wonderlandstock/Alamy

PEOPLE IN SCIENCE NEWS

Jon BOHMER

Cooking with Sunlight

Jon Bohmer isn't the first person to invent an oven that uses sunlight to heat food and water. He's one of many people to use cardboard, foil, and sunlight to build an oven. In some countries, people use firewood for most of their cooking, and must boil all of their water before they drink it. Jon's Kyoto Box oven uses two cardboard boxes painted black on the inside and coated with foil on the outside. It costs only about $5 to make, but it gets hot enough to boil water and cook food.

Scientific Knowledge

ESSENTIAL QUESTION

What are the types of scientific knowledge?

By the end of this lesson, you should be able to differentiate the methods that scientists use to gain empirical evidence in a variety of scientific fields and explain how this leads to scientific change.

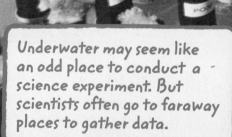

Underwater may seem like an odd place to conduct a science experiment. But scientists often go to faraway places to gather data.

Lesson Labs

Quick Labs
• Pluto on Trial
• Theory or Claim?

Exploration Lab
• Science-Based Commercials

Engage Your Brain

1 Predict Check T or F to show whether you think each statement is true or false.

T F

☐ ☐ All branches of science have scientific theories.

☐ ☐ A scientist can use only one method to investigate.

☐ ☐ Theories are scientific ideas that have not yet been tested.

☐ ☐ Scientific laws describe what happens in the world.

2 Synthesize An aeolipile is a device powered by steam. When heated, water in the bulb produces steam. The bulb rotates as the steam escapes from the nozzles. People were making these devices as long as 2,000 years ago. How do you think they came up with the idea even though they did not have our modern understanding of science?

_____

_____

_____

aeolipile

Active Reading

3 Infer The word *empirical* comes from the Greek word *empeirikos*, meaning "experienced." Based on this information, infer how scientists get empirical evidence.

_____

_____

_____

_____

Vocabulary Terms

• empirical evidence
• theory
• law

4 Apply As you learn the definition of each vocabulary term in this lesson, create your own definition or sketch to help you remember the meaning of the term.

...From the **Beginning**

What is science?

Think Outside the Book Inquiry

5 Define Before you begin reading the lesson, write down what you think science and scientific knowledge are. Reread your definition at the end of the lesson. Has your definition changed?

Science is the study of the natural world. Scientists study everything from the deepest parts of the ocean to the objects in outer space. Some scientists study living things. Others study forces such as gravity and magnetism. Name anything you see around you. Chances are, there is a scientist who studies it.

The natural sciences are divided into three areas: biology or life science, geology or Earth science, and physics or physical science. The three areas differ in the subjects they study and the methods they use. Biology is the study of living things. Biologists study everything from the tiniest organisms to human beings. Geology is the study of Earth: what it's made of and the processes that shape it. Physical science is the study of nonliving matter and energy. Chemistry often is included under physical science. A scientist's work sometimes may overlap two or more areas. For example, a biologist often must know chemistry to understand the processes in living things.

Each of the photographs below relates to one of the areas of science in some way. From the captions, can you identify to which area each belongs?

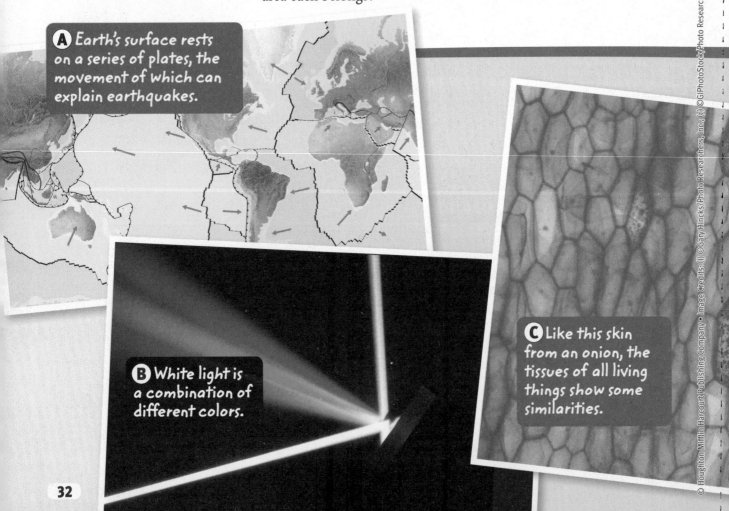

A Earth's surface rests on a series of plates, the movement of which can explain earthquakes.

B White light is a combination of different colors.

C Like this skin from an onion, the tissues of all living things show some similarities.

What does science tell us?

Active Reading 6 **Identify** Underline what a theory is in science.

You may think that what you read in a science book is accepted by everyone and is unchanging. That is not always the case. The "facts" of science are simply the most widely accepted explanations. Scientific knowledge is and probably always will be changing.

What we learn when we study science are what most scientists agree are the best explanations about how things happen. They are *theories* scientists have about the world. Commonly, we think of a theory as a kind of guess or "hunch." In science, a theory is much more. A scientific theory is an explanation supported by a large amount of evidence. Theories are what most scientists agree to be the best explanations based upon what we now know.

The table below lists three important scientific theories. Each theory relates to one of the areas of science described before. Each also corresponds to a photograph on the previous page. Can you think of what kinds of evidence would support each theory?

Visualize It!

7 **Identify** For each of the three theories listed in the table below, write the letter of the corresponding photograph at the left. On the lines provided, describe what might be some evidence that would support the theory.

Scientific Theories

	What scientists think	What is some evidence?
Biology	____Cell theory: Living things are made up of cells that perform the basic functions of life.	
Geology	____Plate tectonics: Earth's surface is made up of plates that move.	
Physics	____Wave theory of light: Each color of visible light has a wave of a specific wavelength.	

You Can't Break

How do scientific theories differ from laws?

Active Reading **8 Identify** As you read, underline a real-world example of Boyle's law.

To understand the nature of scientific knowledge, you must understand how scientists use certain words. Often, the meanings are very specialized. *Law* and *theory* are two familiar words that have very special scientific meanings.

Laws Describe Principles of Nature

A scientific **law** is a description of a specific relationship under given conditions in the natural world. In short, scientific laws describe the way the world works. They hold anywhere in the universe. You can't escape them.

Boyle's law is one scientific law. According to Boyle's law, at a constant temperature, as the pressure on a gas increases, its volume decreases. To get an appreciation of Boyle's law, think of how it would feel to squeeze a partially deflated beach ball. If you apply pressure by squeezing, the volume, or size, of the ball gets smaller.

You can feel the effects of Boyle's law. A membrane or *eardrum* separates your middle ear from outer ear. Normally, the air spaces on either side are at equal pressure. But sometimes, the pressure on the outer ear can change. For example, the scuba diver in the photo feels an increase in pressure on her eardrum as she descends in the water. By holding her nose and blowing gently, she can force more air into her middle ear. The action momentarily opens the *eustachian tube* connecting the middle ear to the throat. This allows more air from the mouth to rush into the middle ear and equalize the pressure between the two spaces.

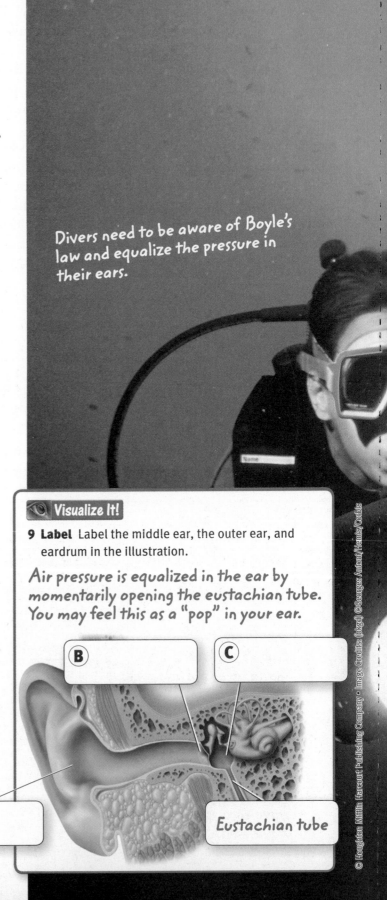

Divers need to be aware of Boyle's law and equalize the pressure in their ears.

Visualize It!

9 Label Label the middle ear, the outer ear, and eardrum in the illustration.

Air pressure is equalized in the ear by momentarily opening the eustachian tube. You may feel this as a "pop" in your ear.

B

C

A

Eustachian tube

a Law!

Theories Describe How Things Happen

While laws describe what happens, scientific theories attempt to explain how things happen. A scientific **theory** is a well-supported explanation of nature. Theories help us understand the laws we observe.

For example, the kinetic theory of gases can explain Boyle's law. The kinetic theory describes a gas as being composed of quickly-moving particles. The particles of gas constantly bounce off of the walls of the container they occupy. The pressure of the gas increases the more frequently the particles bounce off the sides of the container.

Two factors increase how frequently the particles of a gas will bounce off the walls of their container: temperature and volume. If the temperature of a gas increases, the particles move more quickly. The particles, therefore, come into contact with the container's walls more often. Decreasing volume also increases the encounters because the particles have less distance to travel before hitting the wall. The container walls can be anything: a metal cylinder, a beach ball, or your eardrum. The illustration below will give you some of idea of how this works.

 **Visualize It!**

10 Compare In the table below, circle the signs that show the relationships between the volumes, pressures, and temperatures of the gases in the two cylinders. The first is done for you.

Cylinder 1	Relationship			Cylinder 2
Volume	<	=	(>)	Volume
Pressure	<	=	>	Pressure
Temperature	<	=	>	Temperature

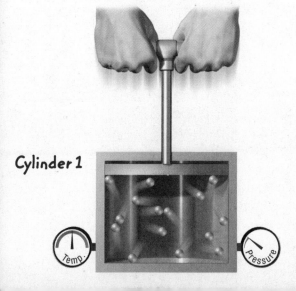

Cylinder 1

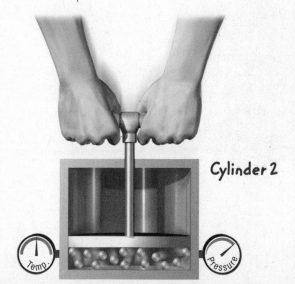

Cylinder 2

What's Your Evidence?

Where do scientists get their evidence?

Scientists are curious. They look at everything going on around them and ask questions. They collect any information that might help them answer these questions.

Scientific knowledge is based on *empirical evidence*. **Empirical evidence** is all the measurements and data scientists gather in support of a scientific explanation. Scientists get empirical evidence in many different places. Generally, scientific work is categorized as field or laboratory work.

This scientist is a paleontologist. A paleontologist looks for fossilized bones. Here, she is carefully excavating the remains of a 10,000 year-old rhinoceros.

Visualize It!

12 Analyze What empirical evidence might the scientist in the photograph be trying to gather?

_____

_____

_____

_____

In the Field

Generally, gathering empirical evidence outdoors or where conditions cannot be controlled is known as working in the field or *fieldwork*. Fieldwork gives scientists the opportunity to collect data in an original setting. Biologists and geologists do fieldwork.

A biologist might observe how animals behave in their natural environment. They may look at how the animals gather food or interact with other animals. A geologist may be interested in the minerals in rocks found in a certain area. They may be trying to determine how the rocks formed.

In the Laboratory

In a laboratory, scientists have the opportunity to collect data in a controlled environment. Unlike in the field, the laboratory allows scientists to control conditions like temperature, lighting, and even what is in the surrounding air. A laboratory is where scientists usually do experiments. In an experiment, scientists try to see what happens under certain conditions. A chemist might be trying to see how two substances react with each other. A physicist might study the energy of a new laser. Even scientists who mainly work in the field, like paleontologists and geologists, may wish to look at a bone or rock in the laboratory.

Laboratories come in many varieties. They can be in the ocean or in the sky. Robotic laboratories even have been sent to Mars!

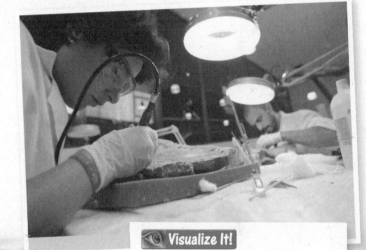

Active Reading

13 Predict What might a scientist look for to collect evidence about the formation of a volcano?

_____

_____

_____

_____

Visualize It!

14 Infer The paleontologists in the photo above have taken a specimen back to the laboratory. What might they be looking for?

_____

_____

_____

The Debate Continues

How do scientific ideas change?

Recall that scientific knowledge is agreed-upon knowledge. It is what scientists think are the most-likely explanations for what we see. Over time, these most-likely explanations can change. Sometimes, these changes are very large. More often, they are very small. Why do scientific ideas and explanations change? It's usually because new evidence was found or someone found a better way of explaining the old evidence.

By New Evidence

The theory of atoms is a good example of how new evidence can modify an established theory. By the mid-1800s, most scientists agreed matter was made of atoms. However, they were not sure what atoms looked like. At first, they thought atoms probably looked like tiny, solid marbles. They assumed atoms of different substances probably differed by their masses.

Later evidence suggested that atoms most likely contained even smaller parts. Scientists observed that these smaller parts carried electric charges and that most of an atom's mass was concentrated at its center. Scientists still saw atoms as extremely small and still often treated them like they were tiny marbles. They came to realize, however, that to explain how atoms interact in the best way, they needed a more complex picture of them.

Today, scientists are still trying to refine the picture of the atom. Much of what they do involves literally smashing atoms into one another. They examine the patterns made by the crashes. It is almost like an atomic game of marbles.

Active Reading

15 **Identify** Underline an example of a scientific idea that was modified after it was first introduced.

Visualize It!

16 **Analyze** How does the early model of the atom differ from the current model? What is similar about the two models?

_____

_____

_____

_____

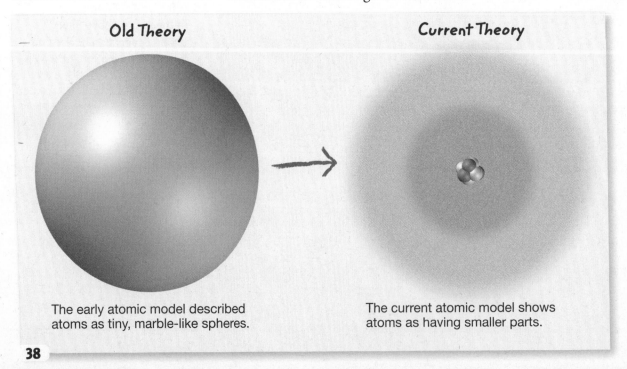

Old Theory

Current Theory

The early atomic model described atoms as tiny, marble-like spheres.

The current atomic model shows atoms as having smaller parts.

By Collaboration and Debate

Most scientists do not work in isolation. They collaborate and share ideas. In a way, all scientists are trying to solve a puzzle. Often, many brains are better than one when solving a puzzle.

Scientists regularly gather at meetings to discuss and debate ideas. This helps them to come to an agreement on their ideas. Many ideas are not accepted at first. It is the nature of science to question every idea. Many times, challenges are even welcomed. This rigorous evaluation ensures that scientific knowledge is solidly supported.

Think Outside the Book Inquiry

17 Evaluate Describe a time when you had to ask someone's help in solving a problem. Why did you ask for help?

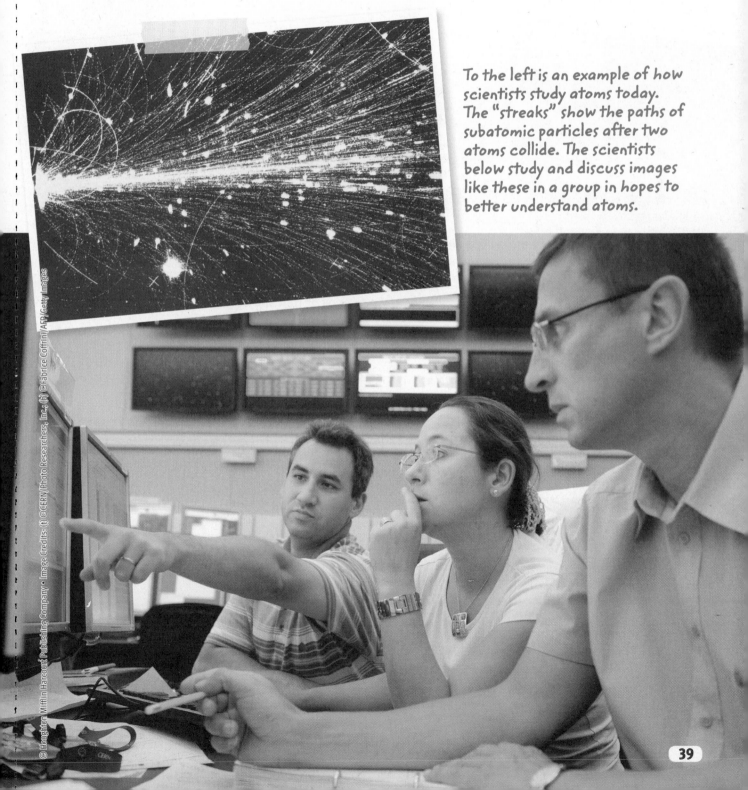

To the left is an example of how scientists study atoms today. The "streaks" show the paths of subatomic particles after two atoms collide. The scientists below study and discuss images like these in a group in hopes to better understand atoms.

Visual Summary

To complete this summary, fill in the blanks with the correct word or phrase. Then, use the key below to check your answers. You can use this page to review the main concepts of the lesson.

The facts we may think of as science are simply the most widely accepted explanations.

18 A scientific_____ describes what happens, but a scientific _____ describes for what reasons it happens.

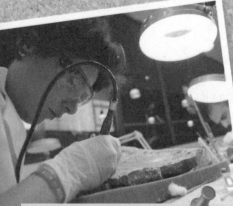

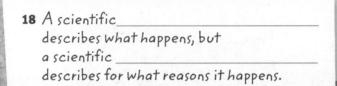
Scientific Knowledge

Empirical evidence is all the measurements and data scientists gather in support of a scientific explanation.

19 Empirical evidence about rocks might be collected by a _____ doing _____

20 Empirical evidence about how substances combine might be collected by a _____ doing work in the _____

Scientific knowledge often changes with new evidence or new interpretations.

21 Scientists often_____ and _____ to help them interpret complex ideas.

22 **Justify** Could a scientific theory be thought of as a scientific law that doesn't have as much evidence supporting it? Explain your answer.

Lesson Review

Vocabulary

Circle the term that best completes each of the following sentences.

1 A scientific *law / theory* is an explanation for how something occurs. It is supported by a great deal of evidence.

2 Scientists look for *empirical evidence / law* either in the field or in the laboratory.

3 A basic principle that applies everywhere and in all situations is best described as a scientific *law / theory*.

Key Concepts

4 List Into what three areas are the natural sciences commonly divided?

_____

_____

5 Distinguish How is the use of the word *theory* in science different from its more common use?

_____

_____

_____

6 Differentiate How would you distinguish a scientific theory from a scientific law?

_____

_____

_____

7 Identify Name two methods scientists use to obtain empirical evidence.

_____

_____

8 Apply What is a difference between research in the field and in the laboratory?

_____

_____

_____

Critical Thinking

Use this picture to answer the following question.

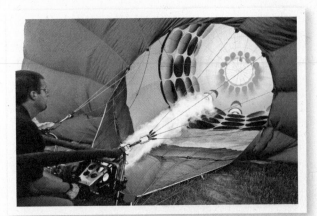

9 Interpret As the flames heat the gases in the balloon, the volume of the gases increases. At constant pressure, the volume of all gases increases with increasing temperature. Is this statement a scientific theory or law? Explain.

_____

_____

_____

10 Defend Someone tells you that scientific knowledge cannot be changed or modified. How would you answer this statement?

_____

_____

_____

11 Conclude Each year, the American Chemical Society holds a national meeting and many regional meetings for chemists. Reports of these meetings are then circulated all over the world. Why do you think this has become standard practice?

_____

_____

_____

_____

My Notes

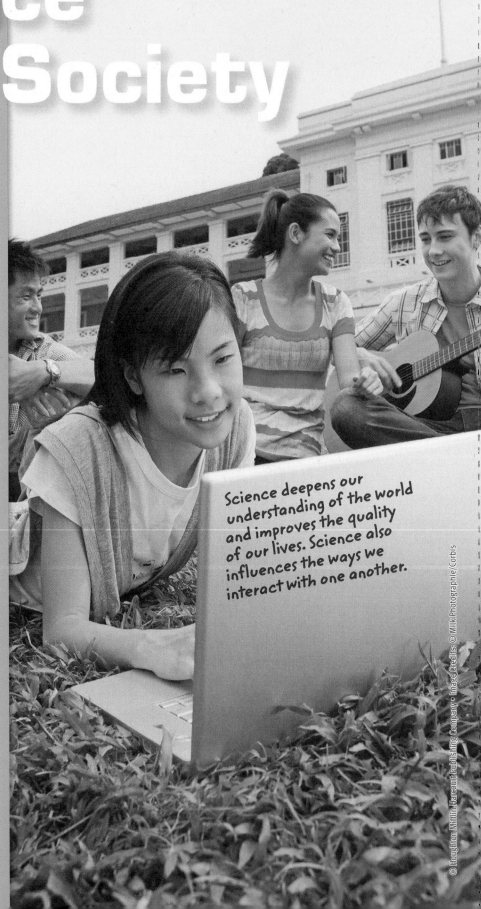

Lesson 4

Science and Society

ESSENTIAL QUESTION

How does science affect our lives?

By the end of this lesson, you should be able to describe the impact that science has had on society and the role of scientists throughout history and today.

Science deepens our understanding of the world and improves the quality of our lives. Science also influences the ways we interact with one another.

Engage Your Brain

1 Predict Check T or F to show whether you think each statement is true or false.

T   F

☐ ☐ Science has very few career opportunities and does not impact our lives.

☐ ☐ Good scientists are creative, logical thinkers and keen observers.

☐ ☐ Only scientists are capable of scientific thinking.

2 Identify List the first five things you did this morning after you woke up. Put a check mark next to any of these things that were made possible by the work of scientists.

_____

_____

_____

_____

_____

Active Reading

3 Derive Many English words have their roots in other languages. Use the Latin word below to make an educated guess about the meaning of the word *scientific*.

Latin word	Meaning
scientia	knowledge

Example sentence
After years of <u>scientific</u> experimentation and observation, the researcher reported a major discovery.

scientific:

_____

_____

Vocabulary

4 Identify As you read, place a question mark next to any words you don't understand. When you finish reading the lesson, go back and review the text that you marked. If the information is still confusing, consult a classmate or a teacher.

A Mighty Impact!

What does science affect?

For centuries, people have been asking questions and seeking answers. Even before there were people known as scientists, people engaged in scientific exploration. Science has had a great impact on all of us. Most likely, you can think of ways science affects your life already. You may be surprised to discover how large the influence of science really is.

The Way We Think

How do you see yourself? People used to think that Earth was the center of the universe. They thought the objects in the sky moved around them. They thought the sky existed only for them to look at. These beliefs made people feel very special.

We now know Earth is just one planet in one solar system. Earth orbits the sun and rotates once each day. When people realized this, they had to rethink their place in the universe. They had to rethink just how special they believed themselves to be. Scientific findings affect how we see ourselves.

© Houghton Mifflin Harcourt Publishing Company • Image Credits: (l) ©Hulton Archive/Getty Images; (r) ©Bob Krist/Corbis

Space science, 100 BCE

Space science, Today

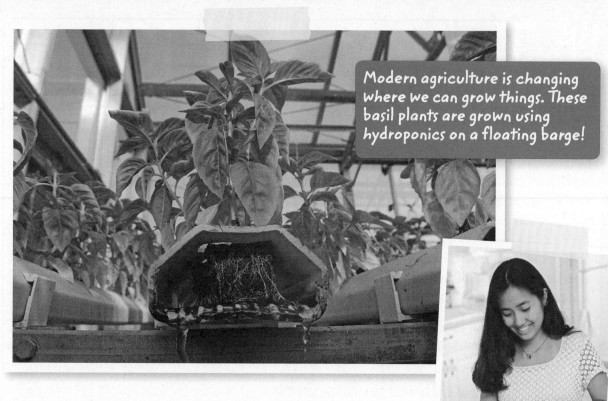

Modern agriculture is changing where we can grow things. These basil plants are grown using hydroponics on a floating barge!

The Way We Live Our Lives

Our daily activities have been affected by advances in science, too. In industrialized countries, many people enjoy clean water and sanitary living conditions. Scientists frequently find new ways for us to conserve and protect resources. Medicines have eliminated many health concerns. Cars, trains, and airplanes take us where we want to go. Weather forecasts tell us what to expect, and then we can dress appropriately. Satellites and cables allow us to communicate with others from all over the world. Most of these things were not even imaginable just 100 years ago.

Society became more complex with the beginning of farming. People joined together to grow crops for the benefit of all. World population has been able to grow so large today because of advances in farming. We can now grow crops in soil once thought to be infertile. Thanks to science, we can even grow plants with no soil at all! Hydroponics (HY•druh•pahn•iks), or growing plants without soil, may one day allow us to live in outer space.

---

7 Compare When your grandparents were growing up, they ate mostly foods grown or produced near them. Describe how the food you eat is different from the food your grandparents ate as a result of science's impact on agriculture and transportation.

_____

_____

_____

_____

It Takes All Kinds

Who contributes to science?

Myra Logan was the first female to perform open-heart surgery. She also played piano and contributed to the civil rights movement. Leonardo da Vinci was a great artist. He also drew designs for flying machines and studied human anatomy. Logan and da Vinci are just two of the many people who have contributed to science. People who contribute to science come from all backgrounds, fields of interest, and skill groups. So who contributes to science?

> **Active Reading** **8 Identify** As you read, underline some characteristics of people who do scientific research.

Those Who Do Scientific Research

Scientists are curious, creative, and enjoy solving problems. Scientists do research to answer questions and to investigate and challenge prevailing ideas. Some scientists work in life science, like immunologist César Milstein, who researches viruses like AIDS. Physicist Chien-Shiung Wu, a physical scientist, spent time in laboratories with radioactive elements. Mary Leakey, an archaeologist and Earth scientist, unearthed ape fossils in the field.

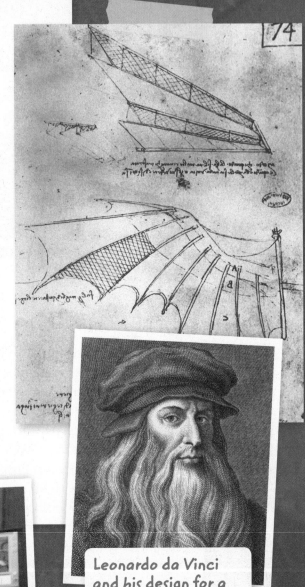

Leonardo da Vinci and his design for a flying machine

Klaus Radermacher uses robots and computers to make custom prosthetics. Prosthetics are artificial body parts that can replace missing, damaged, or diseased parts.

Visualize It!

9 Predict What problem might Radermacher have been trying to solve when he began his research?

_____

_____

_____

_____

People in Many Fields

The number of men and women who get paid to do scientific research is not very high. However, the opportunities open to those who are willing to learn and think like a scientist in other fields are almost limitless.

Many occupations use science. Medical and dental technicians help doctors and dentists keep people in good health. Architects use the laws of physics to design stable homes and offices. People who dye and style hair use chemistry when mixing hair dye and relaxing solutions. In the growing field of forensics, police officers use science to help them solve crimes. Auto engineers use physics to design aerodynamic cars.

Forensic technician

Auto engineers design vehicles.

10 Infer What might motivate someone to study forensics?

_____
_____
_____
_____
_____

11 Describe Fill in the second column with a description of how a person might use science in each of the careers. Fill in the last row of the table with a career you might like to have.

Career	Science applications
Firefighter	
Pharmacist	
Chef	

Anyone Who Asks Scientific Questions and Seeks Answers

Active Reading

12 Identify As you read, underline questions that science can help you answer.

An important point to remember is that anyone can think and act like a scientist and do science. Have you wondered why certain plants always flower at about the same time of year? Have you wondered what the center of Earth is like? Have you wondered why sugar dissolves faster in hot liquids than in cold ones? If you have asked questions and thought about finding the answers, you have acted like a scientist.

Do not be embarrassed to ask impossible questions. A lot of what we take for granted today was once thought impossible. You may even discover that you are asking the same questions many scientists still ask.

Inquiry

13 Relate Questions about the world can pop into your mind at any time. Write down something you've thought about recently as you've gone about your usual activities. Then write how you might investigate it.

_____

_____

_____

_____

_____

_____

Think Outside the Book

14 State What is your daring dream? Write a scientific question you would like to answer, regardless of how impossible it might seem to do.

Let the Games Begin

Robotics tournaments, model car races, and science fairs offer opportunities for you to explore and share your interest in science with others. You may even win a prize doing it!

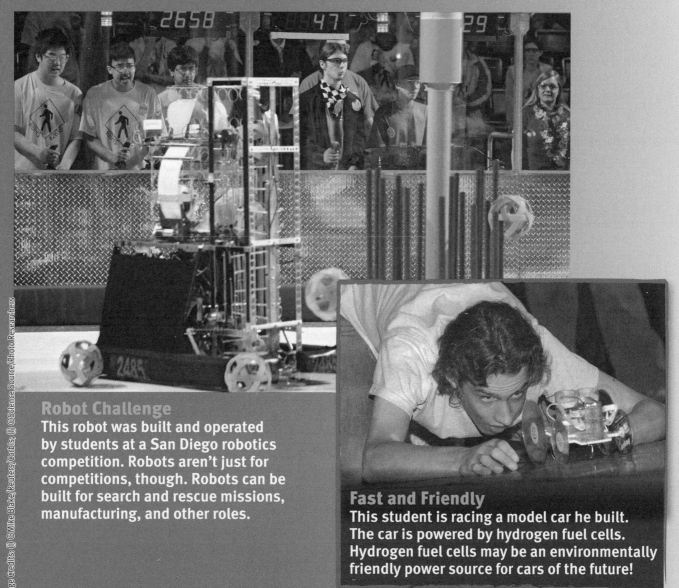

Robot Challenge
This robot was built and operated by students at a San Diego robotics competition. Robots aren't just for competitions, though. Robots can be built for search and rescue missions, manufacturing, and other roles.

Fast and Friendly
This student is racing a model car he built. The car is powered by hydrogen fuel cells. Hydrogen fuel cells may be an environmentally friendly power source for cars of the future!

Extend

Inquiry

15 Select Which would you be most interested in entering: a science fair, a robotics competition, or a model car race? Why?

16 Identify Use the Internet to find a science competition in your area. Consider visiting it!

17 Plan Make a poster, draw a model, or write a paragraph explaining an idea you have for a science competition.

Visual Summary

To complete this summary, check the box that indicates true or false. Then use the key below to check your answers. You can use this page to review the main concepts of the lesson.

Science and Society

Impact of Science

The work of scientists has changed the way we live and think about the world.

	T	F	
18	☐	☐	As science has advanced, technology has advanced.
19	☐	☐	Agriculture and medicine are affected by science.

Who Does Science

Scientists are curious about the world and enjoy exploring it. They may work in laboratories, in the field, or in other locations.

	T	F	
20	☐	☐	Only people who work in science use scientific thinking skills.
21	☐	☐	People from all backgrounds, interests, and cultures can contribute to science.

Answers: 18 T; 19 T; 20 F; 21 T

22 **Predict** Identify two changes in your world that might occur if funding for scientific research were cut drastically.

Lesson Review

Vocabulary

Fill in the blanks with the term or phrase that best completes the following sentences.

1 A(n) _____ may work in a lab or in the field and conducts research to discover new things.

2 The impact of science on _____ includes improvements in medicine, new technology, and more diverse food sources.

Key Concepts

3 Apply Identify two areas of science or technology that make your life easier, safer, or otherwise better than your grandparents' lives were.

_____

_____

_____

_____

_____

4 List Name three characteristics of scientists that are important to their work but are also found in nonscientists.

_____

_____

Critical Thinking

5 Devise Imagine that one tree outside your school looks unhealthy, although all the other trees seem healthy and strong. Describe how you could apply scientific thinking to the situation.

_____

_____

_____

_____

_____

Use this table to answer the following questions.

Scientists and Their Contributions		
When	**Who**	**What**
1660s	Robert Hooke	Identified and coined the word *cells* using early microscopes
Late 1700s	Antoine Lavoisier	Identified oxygen and oxygen's role in respiration and combustion
Early 1900s	Marie Curie	Experimented with radioactivity and identified new chemical elements
Early 1980s	Luis Alvarez	Used geological evidence to show that a meteor struck Earth and proposed that this led to the extinction of dinosaurs

6 Categorize The main branches of science are life science, physical science, and Earth and space science. Identify a branch of science that was affected by each of these scientists.

_____

_____

7 Justify Why do you think the work of scientists cannot be pinned down to a single year?

_____

_____

_____

8 Debate Do you think the contributions of these scientists are still valuable, even though some were made hundreds of years ago? Explain your answer.

_____

_____

_____

_____

My Notes

Unit 1 〔Big Idea〕 Scientists use careful observations and clear reasoning to understand processes and patterns in nature.

Lesson 1
ESSENTIAL QUESTION
What are the characteristics of science?

Distinguish what characterizes science and scientific explanations, and differentiate between science and pseudoscience.

Lesson 3
ESSENTIAL QUESTION
What are the types of scientific knowledge?

Differentiate the methods that scientists use to gain empirical evidence in a variety of scientific fields and explain how this leads to scientific change.

Lesson 2
ESSENTIAL QUESTION
How do scientists discover things?

Summarize the processes and characteristics of different kinds of scientific investigations.

Lesson 4
ESSENTIAL QUESTION
How does science affect our lives?

Describe the impact that science has had on society and the role of scientists throughout history and today.

Connect ESSENTIAL QUESTIONS
Lessons 2 and 3

1 Synthesize In what ways might the type of investigations conducted by physicists and chemists differ from the type of investigations conducted by biologists and geologists?

_____

_____

_____

_____

_____

_____

Think Outside the Book

2 Synthesize Choose one of these activities to help synthesize what you have learned in this unit.

☐ Using what you learned in lessons 1, 2, and 3, draw a flow chart to show how an idea can go from a hypothesis to a theory. In the steps, show how a theory results from many investigations. Include loops for revising ideas.

☐ Using what you learned in lessons 1, 2, and 4, explain the importance of science in society by writing a script for a debate between a scientist and a person selling a fraudulent product for reversing old age. Have the debaters present examples of empirical evidence and examples of pseudoscientific evidence.

Name _____

Vocabulary

Fill in each blank with the term that best completes the following sentences.

1 A(n) _____ is an organized procedure to study something under controlled conditions.

2 A scientific _____ is a well-supported and widely accepted explanation of a natural occurrence.

3 Scientists collect and record _____.

4 The collective body of observations of a natural phenomenon on which scientific explanations are based is called _____.

5 A(n) _____ is deliberately changed in a scientific study.

Key Concepts

Read each question below, and circle the best answer.

6 The graph shows the number of a school's male and female athletes.

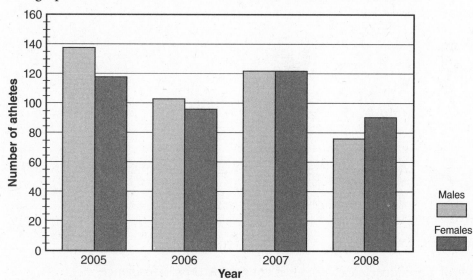

How can the data help the principal increase student participation in athletics?

A She can identify from the data why students like participating in sports.

B She can see why there is a decrease in participation between 2005 and 2006.

C She can tell why there were equal numbers of male and female athletes in 2007.

D Participation data from the previous year can help her set goals for next year.

7 Laboratory experiments allow scientists to make precise observations. Which one of the following is not a laboratory experiment?

A counting the population of a country

B comparing the color of mold in three different Petri dishes

C measuring how much three plants grow with different amounts of light

D making observations about the impact of different kinds of fertilizer on seedlings growing near the windows in the lab

8 What is the description of a specific relationship under given conditions in the natural world known as?

A a tenet of science

B a scientific law

C a theory

D a hypothesis

9 See the drawing of the astrological zodiac signs.

Aquarius   Pisces   Aries   Taurus

Gemini   Cancer   Leo   Virgo

Libra   Scorpio   Sagittarius   Capricorn

Astrology is an example of a pseudoscience. Why is it considered a pseudoscience, unlike astronomy, which is a science?

A because it is based on the scientific method

B because it is not based on the scientific method

C because it can be easily replicated by other scientists

D because it was a much earlier science

10 Which of the following is not a characteristic of a good scientific investigation?

A It can be replicated.

B It is controlled.

C It has a large sample size.

D It has a very small sample size, making it easier for anyone to replicate it.

11 Clara tests a hypothesis that the heavier of two materials will insulate cold drinks better than the lighter material. She adds equal volumes of the same cold drink to two different cup types. One cup type is made of a lightweight plastic foam. The other cup type is a heavier, ceramic material. Her sample size is five cups of each material. She records the average of her results in a chart.

Material	Time for liquid to warm to room temperature (hours)
plastic foam	3.25
ceramic	2.50

How are these experimental results valuable to Clara?

A The results explain why the materials perform differently.

B The results do not support her hypothesis so she should form a new one.

C Clara can use a different heavier material to see if she obtains different results.

D The results can be communicated with others through newspapers, magazines, and the Internet to increase the validity of her results.

12 After many investigations, Dr. Grossman, a geologist, developed an idea about why certain rocks are found in the Rocky Mountains of North America. Many other geologists accept Dr. Grossman's findings and ideas about why these rock types are present in the Rocky Mountains. What has Dr. Grossman developed?

A a law

B a theory

C a set of facts

D a hypothesis

13 Deandra designs an experiment to test how far a rubber band stretches when objects of different mass are suspended from it. She records her data in a chart.

Mass (g)	Stretch (cm)	Mass (g)	Stretch (cm)
10	1	40	4
20	2	50	4.8
30	3	60	5.5

Which variable is independent?

A Band type   **C** Time

B Stretch   **D** Mass

Critical Thinking

Answer the following questions in the space provided.

14 Using an example, explain the difference between a hypothesis and a prediction.

_____

_____

_____

_____

_____

15 Evaluate the strengths and limits of science in terms of scope.

_____

_____

_____

_____

Connect ESSENTIAL QUESTIONS
Lessons 1 and 4

Answer the following question in the space provided.

16 Explain how the work of scientists benefits our society as a whole.

_____

_____

_____

_____

Measurement and Data

The Hubble Space Telescope has provided astronomical data that has greatly expanded our view of the universe.

Big Idea

Scientists use tools to collect, organize, and analyze data while conducting investigations.

What do you think?

Scientists need to have accurate instruments in order to collect useful data. What problems do you think scientists encounter when using instruments to collect data?

A microscope helps collect data about very small objects.

Unit 2
Measurement and Data

CITIZEN SCIENCE

Earth Watch

In order to study the environment, scientists need to collect large amounts of data about plants and animals in the wild. To help collect data, many scientists enlist the help of volunteers through programs like Earthwatch. This nonprofit organization supports many scientific expeditions around the world that allow anyone to participate, even teenage students.

Volunteers work closely with Earthwatch scientists to collect data in the field.

① Think About It

A Search through the expeditions on the Earthwatch web page, and pick one that you would like to participate in. Where is the expedition?

_____

_____

B What is the goal of the expedition?

_____

_____

② Ask a Question

A If you were to go on the Earthwatch expedition you chose, where do you think you would go to collect the data?

_____

_____

_____

B What instruments do you think you would use to collect the data?

_____

_____

_____

C How would you organize the data you collect to make it useful for a scientific study?

_____

_____

_____

③ Apply Your Knowledge

A As a class, select and do one of the lesson plans available on the Earthwatch web page. How does the lesson relate to an actual Earthwatch expedition?

_____

_____

_____

B Think about how to apply the lesson to a scientific study of a location near you. List the steps you would take to carry out the study.

_____

_____

_____

Students count invertebrates collected in their net. The number and types of invertebrates in a sample are good indicators of water quality.

Take It Home

What kind of local scientific organizations might have projects that use volunteers? Contact one of these organizations to find out how you and your class can get involved in a project. See *ScienceSaurus*® for more information about wildlife conservation.

Representing Data

ESSENTIAL QUESTION

How do scientists show the results of investigations?

By the end of this lesson, you should be able to use tables, graphs, and models to display and analyze scientific data.

This clay tablet, which dates back to 2400 BCE, displays accounting records written in cuneiform script. Cuneiform is a picture-writing system that uses symbols. Today the tablet is located in the Louvre, in Paris, France.

✋ Lesson Labs

Quick Labs
- Heart Rate and Exercise
- Modeling Heights of Students

Field Lab
- Investigate Water Usage

🧠 Engage Your Brain

1 Evaluate Check T or F to show whether you think each statement is true or false.

T   F

☐   ☐   A graph should always have a title describing what the graph is about.

☐   ☐   The factor that is manipulated in an experiment is usually plotted on the vertical axis of a graph.

☐   ☐   A model can be used to represent something that is too small to see with the naked eye.

2 Assemble Write a word or phrase beginning with each letter of the word MODEL that is an example or use of a model. Think of a model as anything that represents something else.

M_____

O_____

D_____

E_____

L_____

✏️ Active Reading

3 Apply Use context clues to write your own definition for the words *independent* and *dependent*.

Example sentence
After <u>independent</u> studies, the two scientists reached very different conclusions.

independent:

_____

_____

Example sentence
The cost of the service is <u>dependent</u> on its availability.

dependent:

_____

_____

Vocabulary Terms

- independent variable
- dependent variable
- model

4 Apply As you learn the definition of each vocabulary term in this lesson, create your own definition or sketch to help you remember the meaning of the term.

Modeling Data with Graphs

How do scientists make sense of data?

There are many different kinds of scientific investigations conducted in science, all of which involve the collection of data. *Data* are the facts, figures, and other evidence scientists gather when they conduct an investigation.

Scientists Organize the Data

Scientists use data tables to organize and record the data that they collect. By creating a data table, they can record their observations and measurements in an orderly way.

Data tables often have two columns. One column lists the **independent variable**. This is the variable that is deliberately manipulated in an investigation. The other column lists the **dependent variable**. This is the variable that changes as a result of the manipulation of the independent variable. When creating a data table, any units of measurement, such as seconds or degrees, should be included in the table's column headings and not in the individual cells.

The data table below shows the high temperatures for certain days and the number of cold drinks sold at a concession stand on those days.

Drink Sales

High temperature (°F)	Number of cold drinks sold
25	43
40	55
58	60
70	72
81	70

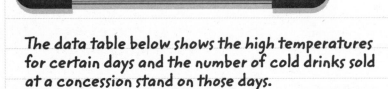 **Visualize It!**

5 Apply Name the independent variable and the dependent variable in the data table. Explain your answer.

_____

_____

_____

_____

Scientists Graph and Analyze the Data

Scientists often analyze data for patterns or trends by constructing graphs of the data. The type of graph they construct depends upon the data they collected and what they want to show.

A *scatter plot* is a graph with points plotted to show a possible relationship between two sets of data. A scatter plot has a horizontal *x*-axis and a vertical *y*-axis. The *x*-axis usually represents the independent variable in the data table. The *y*-axis usually represents the dependent variable.

To show the general relationship between the two variables in the graph, a "line of best fit" is often used. A line of best fit is a line that is drawn to "fit," or come close to, most of the data points.

The graphs below show steps used to construct a scatter plot of the drink sales data at the left.

**Active Reading**

6 Identify Which axis of a graph usually represents the independent variable?

_____

_____

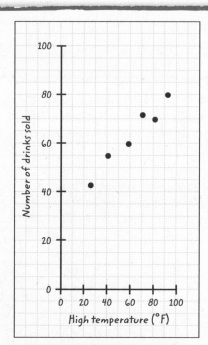

Visualize It!

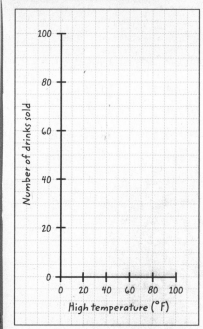

Step 1 Label the Axes Label each axis on a graph with the name of the variable that is represented. Each axis can have its own range and scale so that the data can be seen easily. The range is the difference between the greatest value and the least value of a variable. The scale is the size that is used for each box or grid mark on the graph.

Step 2 Plot the Data Points Plot the data from the table as data points on the graph.

7 Analyze Do you see a trend in these data? Explain.

_____

_____

_____

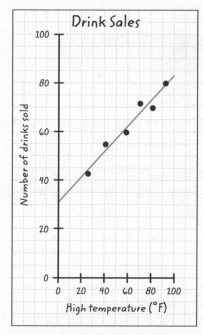

Step 3 Draw a Line of Best Fit Draw a line that comes close to most of the data points. The line shows the pattern described by the data. It also shows how the data differ from the pattern.

More Graphing!

What do graphs show?

Different types of graphs are used to show different types of information about data. On the previous pages, you read about scatter plots. Other graphs include bar graphs and circle graphs. A *bar graph* is used to display and compare data in a number of separate, or distinct, categories. Data about the number of inches it rained each month can be displayed in a bar graph. A *circle graph* is used when you are showing how each group of data relates to all of the data. Data about the number of boys and girls in your class can be displayed in a circle graph.

Active Reading **8 List** Name three different types of graphs.

_____

_____

Visualize It!

Dwayne has been training for several weeks for cross-country tryouts. To make the team, he must be able to run 1 mile in less than 8 minutes. The data at the right shows the amount of time in minutes that it took Dwayne to run a mile each week.

Week 1	11.95 min
Week 2	11.25 min
Week 3	11.40 min
Week 4	10.10 min
Week 5	9.25 min
Week 6	8.60 min

9 Complete Use the empty table below to organize Dwayne's running data. Include a title for the table, the column heads, and all of the data.

Title

Headings

Data

Use the steps below to construct a graph of Dwayne's running data. The horizontal and vertical axes have been drawn for you.

Step 1
Label each axis with the name of the variable that is represented.

Step 2
Find the range for each axis. For the running data, the range of the independent variable is 6 weeks. Thus, the *x*-axis must cover at least 6 weeks.

Step 3
Decide the scale for each axis. For the running data, use a scale of 1 week for each grid mark on the *x*-axis.

Step 4
Graph the points by putting a dot on the graph for each pair of data in the data table.

Step 5
Title the graph. A good title tells a reader what the graph is all about.

10 Graph Use the steps at the left to construct a scatter plot of the running data given.

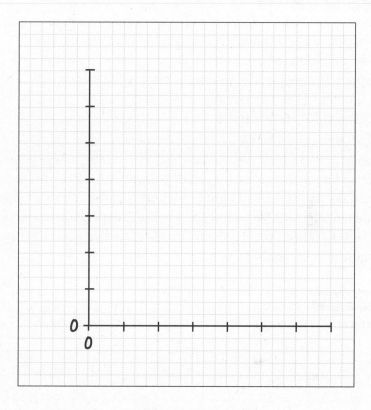

11 Assess Explain how you could use the graph to predict whether Dwayne will run 1 mile in less than 8 minutes.

_____

_____

_____

_____

_____

_____

_____

_____

_____

_____

Throw Me a Curve!

What kinds of patterns can be shown using graphs?

When you graph data, you can identify what the pattern, or *trend*, of the data is. A trend shows the relationship between the two variables studied in the experiment. Graphs make it easy to tell if something is increasing, decreasing, or staying the same.

Linear Relationships

A line can sometimes be used to show the trend of data on a graph. A graph in which the relationship between the independent variable and dependent variable can be shown with a straight line is called a *linear graph*. A straight line shows that the rate of change of the dependent variable with respect to the independent variable is constant. In other words, *y* always increases or decreases by the same value in relation to *x*.

Visualize It!

12 Interpret Use the graph to determine the mass of 7 cm³ of water.

_____

_____

_____

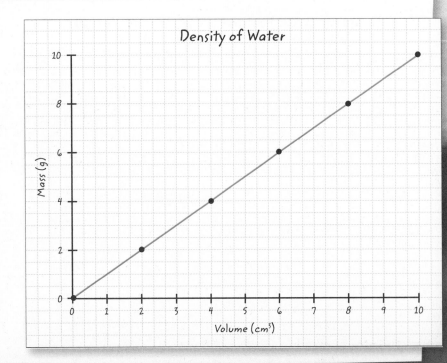

Density of Water

Mass (g) vs. Volume (cm³)

The density of water is an example of a linear relationship.

Nonlinear Relationships

Sometimes, the graph of the relationship between the independent variable and dependent variable studied is not a straight line but a smooth curve. Any graph in which the relationship between the variables cannot be shown with a straight line is called a *nonlinear graph*.

Graphs allow scientists to determine the relationship between variables. In a direct relationship, the value of one variable increases as the value of the other variable increases. In contrast, an inverse relationship is one in which the value of one variable decreases as the other increases. The graph of a direct relationship is an upward sloping line. The graph of an inverse relationship is a downward sloping line.

Active Reading **13 Apply** Describe the difference between linear and nonlinear relationships on a graph.

_____

_____

_____

_____

_____

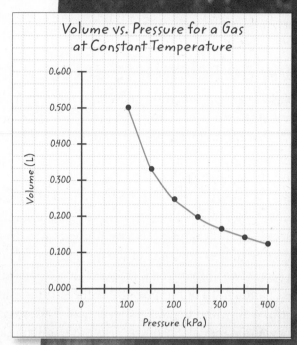

Both of these graphs show nonlinear relationships.

Visualize It!

14 Infer Describe the relationship shown in the graph of Suzi's Surf Shop Sales. Then use the graph to find the approximate sales of the surf shop in 2007.

_____

_____

_____

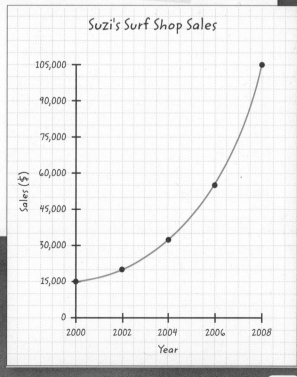

The Perfect Model

How do scientists select a model?

A **model** is a representation of an object or a process that allows scientists to study something in greater detail. The best models are those that most closely resemble the system, process, or object they represent.

By the Kind of Information It Shows

Scientists use many different kinds of physical and mathematical models. A physical model is something that is drawn or built. Maps and globes are some of the oldest types of physical models. These are two-dimensional models. Two-dimensional models have length and width but not height. A three-dimensional model has length, width, and height. A diorama of a classroom is a three-dimensional model. Scientists also use mathematical models to represent how the natural world functions. With mathematical models, you can predict the results of changes in a system. A computer simulation is one type of mathematical model.

Active Reading

15 Apply As you read, underline some examples of models.

Visualize It!

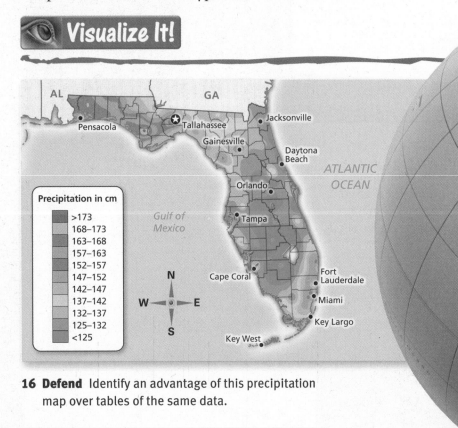

16 Defend Identify an advantage of this precipitation map over tables of the same data.

_____

_____

_____

By How It Can Be Used

A two-dimensional floor plan of a building would give you a good idea of the building's layout. You could add furniture to the floor plan to see how you would use the space, but you would not be able to determine anything about the height of the furniture in the room. A three-dimensional model would allow you to see the walls and windows, and get a better feeling for how objects fit in the room. A computerized simulation of the building could enable you to see what it would be like to move through the building.

Similar models could be made of a molecule such as DNA. A two-dimensional drawing of the molecule would show the atoms that make up the molecule and how those atoms are arranged. A three-dimensional model would enable you to study the molecule from different angles. A simulation would enable you to see how the molecule functions. Today, many processes in science can be modeled in great detail. The information needed from the model determines the type of model that is used.

Think Outside the Book Inquiry

19 Criticize Many advertisements feature models. Find an example of a nonhuman model in a magazine. Write a critique of the model. Consider the following questions: "How useful is the model? What has been left out or exaggerated? How could the model be improved?"

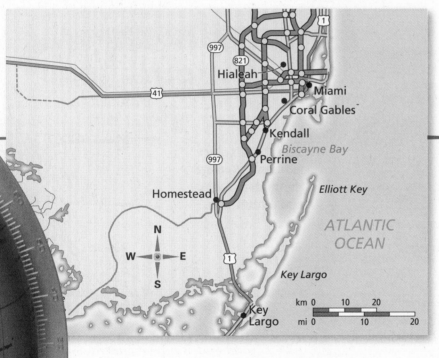

18 Predict Scale is the relationship between the dimensions of a model and the dimensions of the real object. How could the scale on this map be helpful when taking a trip?

_____

_____

_____

_____

_____

Inquiry

17 Infer What are two advantages of the globe over the precipitation map of Florida for understanding characteristics of Florida? What are two advantages of the map over the globe?

_____

_____

_____

Visual Summary

To complete this summary, circle the correct word. Then use the key below to check your answers. You can use this page to review the main concepts of the lesson.

A graph in which the relationship between the independent and dependent variable can be shown with a straight line is a linear graph.

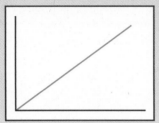

20 The dependent / independent variable is usually found on the x-axis of a graph.

A graph in which the relationship between the variables cannot be shown with a straight line is called a nonlinear graph.

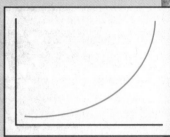

21 If the rate of change of the dependent variable with respect to the independent variable is not constant, then the relationship between the variables is linear / nonlinear.

Representing Data

A scientific model is a representation of an object or system.

22 A globe is an example of a mathematical / physical model.

23 An equation is an example of a mathematical / physical model.

Scientists select models based on their advantages and limitations.

24 A road map is a two-dimensional / three-dimensional model.

25 Conclude You and a friend each decide to build the same model airplane. After the airplanes are built, you decide to conduct an investigation to determine which airplane can glide through the air the longest. Outline a plan to conduct your investigation.

Lesson Review

Vocabulary

Fill in the blank with the term that best completes the following sentences.

1 The _____ variable in an investigation is the variable that is deliberately manipulated.

2 The _____ variable in an investigation is the variable that changes in response to changes in the investigation.

3 A(n) _____ can be a physical or mathematical representation of an object or a process.

Key Concepts

4 Identify Alfonso is conducting an experiment to determine whether temperature affects how fast earthworms move. What are the independent and dependent variables in his experiment?

_____

_____

_____

_____

5 Apply When creating a graph, why is an appropriate title for a graph important?

_____

_____

_____

6 Provide Give an example of a model used in science that is larger than the real object and an example of a model that is smaller than the real object.

_____

_____

_____

Critical Thinking

Use this graph to answer the following questions.

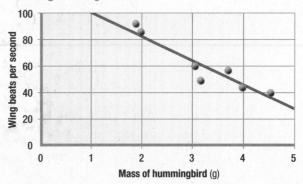

Hummingbird Wing Beats

7 Interpret In this graph, what are the independent and dependent variables?

_____

_____

_____

_____

8 Describe Explain a trend or pattern you observe in the graph.

_____

_____

_____

_____

_____

_____

9 Analyze Both a globe and a flat world map can model features of Earth. Give an example of when you would use each of these models.

_____

_____

_____

_____

_____

_____

_____

My Notes

Making Conclusions from Evidence

In scientific investigations, you will be asked to collect data and summarize your findings. Sometimes, a set of data can be interpreted in more than one way and lead to more than one conclusion. A reliable investigation will allow you to make conclusions that are supported by the data you have collected, and that reflect the findings of other scientists.

Tutorial

Take these steps as you analyze findings and evaluate a conclusion made from the findings.

Flu Prevention Breakthrough

A medical study has shown that a new drug, Compound Z, protected children from the flu. The results of the study that was conducted last year showed that only 5% of students who were taking Compound Z were affected by the flu. During the same period of time, 20% of the general population was affected by the flu.

Researchers do not know exactly how Compound Z protects children from the flu.

1 What conclusion is made by the study? Identify the conclusion or interpretation of the data that is being made in the study.

2 What evidence or data is given and does the data support the conclusion? Identify all the observations and findings that are presented to support the conclusion. Decide whether the findings support the conclusion. Look for information and data in other studies that replicate the experiments and verify the conclusion.

3 Should other data be considered before accepting the conclusion as true? There may be more than one way to interpret findings of scientific work, and important questions left unanswered. When this happens, plan to make observations, look for more information, or do further experiments that could eliminate one explanation as a possibility.

Other data should be considered before the conclusion above can be supported. For example, data should be gathered to determine the percentage of children who were not taking Compound Z and got the flu. And, within the 20% of the general population who got the flu, what percentage were children?

You Try It!

Climate change is one of the most debated issues in modern science.

In the past 100 years, Earth's average global temperature has risen more than 0.74 °C. In 2008, the cold La Niña current in the Pacific caused the average global temperature to drop, but the global average was still warmer than any year from 1880 to 1996. The concentration of the greenhouse gas carbon dioxide (CO_2), rose from by about 76 parts per million from 1958 to 2008. Many people interpret this to mean that human activity is causing global climate change. However, evidence from the geologic record shows that Earth's climate has experienced even larger climate changes in the past.

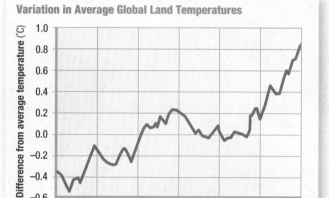

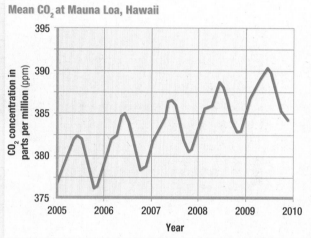

1 Gathering Data The graphs shown above are taken from a study on climate change. Identify trends or patterns that you observe in the graphs.

_____

_____

_____

_____

2 Making a Conclusion Draw a conclusion that is supported by the data you describe. Summarize your conclusion in a single paragraph.

_____

_____

_____

_____

_____

_____

3 Analyzing Data Which conclusions are supported by the data in the graphs? Which conclusions are not supported by the data?

_____

_____

_____

_____

4 Making Predictions What other data do you need to further support your conclusion?

_____

_____

_____

Take It Home

Find an article that makes a conclusion based on a scientific study. Evaluate the conclusion and determine whether the evidence given supports the conclusion. Bring the article to class and be prepared to discuss.

Scientific Tools & Measurement

ESSENTIAL QUESTION

What are the tools and units used in science?

By the end of this lesson, you should be able to describe the different tools and units of measurement used in scientific investigations.

An important part of a scientist's job is picking the right tool for a measurement. For this measurement, calipers are more accurate than a metric ruler.

© Houghton Mifflin Harcourt Publishing Company • Image Credits: (bg) ©Jim Zipp/Photo Researchers, Inc.

Lesson Labs

Quick Labs
- Investigate Making Measurements
- Investigating Density

Field Lab
- Use a Sextant to Make a Map

 Engage Your Brain

1 Predict Check T or F to show whether you think each statement is true or false.

T   F

☐ ☐ A lab journal or notebook is considered a scientific tool.

☐ ☐ Scientists worldwide use the same units of measurement.

☐ ☐ It is sometimes appropriate for scientists to estimate measurements.

☐ ☐ Precision describes how close a measured value comes to the true value of the measurement.

2 Infer Describe how the scientist might use this electron microscope for a scientific investigation.

_____

_____

_____

 Active Reading

3 Apply Use context clues to write your own definition for the term *standard*.

Example sentence
A scientist uses a <u>standard</u> unit of measurement to compare the lengths of different bacteria.

standard:

_____

_____

_____

Vocabulary Terms
- measurement
- scientific notation
- accuracy
- precision

4 Apply As you learn the definition of each vocabulary term in this lesson, create your own definition or sketch to help you remember the meaning of the term.

For Good Measure

What is measurement?

In science, the ability to describe an observation is an important skill. A description is a statement that reports what has been observed. Often, a scientist uses a measurement to describe an observation. A **measurement** is a description that includes a number and a unit.

Why do we use standard units of measurement?

Measurements were once based on parts of the body, such as arms or feet, but this method caused problems with accuracy. Body parts vary in size from one person to another, which made it difficult for two people to get the same measurement for an object.

Over time, societies realized that they needed to make units of measurement standard. Using standard units makes it possible for a person in one place to work with the same quantity as someone many kilometers away. Standard units also allow scientists to repeat one another's experiments. Experiments must be repeatable to determine if the results are valid.

ggs
dash of vanilla
pinch of salt
3 cups all-purpo
1 teaspoon bak

Whether you are in the kitchen or the laboratory, it is difficult to work with nonstandard units of measurement.

5 Compare What is the difference between a description and a measurement?

_____

_____

_____

_____

Visualize It!

6 List Which units of measurement in this recipe are not standard?

_____

_____

_____

What is the International System of Units?

In the late 1700s, the French government requested that the French Academy of Sciences improve their own existing official measurement system. The academy responded by creating the original metric system. The system has undergone several changes over the years. The modern metric system is now called the International System of Units (SI). The SI units are the language for all scientific measurement. There are seven base SI units. They are used to express the following quantities: length, mass, time, temperature, amount of substance, electric current, and light intensity. Each SI unit is represented by a symbol. Each quantity can also be measured with a specific tool or set of tools.

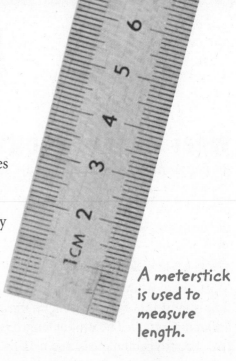

A meterstick is used to measure length.

A spring scale is used to measure weight.

A brass weight may be used when measuring the mass of an object.

A volumetric flask can be used to measure liquid volume.

What are the advantages of using the SI?

There are many advantages of using the SI rather than other systems of measurement. One advantage is that SI measurements provide a common international language for scientists. Scientists worldwide can share and compare their observations and results. A second advantage is that changing from one unit to another is easier in SI than in other systems. Almost all SI units are based on the number 10. You can convert from one unit to another by multiplying or dividing by a multiple of 10. Conversions in non-SI systems are more complicated, as when converting between inches, feet, and yards.

Think Outside the Book

7 Apply Do ONE of the following: Write a blog entry from the viewpoint of a member of the 1790 French National Assembly on the need for a standard measurement system. OR Research the history of a common measurement, such as the yard, and write a report explaining how it came into use.

Made to Measure

What are the SI units?

Earlier we mentioned that there are seven base SI units. There are also units that are derived, or formed from, these base units. Let's take a look at the units you will use in the lab.

SI Base Units

Most often, you will use the base units for these four quantities in the lab: *length*, *mass*, *time*, and *temperature*. The unit of length is the *meter* (m). Length can be measured using a meterstick, ruler, or measuring tape. The *kilogram* (kg) is the SI unit for mass. Mass is measured using a balance. The SI unit for time is the *second* (s). Time can be measured using a stopwatch. The *kelvin* (K) is the SI unit used for temperature. Temperature is measured using a thermometer.

Derived Units

The unit for volume is an example of a derived unit because it is calculated from a base unit, length. Volume is the amount of space that something occupies. The SI unit for volume is the cubic meter (m^3), but liquid volume is often expressed in *liters* (L), which is not an SI unit. One liter is equal to one cubic decimeter. One *milliliter* (mL) is equal to one cubic centimeter (cm^3). Liquid volume can be measured using graduated cylinders and beakers.

The SI unit for weight is the *newton* (N). Weight is a measurement of the gravitational force on an object. It depends on the object's mass. Weight is measured using a spring scale. Measurements such as density must be calculated. Density is the amount of matter in a given volume. Density is calculated by dividing an object's mass by its volume.

Visualize It!

8 Label Using the table, identify the measurement associated with each tool in the image below.

Measurement	Base unit	Symbol
length	meter	m
mass	kilogram	kg
time	second	s
temperature	kelvin	K

Measurement	Derived unit	Symbol
volume	cubic decimeter (liter)	dm³ or L
weight	newton	N
density	grams per cubic centimeter (milliliter)	g/cm³ or g/mL

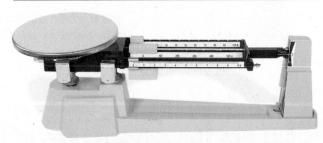

triple beam balance

A _____

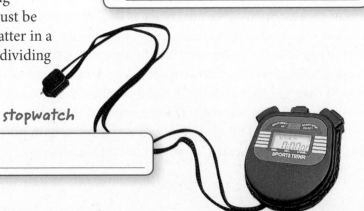

stopwatch

B _____

How can we make very large or small measurements easy to work with?

Some scientific numbers are much smaller or much larger than those we use in everyday life. Measurements that are very big or very small can be confusing to work with. There are two ways that scientists can make working with very large or very small numbers easier: using prefixes and scientific notation.

9 Identify As you read, underline the prefix that means "1/1,000."

We Can Use Prefixes

A prefix is one or more letters or syllables added to the beginning of a word to change its meaning. In the SI, a prefix is used to express an SI unit that is larger or smaller than a base unit. For example, *kilo-* means 1,000 times, so a kilometer is 1,000 meters. The prefix *milli-* indicates 1/1,000 times, so a millimeter is 1/1,000 of a meter. The prefix used depends on the size of the object being measured. The table below shows common SI prefixes.

SI Prefixes		
Prefix	**Symbol**	**Factor**
kilo–	k	1,000
hecto–	h	100
deca–	da	10
		1
deci–	d	0.1
centi–	c	0.01
milli–	m	0.001
micro–	μ	0.000001

10 Apply The table below shows how prefixes can be used with the unit for length. Complete the table by filling in the blanks.

Prefix with the base unit meter	Symbol	Number of meters
kilometer	km	
	hm	100
decameter	dam	
millimeter		0.001

We Can Use Scientific Notation

Scientific notation is a short way of representing very large numbers or very small numbers. Numbers in scientific notation are written in the form $a \times 10^b$. For example, the speed of light in standard notation is 300,000,000 m/s. It is 3×10^8 m/s in scientific notation.

The value for a is usually a number between 1 and 10. To find a, first locate the decimal point. For 300,000,000 m/s, the decimal point is at the right of the last 0. Then move the decimal point to the left until it is to the right of the number 3. The exponent b tells how many places the decimal is moved. When the decimal moves to the left, b is a positive number. For numbers less than 0, the decimal moves to the right, so b is a negative number.

To convert from scientific notation to standard notation, look at the exponent. If the exponent is positive, move the decimal point b places to the right. If the exponent is negative, move the decimal point b places to the left. For the speed of light, 3×10^8 m/s, the exponent is 8, and is positive, so move the decimal eight places to the right to write it as 300,000,000 m/s again.

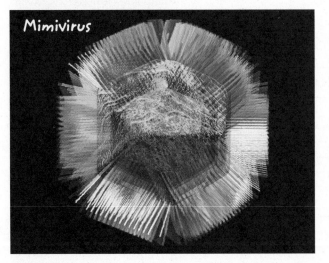

Mimivirus

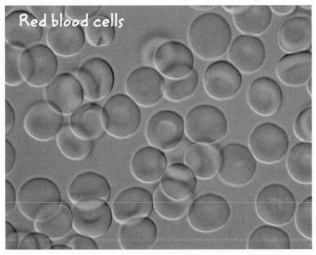

Red blood cells

Sample Problem

The diameter of this mimivirus is 0.000000750 m. Write this number in scientific notation.

Use the form $a \times 10^b$. The first nonzero number(s) given = a. The number of decimal places to move = b.

To get a, move the decimal 7 places to the right.

$$a = 7.5, b = -7$$

$$0.000000750 \text{ m} = 7.5 \times 10^{-7} \text{ m}$$

You Try It

11 Calculate The diameter of a human red blood cell is 0.000006 m. Write the diameter in scientific notation.

Why are accuracy and precision important?

A scientist wants to use tools that can provide a measurement very close to the actual value. **Accuracy** is a description of how close a measurement is to the true value of the quantity measured. The smaller the difference between the measurement and the true value, the more accurate the measurement is.

Precision is the exactness of a measurement. A precise measurement is repeatable and reliable. If a high-precision measurement is repeated, the number obtained will be the same or very nearly the same.

In a game of horseshoes, the most accurate and precise player wins. Accurate throws are close to the stake. Precise throws are close together.

Visualize It!

12 Illustrate Draw a fourth set of horseshoes that represents low accuracy and low precision.

Low accuracy, high precision

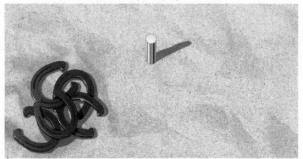

High accuracy, low precision

High accuracy, high precision

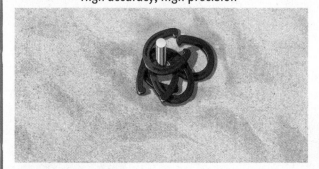

Low accuracy, low precision

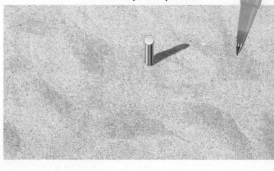

Why do scientists sometimes estimate measurements?

People estimate measurements doing everyday tasks such as making salsa or rearranging furniture. Scientists also make estimates of measurements. Scientists may use estimates to see if the data they collected are reasonable. Scientists may also use estimates to determine which tool is best suited for making the measurements they need.

Think Outside the Book   Inquiry

13 Apply Choose an everyday object, and design a method to measure that object that is both accurate and precise. What tool or tools would you use? Explain your answer.

Tools of the Trade

How are tools used in science?

A scientist needs tools to perform experiments. Hot plates can be used to increase the temperature of a substance. Test tubes are common containers for holding samples of materials. Test-tube racks hold test tubes upright. Pipettes can be used to transfer liquids. Lab journals or lab notebooks and pencils are tools that scientists use to record data and observations.

Scientists also need tools to make observations or measurements that cannot be detected by senses alone. A hand lens can be used to magnify small objects. For very small objects, compound light microscopes or electron microscopes can be used. Light microscopes use a series of lenses to magnify objects. Electron microscopes use tiny particles called electrons to produce clearer and more detailed images than light microscopes. Two types of electron microscopes are scanning electron microscopes and transmission electron microscopes.

Scientists also use digital cameras to record images of objects or environments. These images can be used later to discover details that they did not notice or remember.

Active Reading

14 Distinguish What is the difference between a compound light microscope and an electron microscope?

_____

_____

_____

_____

Visualize It!

15 Identify List the tools in this image that are necessary for performing an experiment.

_____

_____

_____

_____

_____

_____

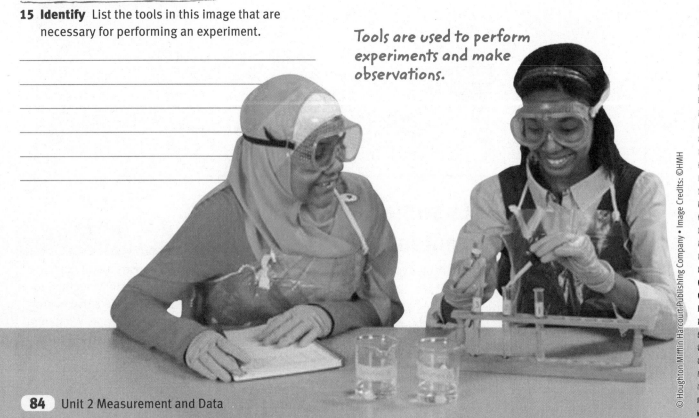

Tools are used to perform experiments and make observations.

How are computers and technology used by scientists?

The use of science for practical purposes is called technology. Scientists use technology to find information and solve problems. Technology also contributes to the progress of science. Calculators and computers are two types of technological devices. They allow scientists to make quick and accurate calculations. They can also analyze data by creating graphs and solving complex equations. Scientists use computers to make spreadsheets, create models, or run simulations. Computers also help scientists share data and ideas with one another and publish reports about their research.

Scientists may also use probeware, which is a measuring tool linked to a computer. Probeware can be used to obtain and display the values of a quantity such as temperature, oxygen concentration, or pH. Probeware also allows scientists to interpret and analyze data. It is often used in long-term projects such as environmental quality monitoring.

When new technology is developed, scientists often learn new information. For example, cells were not discovered until the light microscope was developed. Now electron microscopes can make images of individual atoms. Just as technology leads to new scientific discoveries, new scientific discoveries lead to the development of new technologies. Thanks to the discovery of semiconductors, you can put an entire computer in your lap. The first computers filled up large rooms!

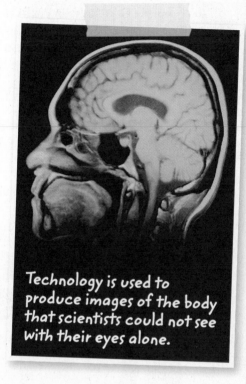

Technology is used to produce images of the body that scientists could not see with their eyes alone.

Magnetic resonance imaging

16 Hypothesize Magnetic resonance imaging (MRI) scanners use electromagnetic waves to generate images of the inside of a person's body. How might MRI technology be used to investigate how the brain works?

_____

_____

_____

_____

_____

_____

_____

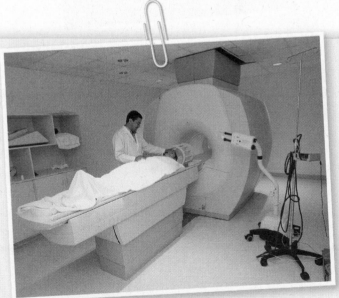

MRI scans allow the inside of a body to be seen in great detail.

Visual Summary

To complete this summary, circle the correct word or phrase. Then, use the key below to check your answers. You can use this page to review the main concepts of the lesson.

Scientific Tools & Measurement

The International System of Units (SI) is the standard system of measurement used in science.

17 The SI unit for mass is the kilogram / newton.

18 The SI unit for time is the hour / second.

Scientific tools are used to make observations, collect and analyze data, and share results.

19 A series of lenses is used to magnify small objects in a compound light microscope / scanning electron microscope.

20 A common container in the laboratory used for holding small samples of liquid is a hot plate / test tube.

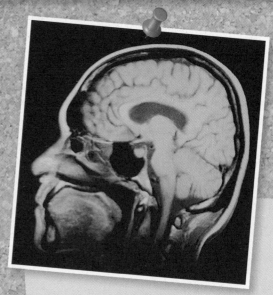

21 Computers may be used at every stage / only to calculate results of a scientific investigation.

22 A sensor that connects directly to a computer to collect data is called a calculator / probeware.

Technology is used to conduct research and to share ideas and results.

Answers: 17 kilogram; 18 second; 19 compound light microscope; 20 test tube; 21 at every stage; 22 probeware

23 Summarize Why are tools and technology important for scientific investigations?

Lesson Review

Vocabulary

Draw a line to connect the following terms to their definitions.

1 precision   **A** closeness to the true value

2 accuracy   **B** description with a unit

3 measurement   **C** way to write very large or small numbers

4 scientific notation   **D** the repeatability of a measurement

Key Concepts

5 Summarize Which of the following is not an advantage of using SI units?

A allows scientists to compare observations and results

B can compare measurements made years apart

C based on the number 5, which is easy to use in calculations

D uses prefixes to express measurements that are small or large

6 Calculate What is 0.003 in scientific notation?

A 10×10^3

B 3×10^{-3}

C 3×10^3

D 10×3^{-10}

7 Identify What is the SI unit for temperature?

A the kelvin

B degrees Celsius

C degrees Fahrenheit

D the newton

Critical Thinking

Use this photo to answer the following questions.

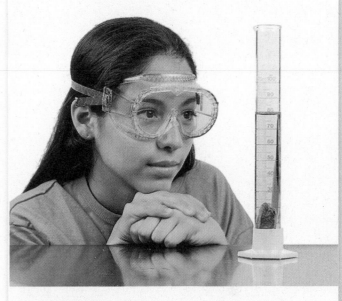

8 Conclude Name the type of measurement the student in the photo is making.

_____

9 Apply The prefix for the measurement the student is making is *milli–*. What does *milli–* mean?

_____

10 Evaluate The student measured the volume of water as 80.0 mL. She discovered that the actual volume was 80.1 mL. Is her measurement accurate? Explain.

_____

_____

_____

11 Compare How might the student's recorded data differ if she were simply describing the liquid instead of measuring it?

_____

_____

_____

My Notes

Engineering Design Process

Skills	Objectives
✓ Identify a need	• Identify a need for a bridge.
✓ Conduct research	• Analyze constraints that affect a bridge design.
✓ Brainstorm solutions	• Draw a detailed blueprint for a bridge.
✓ Select a solution	
Design a prototype	
Build a prototype	
Test and evaluate	
Redesign to improve	
✓ Communicate results	

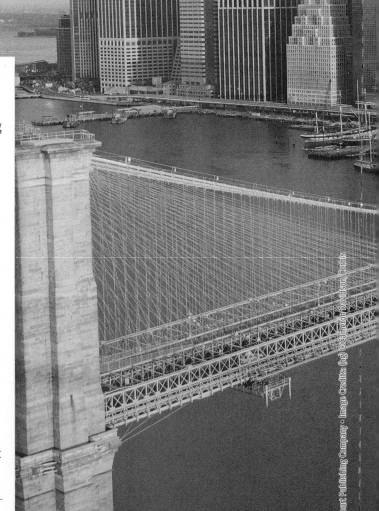

Designing a Bridge

Many steps are involved in planning and building a large engineering project such as a bridge. The first step in designing a bridge is to identify the constraints that affect the design. A constraint may be a physical or a financial factor that places limits on a design or project. Often, in order to work within the constraints, architects and engineers make trade-offs. Making a trade-off means giving up one thing in exchange for another. There are several questions that help determine which constraints affect the design of the bridge. How much money can be spent to build the bridge? How long and how tall does the bridge need to be? How much weight must it support? Once these questions are answered, engineers can begin making a plan.

1 Examine How might constraints and trade-offs affect the final design of a bridge?

_____

_____

_____

Making a Plan

Today, engineers and architects use computer programs to make a plan for a bridge. Because it would be impractical to have a drawing that is the same size as the actual bridge, scale drawings are used. In a scale drawing, the measurements in the drawing are exactly proportional to the full-sized bridge. To make a scale drawing, a ratio is used that is consistent throughout the drawing. For example, 1 cm on the drawing may represent 1 m on the actual bridge. All parts of the bridge are drawn to that scale so that the pieces of the bridge can be made to fit together correctly. The final scale drawing that is used to build the bridge is called a *blueprint* because such scale drawings used to be printed using a light-sensitive blue dye. The blueprint shows all the details and measurements that the construction company needs to build the bridge.

SECTION OF EAST PIER AND CAISSON
ON LINE AB, PLATE VII.
SHOWING THE INTERIOR OF THE MAIN ENTRANCE SHAFT AND AIR CHAMBER AND THE WORKING OF ONE OF THE SAND PUMPS.

This is an original blueprint for part of the Brooklyn Bridge shown below.

2 Predict What might happen if a blueprint were not drawn to scale?

_____

_____

_____

_____

 You Try It! ⟶

Now it's your turn to design a bridge and draw a blueprint.

You Try It!

Now it's your turn to design a bridge and draw a blueprint for it. You will need to research the physical constraints for your bridge. Then you will choose a design and make a scale drawing of your bridge.

You Will Need

✓ calculator
✓ graph paper
✓ pencils
✓ pens
✓ ruler

(1) Identify a Need

Think of a place around your school building where a small, wooden bridge might be helpful. In the space below, describe the location of your bridge and explain why you chose the location.

_____

_____

(2) Conduct Research

Next, conduct research to determine the measurements for your bridge. Make measurements for the bridge in meters. Measure the distance of the gap that your bridge needs to span. How tall does the bridge need to be? How wide should the bridge be? What other information will you need to design a bridge? Record all of your data in the table at the right.

Characteristic	Actual Measurement (m)
Length of bridge	
Height of bridge	
Width of bridge	

(3) Brainstorm a Solution

Research examples of different types of bridges. Consider the various designs you found, and select one that you like that looks like it will meet the need for your bridge. In the space below, make a sketch of the type of bridge you plan to design.

(4) Select a Solution

Use the table below to calculate the scale for your drawing. First, determine how many squares wide the graph paper below is. Your scale drawing will need to fit within this space. Next, divide the longest measurement on your bridge by the number of squares wide the graph paper is. The result gives you the ratio of meters to graph paper squares.

Example

Imagine that your bridge needs to be 40 m long, and your paper is 20 squares long. 40 m divided by 20 squares = 2 m/square. The ratio for your bridge's scale would be 1 square = 2 m.

	Actual measurement (m)	Squares : meters	Number of squares
Length of bridge			
Height of bridge			
Width of bridge			

(5) Communicate Results

Draw a blueprint for your bridge in the space below. Use the ratio you calculated to translate each measurement to the correct number of graph paper squares. Be sure to indicate on your blueprint all the measurements, and include a key to the scale. Present your blueprint to the class, describing the bridge's purpose, how you chose the design, and how you calculated the scale.

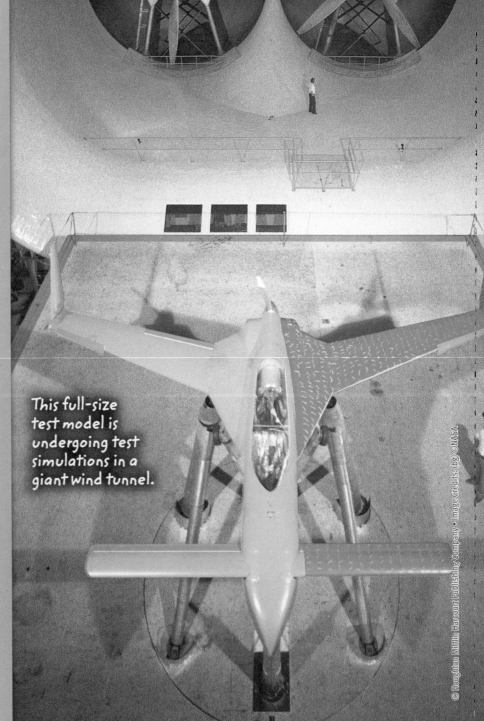

Models and Simulations

ESSENTIAL QUESTION

How do scientists use models and simulations?

By the end of this lesson, you should be able to explain how scientists use models and simulations to represent systems, explain phenomena, and make predictions.

This full-size test model is undergoing test simulations in a giant wind tunnel.

Lesson Labs

Quick Labs
- Modeling Eye Images
- Interpreting Models

S.T.E.M. Lab
- Exploring Convection

 Engage Your Brain

1 Predict Check T or F to show whether you think each statement is true or false.

T   F

☐ ☐ Models can have the same general appearance as real-life objects.

☐ ☐ Models of airplanes have all of the same operating parts as real airplanes do.

☐ ☐ Models can represent systems and processes.

2 Describe Write your own caption to this photo.

_____

_____

_____

_____

 Active Reading

3 Synthesize Many English words have their roots in other languages. Use the Latin word below to make an educated guess about the meaning of the word *simulation*.

Latin word	Meaning
simulatio	make-believe

Example sentence:
A flight simulation lets pilots practice flying an airplane in dangerous conditions.

simulation:

_____

_____

_____

_____

Vocabulary Terms

- **model**
- **simulation**
- **physical model**
- **mathematical model**
- **conceptual model**

4 Identify As you read, create a reference card for each vocabulary term. On one side of the card, write the term and its meaning. On the other side, draw an image that illustrates or makes a connection to the term. These cards can be used as bookmarks in the text so that you can refer to them while studying.

To Be a Model Scientist...

Why do scientists use models and simulations?

Models and simulations help us to understand the world around us. A scientific **model** shows the structure of an object, system, or concept. **Simulations** use models to imitate the function, behavior, or process of whatever the models represent.

To Answer Difficult Questions

What is the structure of an atom? How much fuel do we need to reach the moon? How many fish can we catch each year without reducing the fish population? These questions are all difficult to answer. A difficult question is a question that cannot be answered quickly by direct observation. Models and simulations are tools that can help answer these questions. Models let us test many possible ideas to find the solutions to difficult questions.

To Represent Complex Systems

In the real world, systems are complex and made up of many interacting parts. Scientists can use models to represent these systems. For example, a building is a complex system that has many parts that interact. Scientists can study the way a model building will behave during an earthquake. Data from simulations on a model building can help to produce an earthquake-resistant building design.

Active Reading **5 Identify** What is one example of a complex system that can be represented by a model?

_____

_____

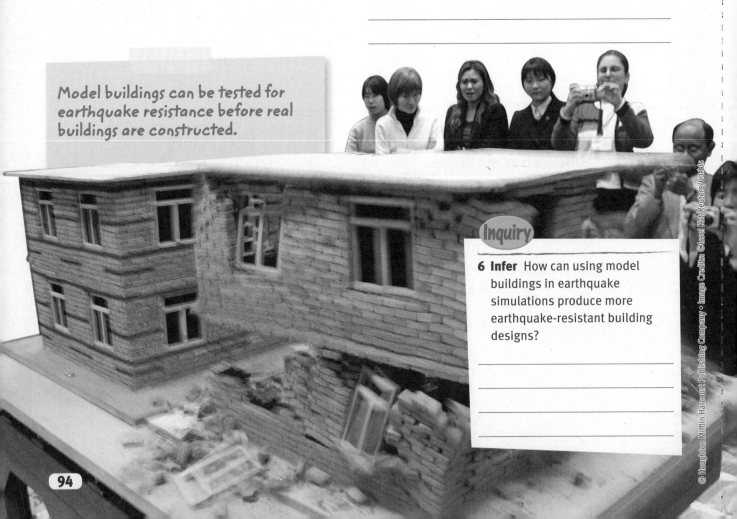

Model buildings can be tested for earthquake resistance before real buildings are constructed.

Inquiry

6 Infer How can using model buildings in earthquake simulations produce more earthquake-resistant building designs?

_____

_____

_____

...Use Models!

To Test New Ideas

People have new ideas all the time. Some ideas are good and lead to useful technologies. Other ideas are never developed. Modeling can separate good ideas from ideas that will never be developed.

Testing is needed before time and money are spent developing new ideas. For example, someone might propose using wind turbines and solar cells as an environmentally friendly way to generate electrical energy in a community. However, before building these expensive systems, computer modeling can be used to determine if these technologies will actually be energy efficient.

Computer models can test designs, such as this turbine, before they are built.

To Make Predictions

Models are used to make predictions that affect our everyday lives. For example, meteorologists make weather predictions by entering data for different weather elements into complex computer programs. Models are also used to make predictions about phenomena that occur far from Earth. For example, the sun has periods of intense magnetic activity. These periods are identified by the number of sunspots that appear on the sun's surface. Solar activity can damage satellites and affect communications. Models of sunspot activity can be built using past sunspot activity. With these models, researchers can predict future sunspot activity and minimize satellite damage and communications interruptions.

Visualize It!

7 Analyze Use the graph to predict sunspot activity in 2020.

_____
_____
_____
_____
_____
_____
_____
_____
_____
_____

Mathematical models are used to make predictions.

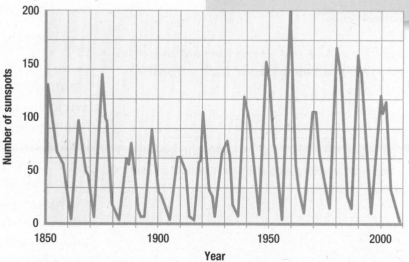

Sunspot Activity

It's a Matter of Scale

Molecular models help us to imagine the structure of tiny molecules.

Life-size models of human organs are often used when learning about their structure.

9 Compare What are some advantages of using a model for teaching about organs rather than using an actual organ?

What are some types of physical models?

Toy cars are physical models that represent real cars. A **physical model** represents the physical structure of an object or system. Physical models often look and act like the object or system they represent. Toy cars look like real cars and roll like real cars. However, toy cars usually don't have working engines.

Scale Models

Scale models are used to estimate distance, volume, or quantity. Scale models are also used to study objects or systems that are too small to see or are too big to see completely. *Scale* is the relationship between a model's measurements and the real object's measurements. A one-eighth scale model of a boat is one-eighth the size of the real boat. Scientists use scale models to estimate the properties of actual objects or systems. For example, the internal structure of atoms is simply too small to see, so we study atoms using models.

Inquiry

8 What are three examples of objects that are too large to easily study without using models?

Life-Size Models

Sometimes models are made to be life-size. This means that the model is the same size as a real-world object. Life-size models are useful for studying objects that are rare or are difficult to find in the natural world. For example, students often learn by using models of human organs and fossils. Before performing surgery on a living person, surgeons practice their technique on life-size models of human organs. Museums use life-size models of dinosaurs to show how large these creatures were when they were alive.

What are some advantages and disadvantages of physical models?

Physical models allow scientists to study objects or systems that are too small to see or too big to see completely. They are also used when objects are too far away, too dangerous, or too expensive to study, or when they no longer exist. Like other models, physical models do not always behave like the real thing.

Physical Models Are Easier and Safer to Work With

Physical models are often easier and less dangerous to work with than the objects that they represent. For example, scale models of ships are used for training shiphandlers and for testing the hydraulic systems that control the ships. For accuracy, the models must consider different variables such as wind, currents, and water depth. Flight simulators on the ground are used to train pilots to fly. The same instruments that are found in a real airplane are used in a flight simulator. Using a simulator is easier, cheaper, and much safer than training pilots in a real plane.

Physical Models Are Not Always Like the Real Thing

Ideally, physical models should work exactly like the objects that they represent. In reality, physical models have limitations. They may not behave in the exact same way as the object or system that they have been made to represent. This may occur if a model is being studied outside of its natural environment. For instance, a model may not function the same way in a laboratory as it would in the real world. Also, a physical model may not be the best way to represent a complex system. It may be impossible to account for every variable in a complex model.

Wind tunnels are used to test the way that air moves around scale-model aircraft.

Visualize It!

10 Predict What is the role of the smoke that is moving over the model aircraft?

_____

_____

_____

It's All in the Numbers

What are some types of mathematical models?

Models that represent processes are more abstract than models that represent objects. Some of the most useful process models are mathematical models. A **mathematical model** uses different forms of data to represent the way a system or process works.

Equations and Graphs

Mathematical models are made up of numbers and equations. These models can often be shown as graphs and are used to predict future trends. For example, in order to plan for future services, a city needs to predict future populations. Based on past data, it is known that populations tend to grow at a faster and faster rate. Such growth is called *exponential* (ek•spuh•NEN•shuhl). When population data are illustrated on a graph, future populations can be predicted by extending the curve. As with all models, assumptions have been made. In this case, the model assumes that the rate of growth remains the same.

Model of Exponential Growth

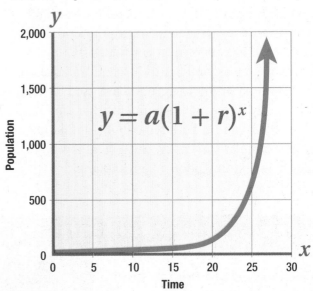

$$y = a(1 + r)^x$$

The process of photosynthesis can be shown as a mathematical model.

$$6CO_2 + 6H_2O \xrightarrow{\text{sunlight}} C_6H_{12}O_6 + 6O_2$$

---

11 Interpret What do the large and small numbers represent in a chemical equation?

_____

_____

_____

_____

Chemical Formulas and Equations

Drawing the chemical structure of each molecule when writing chemical reactions would take too long and use a lot of space. Using words would also be difficult. Instead, chemical symbols from the periodic table are used to represent atoms, just as x and y represent variables in an equation. A number to the right of and below the atom's symbol shows how many of each atom are in a molecule. This number is called the *subscript*. A number before the molecule shows how many of each molecule are in the reaction. This number is called the *coefficient*.

What are some advantages and disadvantages of mathematical models?

Mathematical models are useful for showing patterns and making predictions. They are easy to change and adjust. But some systems that have many variables are too complex to model easily. If key variables are not considered, the model could contain errors.

Mathematical Models are Powerful Predictors

One advantage of mathematical models is that they are useful in making predictions. For obtaining the detailed predictions of a mathematical model, computers are often essential. Computers can process many variables quickly using complex mathematical equations. And they can do so without making the calculation errors that humans often make. Computer modeling is useful for determining how a large number of objects interact or change. For example, weather predictions are made using computer models. Economic forecasts are also made using computer models. Computer models can even be used to predict the sizes and shapes of spots on giraffes.

Mathematical Models Can Be Oversimplified

Mathematical models also have limitations. They are based on current data, which might not be of use in the future. Also, they may exclude variables that did not seem to be important. Sometimes systems are too large or too complex for mathematical modeling, even using computers. To save computer processing time, some variables might need to be left out of a model. Or, to simplify a calculation, only a small portion of the system might be studied. Taking these steps could result in a model that gives misleading results.

Active Reading **12 Explain** What are two ways in which a computer model might be oversimplified?

_____

_____

Mathematical models can be used to predict the size of spots on animals.

It's Kind of Abstract

What are some characteristics of conceptual models?

Another type of model used in science is the conceptual model. A **conceptual model** is a representation of how parts of a system are related or organized. Conceptual models can be used to simplify complex relationships.

Conceptual Models Have Different Uses

Active Reading **13 List** As you read, underline the uses of conceptual models.

Conceptual models are useful in identifying patterns and similarities for classifications. The periodic table is a type of conceptual model. The elements in each horizontal row of the periodic table have the same number of electron shells. The elements in each vertical row have similar chemical properties.

Conceptual models are often used to represent processes that cannot be directly observed. The rock cycle, which is shown below, is an example. Because conceptual models represent how parts of a system are related, they can help predict the effect that changing one part of a system will have on the whole system.

Conceptual Models May Have Limitations

Like all models, conceptual models may have limitations. Models may not be able to take certain data or ideas into account. Therefore, one limitation of conceptual models is that they may be oversimplified. In this case, a model may not be a true representation of the complex relationships that exist in a system. This leads us to a second limitation of conceptual models. If a model is not a true representation of the relationships that exist in a system, then the model can lead to misconceptions. A model that is oversimplified and that can lead to misconceptions can produce incomplete predictions.

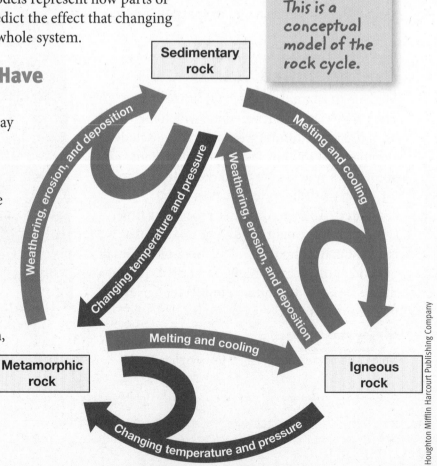

This is a conceptual model of the rock cycle.

Sedimentary rock

Weathering, erosion, and deposition

Melting and cooling

Changing temperature and pressure

Weathering, erosion, and deposition

Metamorphic rock

Melting and cooling

Igneous rock

Changing temperature and pressure

How are simulations used?

Simulations use models to show how an object or system works. Simulations can be used to improve the performance of a piece of technology. Quality control, safety, training, and education are other reasons for using simulations. In research, simulations allow scientists to control variables when conducting tests and to determine what happens when variables are changed.

To Test Designs in a Controlled Environment

Simulations may show how an event would occur under specific circumstances to test a hypothesis. Simulations can test hypotheses by changing certain conditions. Complex technologies can be tested in a variety of environments before they are put in use. For example, the *Mars Exploration Rovers* were designed based on the experiences of previous space expeditions. So, before sending the rovers to Mars, extensive tests were conducted using models on Earth. In this way, researchers could change variables to determine an outcome. During testing, design flaws may be found that can be corrected. This can prevent damage to an expensive piece of equipment or people being injured because of faulty design.

To Test Designs in a Safer, Less Expensive Way

Simulations can prevent costly and dangerous errors in design. Imagine building an expensive rocket, then launching it without knowing if it would work. That's how early rocket designs were tested. Today, new rocket designs are first tested in simulations.

Simulations can also be used to predict future events. Astronauts train in an underwater environment that simulates the weightlessness of space. The astronauts "spacewalk" inside a tank that is 12 m deep and holds 23.5 million liters of water. They put on their spacesuits and practice working on a model of the *Hubble Space Telescope* to prepare for future missions in space.

To improve vehicle safety, crashes are simulated in controlled environments.

Procedures planned for space are always simulated first on Earth.

15 Explain Why is an actual car with realistic passengers needed to simulate the effects of a crash in safety tests?

_____

_____

16 Infer Why do astronauts train using underwater simulations?

_____

_____

Visual Summary

To complete this summary, answer the following True or False questions. Then, use the key below to check your answers. You can use this page to review the main concepts of the lesson.

Models and Simulations

A physical model represents an object or system.

	T	F	
17	☐	☐	Models always behave exactly like the thing they represent.

Mathematical models use numbers and equations to represent the way a system or process works.

	T	F	
18	☐	☐	Computer modeling is useful for determining how objects interact with one another or change.

A simulation uses a model to imitate the function, behavior, or process of the thing it represents.

	T	F	
19	☐	☐	Complex objects or processes are easier to simulate.

A conceptual model shows how parts of a system are related or organized.

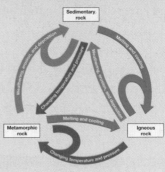

	T	F	
20	☐	☐	Conceptual models can represent a process that cannot be observed directly.

Answers: 17 F; 18 T; 19 F; 20 T

21 Synthesize How can models and simulations be used to build safer cars?

Lesson Review

Vocabulary

Draw a line to connect each type of model to its matching examples.

1 physical model

2 conceptual model

3 mathematical model

A water cycle, rock cycle, family tree

B chemical reaction, population growth, sunspot activity

C architectural model, atomic structure, an artificial organ

Key Concepts

4 Identify What are three advantages of using conceptual models?

_____

_____

_____

_____

_____

5 Explain Models are often used to represent very small objects or very large objects. Why is it also useful to create life-size models of some objects?

_____

_____

_____

_____

_____

_____

6 List What are two advantages and two limitations of physical models?

_____

_____

_____

_____

Critical Thinking

Use this graph to answer the following questions.

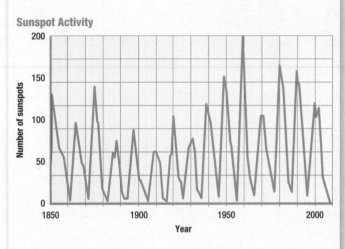

Sunspot Activity

7 Analyze What is the length of time between peaks in sunspot activity?

_____

_____

8 Evaluate Evaluate the following statement. *By using the sunspot graph above, you can predict the exact number of sunspots for any year in the future.*

_____

_____

_____

_____

_____

9 Infer Computers are fast and do not make errors when doing calculations. Does this mean that computer models are always correct? Explain your answer.

_____

_____

_____

_____

_____

My Notes

Unit 2 ▸Big Idea◂ Scientists use tools to collect, organize, and analyze data while conducting investigations.

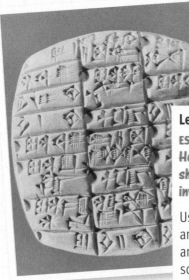

Lesson 1

ESSENTIAL QUESTION
How do scientists show the results of investigations?

Use tables, graphs, and models to display and analyze scientific data.

Lesson 2

ESSENTIAL QUESTION
What are the tools and units used in science?

Describe the different tools and units of measurement used in scientific investigations.

Lesson 3

ESSENTIAL QUESTION
How do scientists use models and simulations?

Explain how scientists use models and simulations to represent systems, explain phenomena, and make predictions.

Connect ESSENTIAL QUESTIONS
Lessons 1 and 3

1 Synthesize Compare the ways in which a scientist would use a graph and a model in investigations.

_____

_____

_____

_____

_____

Think Outside the Book

2 Synthesize Choose one of these activities to help synthesize what you have learned in this unit.

☐ Using what you learned in lessons 1 and 2, graph how air temperature changes during the day. Include data points for every hour between 6:00 a.m. and 6:00 p.m.

☐ Using what you learned in lessons 2 and 3, describe the measurements and the type of model that a meteorologist would use to predict the weather created by a developing storm.

Unit 2 Review

Name _____

Vocabulary

Fill in each blank with the term that best completes the following sentences.

1 Visual or mathematical representations used to develop scientific explanations are called _____.

2 A _____ is a description of something that includes a number and a unit.

3 A toy car is an example of a _____ that represents a real car.

4 The data for the _____ are usually found in the first column of a data table.

5 Scientists use _____ to understand how systems work.

Key Concepts

Read each question below, and circle the best answer.

6 This line graph shows a company's average annual salary over nine years.

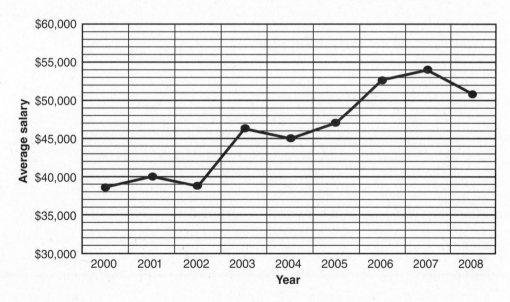

From 2000 to 2008, how many times did the average annual salary decrease?

A once

B twice

C three times

D four times

7 Mrs. Rehak shows her students a model of the three states of matter.

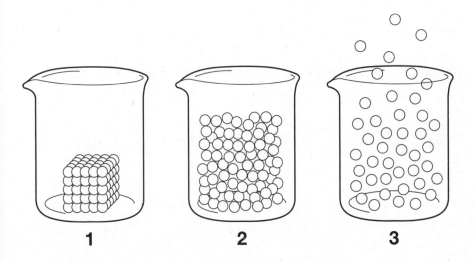

Which part(s) of Mrs. Rehak's model represents a gas?

A 1 and 2

C 2

B 3

D 1

8 Scientists use which one of the following units to measure mass?

A pounds

C kilograms

B meters

D ounces

9 Which is a tool that scientists would not likely use in a lab?

A test tube

B hot plate

C electron microscope

D yard stick

10 How should scientists express very large numbers when reporting data?

A in scientific notation

B to the tenth decimal point

C as a fraction

D in inches

11 Scientists use models and simulations in their work. Which one of the following does a simulation not do?

A imitates the function of the thing it represents

B imitates the behavior of the thing it represents

C imitates the process of the thing it represents

D takes the place of the thing it represents

12 Look at the diagram below of the rock cycle.

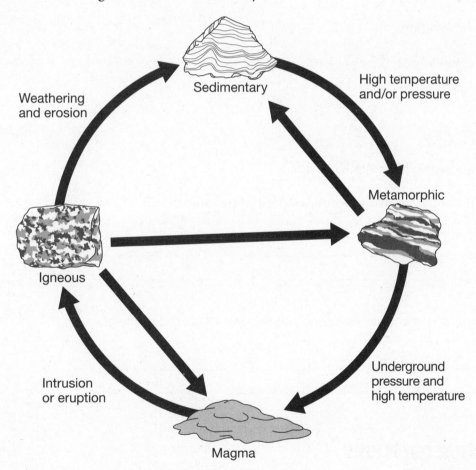

What does the diagram represent?

A mathematical model

B simulation

C conceptual model

D physical model

13 Emmanuel compared the growth of plants in full sun and part shade.

Plant Growth

Conditions	Initial height (cm)	Height after 10 days (cm)	Height after 20 days (cm)	Height after 30 days (cm)
Full sun	20	24	27	31
Part shade	20	22	23	25

Emmanuel decides to create a line graph to show the growth of the plant grown in full sun. What would be the correct labels for the axes of the line graph?

A Full sun and Number of days

B Height (cm) and Conditions

C Conditions and Number of days

D Number of days and Height (cm)

Critical Thinking

Answer the following questions in the space provided.

14 What advantage do computers give scientists as tools for investigations?

_____

_____

_____

15 Explain what a model is. What disadvantage could there be in using a model to represent data?

_____

_____

_____

Connect **ESSENTIAL QUESTIONS**
Lessons 1 and 3

Answer the following question in the space provided.

Define mathematical model and conceptual model. Give at least one example of each. What kind of data would each represent?

_____

_____

_____

_____

Engineering, Technology, and Society

This storm surge barrier in Rotterdam, the Netherlands, can be closed like a gate to protect the city from flooding during a storm.

Humans design and use systems, products, and processes to meet a variety of needs.

What do you think?

Large engineering projects require a great deal of planning and community involvement. What issues do you think need to be considered when planning a major project?

Engineers must work in teams.

Civil Engineering

Large civil-engineering projects, such as a major bridge or dam, obviously require a great deal of money, work, and careful planning. Similar factors must be considered even for smaller engineering projects that may be going on in your own community right now. Whether large or small, civil-engineering projects are meant to address problems faced by the community.

① Define the Problem

Find a construction or engineering project that is going on in your community. What is the problem that this project addresses?

_____

_____

_____

_____

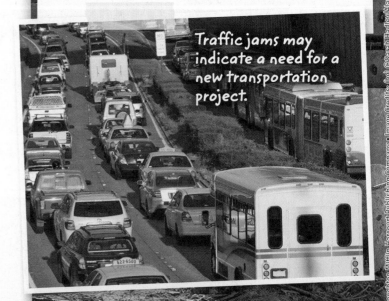

Traffic jams may indicate a need for a new transportation project.

② Ask a Question

Interview local officials or the construction company to find out more about the project. You can also research newspapers, government web pages, or minutes from city council meetings.

A What issues had to be considered in the planning of this project?

_____

_____

_____

_____

_____

B Who made the decisions? How?

_____

_____

_____

③ Propose an Alternative

A What parts of the project do you think could have been improved?

_____

_____

_____

_____

B Propose a way to improve the current project. If you don't agree with the project, propose an alternative project that you think would be better.

_____

_____

_____

_____

Construction projects might cause temporary inconvenience but are meant to solve a problem.

Take It Home

What kinds of engineering projects are going on around your home? Research news stories or other sources to find out what's being done and why. See *ScienceSaurus*® for more information about science and engineering.

The Engineering Design Process

ESSENTIAL QUESTION

What is the engineering design process?

By the end of this lesson, you should be able to explain how the engineering design process develops technical solutions to meet people's needs.

Every part of a rocket and its launching platform is carefully engineered. All the parts are designed to work together to make sure the rocket launch is a success.

Lesson Labs

Quick Labs
- Designing a Consumer Product
- Technology, Engineering, and Science

S.T.E.M. Lab
- Earthquake Engineering Design Challenge

 Engage Your Brain

1 Predict Check T or F to show whether you think each statement is true or false.

T   F

☐ ☐ New designs are always complicated.

☐ ☐ Changes in design can make products easier to use.

☐ ☐ Cost has no influence on the way objects are designed.

2 Compare The round broom was redesigned into a flat broom. How does the flatter design make sweeping the floor easier?

_____

_____

_____

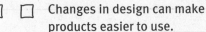 Active Reading

3 Synthesize You can often define an unknown word if you know the meaning of its word parts. Use the word parts and sentence below to make an educated guess about the meaning of the word *prototype*.

Word part	Meaning
proto	first
type	kind or form

Example sentence:
Electrical engineers design a headlight prototype before making it in large numbers.

prototype:

_____

_____

Vocabulary Terms

- technology
- engineering
- trade-off
- prototype

4 Apply This list contains the vocabulary terms you'll learn in this lesson. As you read, circle the definition of each term.

Technology BREAKS Barriers

What is technology?

Science is the study of the natural world. Scientific discoveries are used to solve everyday problems. **Technology** is the application of science for practical purposes. Technology can include products, processes, and systems. The method used to develop new technology is called the *engineering design process.* By this process, people identify a need and then look for ways to meet that need. For example, all living things need nutrients. Early humans developed technology, such as spears, to help them hunt for food. Since that time, many technologies have been developed to improve the way that people get, grow, and process food.

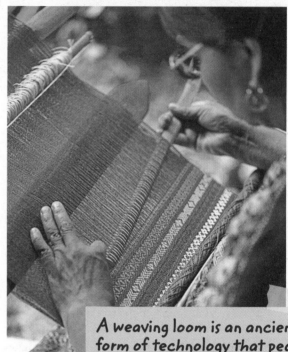

A weaving loom is an ancient form of technology that people still use to make cloth.

Active Reading

5 Explain How are science and technology related?

_____

_____

_____

Tape is a simple technology!

A trebuchet (treb-yuh-SHET) is a kind of catapult. Catapults began as a weapons technology that enabled armies to hurl objects through the air.

6 Relate Catapults developed at the same time as high-walled cities. Why do you think this weapons technology and building technology developed together?

_____

_____

_____

© Houghton Mifflin Harcourt Publishing Company • Image Credits: (t) ©PictureNet/Corbis; (b) ©Chris Hellier/Corbis

Is all technology complicated?

When you think of technology, you might think of lasers, satellites, or solar-powered cars, but even simple things we use every day are examples of technology. Technology is not necessarily complicated, expensive, or something that needs to be plugged in.

Technology Can Be Simple

Zippers use simple but effective technology. Why is the technology considered simple? Zippers are relatively simple to make and are inexpensive. They require no electrical energy to operate and are easy to use and understand.

If you look at a zipper closely, you will see that it has two rows of interlocking teeth and a metal slider. The shape of the slider joins or separates the rows of teeth as it moves. The slider has been designed to work perfectly with the rows of teeth. The technology is very effective, but it's so simple that you may not have noticed it.

Technology Can Be Complex

Many newer technologies are much more complex than zippers. For example, making electronic devices, such as computers and MP3 players, is a complex process that requires knowledge of physics, electronics, microprocessors, and software. Complex technologies often use electrical energy and are often expensive. Usually you cannot see how complex technologies work just by looking at them. But complex devices like computers perform many useful functions. Life would be very different without them.

zipper

MP3 player

7 Contrast Fill in the Venn diagram to compare characteristics of simple and complex technology.

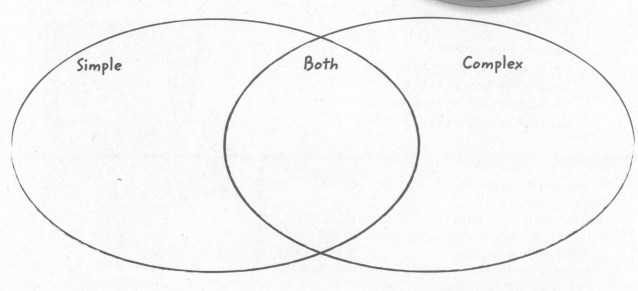

Simple   Both   Complex

BRIDGING the Gap

What do engineers do?

Much of the technology we use today is the result of engineering. **Engineering** is the application of science and mathematics to solve real-life problems. There are many types of engineers. For example, chemical engineers use their knowledge of chemistry and math to develop chemical products. Electrical and mechanical engineers work with computers and machines. Biomedical engineers design medical devices such as prosthetics and x-ray machines.

Apply Science and Math

When working on problems, engineers first conduct research. They may improve on a solution that was used before or build on a new scientific discovery. For example, suppose a chemist discovers a new solvent. Chemical engineers might use that solvent to develop a new floor cleaner. Scientific discoveries can lead to new products through engineering.

Math is also important to all fields of engineering. For example, the engineers developing the new floor cleaner would need to make a large amount of the cleaner to sell. Using their original process as a model, the engineers use math to calculate how to make large amounts of the cleaner with the same proportion of ingredients.

Active Reading

8 Explain Why do engineers need to know about new discoveries in science?

_____

_____

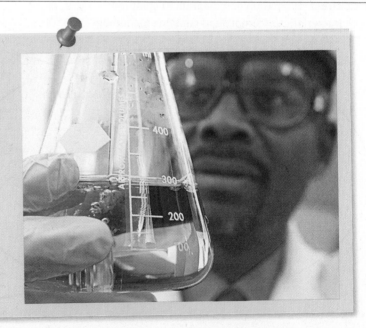

Chemical engineers apply math and scientific knowledge to make useful chemicals such as cleaners, medicines, and fuels.

Think Outside the Book Inquiry

9 Research What kinds of engineers are involved in the process of growing and delivering vegetables to stores in a city?

Civil engineers use math and their knowledge of materials to design bridges such as these in Japan.

Solve Real-World Problems

Transportation is a vital part of modern life. But meeting the transportation needs of a community can be difficult. Extreme landscapes, rough terrain, and the need to preserve sensitive ecosystems all add to that challenge.

Civil engineers design solutions to transportation problems. When engineers design a new bridge, they first identify the problem they are trying to solve. Then, they investigate how other engineers have solved similar problems before. They research new materials and processes, too. Then, they carefully plan and calculate how to build a structure that will solve their problem.

The real world also has *constraints*. Constraints are limitations. For example, when a team of civil engineers plans a bridge, the goal is to solve a transportation problem. But the engineers have to work within the laws of physics and the properties of their materials. The bridge has to be affordable and must meet safety and environmental regulations. These are the bridge's constraints.

To work within constraints, engineers often make trade-offs. A **trade-off** is the act of giving up one advantage to keep another. For example, keeping costs low is important on any project. But using more steel in a bridge may help make the bridge stronger and last longer. So spending more money but building a stronger, more durable bridge is a trade-off.

Do the Math

You Try It

10 **Calculate** In 1919, a twin-propeller airplane made the first nonstop flight across the Atlantic Ocean, traveling 3,630 km in about 16 hours. Today, modern jets can travel the same distance in about 5 hours. What is the difference in speed between the 1919 twin-propeller plane and a modern jet plane? Show your work below.

What skills are needed for engineering design?

The engineering design process is a series of steps that lead to a new product, process, or technique. Any product you can think of was designed this way. New soaps, cars, fuels, fabrics, and even roller coasters are developed using these steps. The engineering design process leads engineers from problems to solutions. And to get through the steps of the process, engineers need some important skills.

Active Reading

11 Identify As you read, underline the reasons that engineers need each of the skills on this page.

Engineers use many skills when they design complex structures like a roller coaster.

Thinking Creatively

It's easy to keep doing things the same old way. Creativity leads to new ways of doing things that are more efficient or more enjoyable or that improve quality of life. But creativity has limitations. For example, adding loops makes this roller coaster more exciting, but the ride still has to be safe.

Thinking Methodically

Methodical thinking means thinking in an organized way and paying close attention to details. Engineers consider the constraints and requirements of a design before building it. Following a careful process ensures that this roller coaster is both safe and exciting.

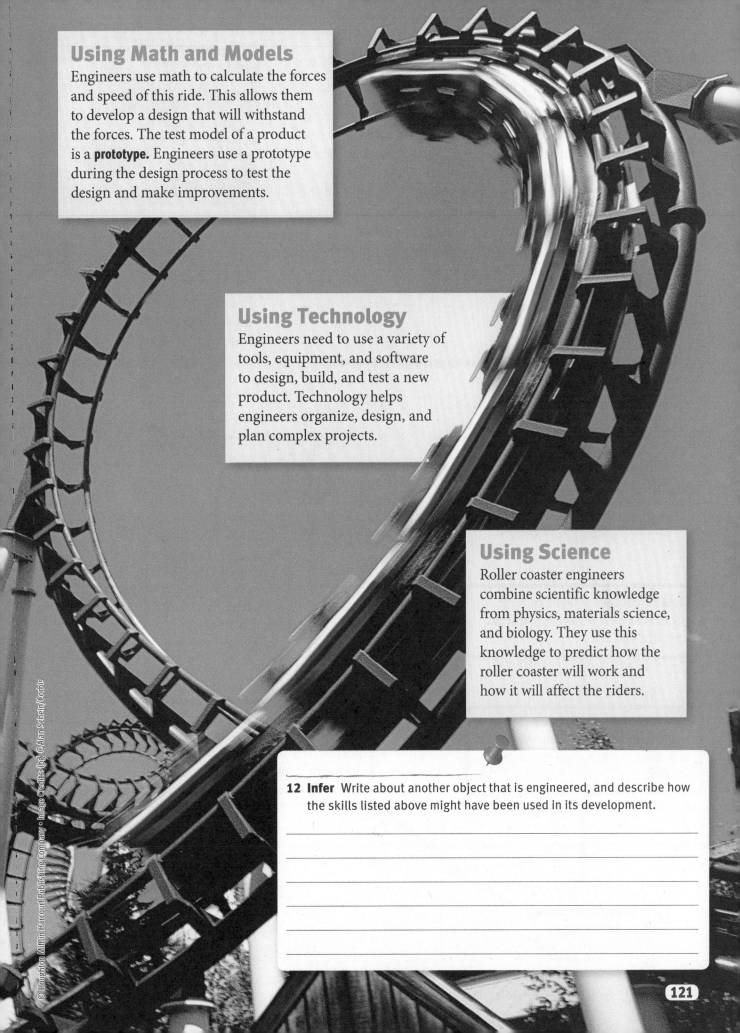

Using Math and Models

Engineers use math to calculate the forces and speed of this ride. This allows them to develop a design that will withstand the forces. The test model of a product is a **prototype.** Engineers use a prototype during the design process to test the design and make improvements.

Using Technology

Engineers need to use a variety of tools, equipment, and software to design, build, and test a new product. Technology helps engineers organize, design, and plan complex projects.

Using Science

Roller coaster engineers combine scientific knowledge from physics, materials science, and biology. They use this knowledge to predict how the roller coaster will work and how it will affect the riders.

12 Infer Write about another object that is engineered, and describe how the skills listed above might have been used in its development.

_____

_____

_____

_____

_____

_____

How does the engineering design process work?

Engineers put their skills to work in the steps of the engineering design process. The process always begins with identifying a need for a new or improved product or technology. Then, engineers work in teams to brainstorm solutions. After a plan of action is chosen, a prototype is made, tested, and revised. Throughout the process, constraints always limit the options for change. And many changes involve a trade-off of one advantage for another.

In the chart below, the rectangles contain steps, and the diamonds contain questions. The path you follow through the process depends on the answers to the questions.

Prototypes are almost always revised to make improvements.

 **Active Reading**

13 Identify What is the beginning of the engineering design process?

_____

_____

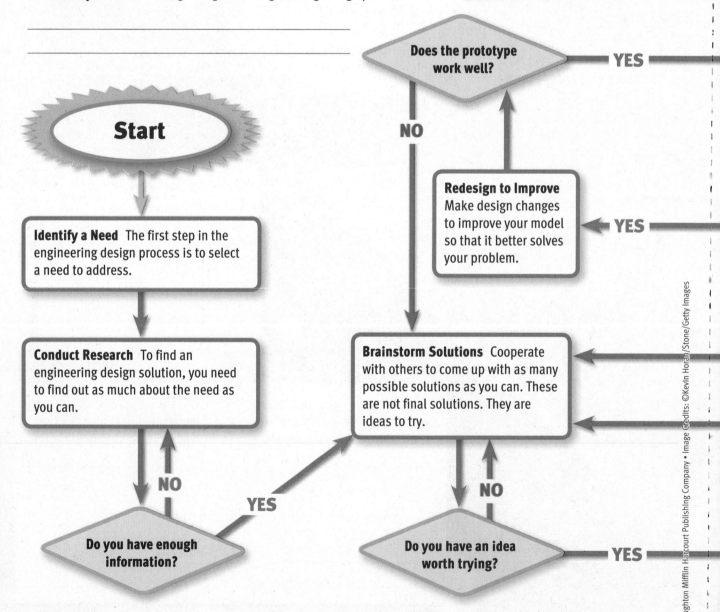

Start

Identify a Need The first step in the engineering design process is to select a need to address.

Conduct Research To find an engineering design solution, you need to find out as much about the need as you can.

Do you have enough information?

NO

YES

Does the prototype work well?

YES

NO

Redesign to Improve Make design changes to improve your model so that it better solves your problem.

YES

Brainstorm Solutions Cooperate with others to come up with as many possible solutions as you can. These are not final solutions. They are ideas to try.

NO

Do you have an idea worth trying?

YES

The complex technology found in automobiles is only possible because engineers follow the engineering design process for every part of the car.

Communicate Your Results When your prototype is finished, you have designed a solution to your problem. Tell others how you did it!

End!

Test and Evaluate Your prototype probably won't be perfect the first time, but it should be on the right track.

Does the prototype show promise?

NO

Build a Prototype Your prototype should be a working model of your solution.

YES

NO Can you make a prototype?

Select a Solution Which of your ideas do you want to try? Pick one, and plan how you want to try it.

Visualize It!

14 Organize List the eight steps of the engineering design process, assuming that the answer to all of the questions is "yes."

_____

_____

_____

_____

_____

_____

_____

Visual Summary

To complete this summary, fill in the correct word or phrase. Then, use the key below to check your answers. You can use this page to review the main concepts of the lesson.

The Engineering Design Process

Technology is the application of science for practical purposes.

The goal of technology is to meet human needs.

15 A _____ uses simple technology. A computer is an example of _____ technology.

Engineers apply science and math.

Engineers solve real-world problems.

16 Five skills engineers need are creative thinking, methodological thinking, using math and models, using technology, and and using _____

The design process follows a series of steps.

The path through the process leads to new technology.

17 _____ is a creative process where groups of people work together to find potential solutions.

15 zipper, complex; 16 science; 17 brainstorming

18 Synthesize How are technology, engineering, and science related?

Lesson Review

Vocabulary

Draw a line to connect the following terms to their definitions.

1 prototype   **A** The application of science and math to solve real-life problems.

2 engineering   **B** The application of science for practical purposes.

3 technology   **C** A model made and modified during the engineering design process.

Key Concepts

4 Identify Why is methodical thinking important to engineers?

_____

_____

_____

_____

5 Describe What are two characteristics of simple technology and two characteristics of complex technology?

_____

_____

_____

_____

_____

6 Apply What are three constraints that limit the design of a car?

_____

_____

_____

_____

_____

_____

Use this diagram to answer the following questions.

7 Sequence Fill in the missing steps of the engineering design process.

| Identify a need |
| Conduct research |
| |
| Select a solution |
| |
| Test and evaluate |
| Redesign to improve |
| Communicate results |

Critical Thinking

8 Explain At what steps should arrows also be drawn in the opposite direction? Explain your answer.

_____

_____

_____

_____

_____

_____

My Notes

Analyzing Technology

Skills
✓ Identify benefits and risks
✓ Evaluate cost of technology
✓ Evaluate environmental impact
Propose improvements
Propose risk reduction
Compare technology
✓ Communicate results

Objectives
• Identify the benefits of a specific technology.
• Identify the risks of a specific technology.
• Conduct a risk-benefit analysis of a specific technology.

Risks and Benefits of Electric Transportation

The growing population in many areas has led to significant transportation problems. People need to move around to get to work, school, or shopping areas. However, without other options, they often end up driving around in cars all by themselves. This contributes to traffic problems, wear and tear on the roads, pollution, and wasted fuel.

Many traffic problems are caused by too many cars on the roads.

1 Observe From a safe place, observe the number of cars driving by your school or driving on a main street in your neighborhood. Record how many cars drive by in a certain amount of time and also how many of those cars contain only the driver.

Cars	Only driver

2 Infer What are some of the benefits of people driving around in cars, even though they may often be by themselves?

_____

_____

_____

_____

_____

Electric Scooters

Electric scooters are small, open vehicles that use a battery-operated electric motor to propel the rider. Some people say electric scooters are the solution to modern transportation problems. A benefit is something that provides an advantage. Some benefits are that electric scooters take up less space on the road and in parking lots. Electric scooters also do not emit exhaust and can be cheaper to own and operate than cars. A risk is the chance of a dangerous or undesirable outcome.

3 Infer What are some of the problems or risks that could result from the widespread use of electric scooters?

_____

_____

_____

_____

Risk
Even though electric vehicles don't emit exhaust, the power plants that deliver their electricity do have negative environmental effects.

Benefit
Electric scooters take up less room on the road than cars.

You Try It!

Now it's your turn to evaluate the risks and benefits of students using electric scooters to travel to and from your school.

 You Try It!

Now it's your turn to evaluate the risks and benefits of students using electric scooters to travel to and from your school.

① Identify Risks and Benefits

Suppose all of the students at your school used electric scooters to ride from home to school and back. Think of all the positive and negative aspects of all students riding electric scooters. In the table below, list all of these risks and benefits. List any negative aspects under the "Risks" heading and list any positive aspects under the "Benefits" heading. You may need to add to the table as you complete the rest of this activity.

Risks	Benefits

② Evaluate Cost of Technology

A Imagine that every student in your school rides the school bus. Research the cost per student per year of your school's bus system. To do this, estimate how many miles the students have to ride to and from school and how much gas is needed to travel that distance.

_____

_____

_____

B Research the cost of electric scooters that students might be able to use to get to and from your school. How much would it cost each student to buy a scooter? What other costs do you need to consider?

_____

_____

_____

(3) Evaluate Environmental Impact

In what specific ways would the environment be affected by all students riding electric scooters to and from your school? Be sure to think about both positive and negative effects on the environment.

_____

_____

_____

_____

_____

(4) Communicate Results

A Based on all the risks and benefits you listed, what conclusion would you make about whether all students should drive electric scooters to and from your school? Explain your answer.

_____

_____

_____

_____

_____

_____

B Write a persuasive letter to your local school board attempting to convince members to adopt your conclusion about the use of electric scooters at your school. Be sure to support your argument with facts from your risk-benefit analysis.

_____

_____

_____

_____

_____

_____

_____

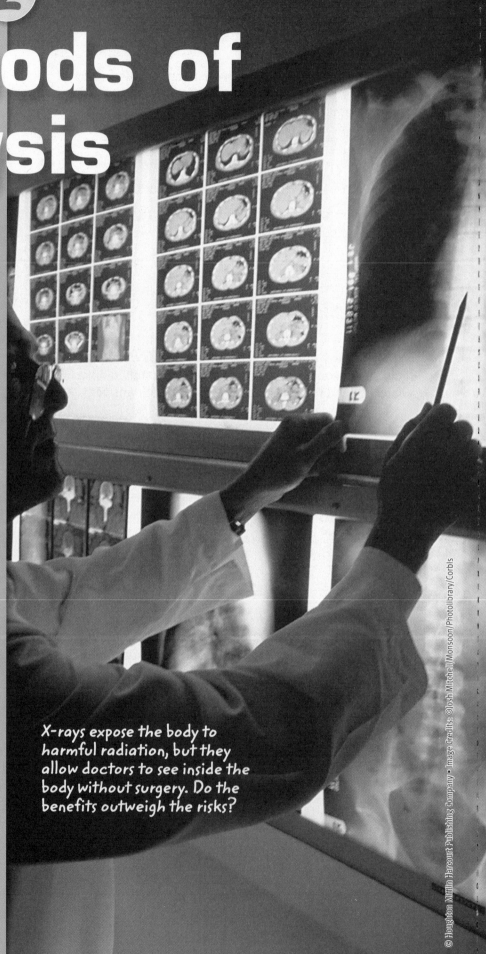

Methods of Analysis

ESSENTIAL QUESTION

How can we evaluate technology?

By the end of this lesson you should be able to explain how scientists and engineers determine the costs, benefits, and risks of a new technology.

X-rays expose the body to harmful radiation, but they allow doctors to see inside the body without surgery. Do the benefits outweigh the risks?

Engage Your Brain

1 Predict Check T or F to show whether you think each statement is true or false.

T   F

☐   ☐   Sometimes people accept certain risks in exchange for other benefits.

☐   ☐   Technology never causes problems.

☐   ☐   When comparing technology, you need to examine each feature.

☐   ☐   A product only affects the environment when it is thrown away.

2 Identify List advantages and disadvantages of each of the writing utensils shown here.

	Advantages	Disadvantages
A		
B		

 Active Reading

3 Infer The term *life cycle* often describes the stages an organism goes through from birth to death. What do you think *life cycle* means when it is used to talk about a product?

_____

_____

_____

_____

_____

Vocabulary Terms

- trade-off
- risk-benefit analysis
- life cycle analysis
- Pugh chart

4 Apply As you learn the definition of each vocabulary term in this lesson, create your own definition or sketch to help you remember the meaning of the term.

Better or Worse

How can the effects of technology be described?

Technology is the application of science for practical purposes and can include products, processes, and systems. New technology may affect society, the environment, or the economy in several ways. The effects of a new technology can be classified in four ways:

- expected and favorable
- expected and unfavorable
- unexpected and favorable
- unexpected and unfavorable

Expected Effects

When people develop technology, they try to predict the effects that it may have. The goal for any new technology is to keep the expected favorable effects greater than any expected unfavorable effects. People make trade-offs when they adopt new technology. A **trade-off** means accepting risks in exchange for benefits or giving up one benefit to gain another. The control of fire is one of the earliest human technologies. Fire improves food and increases the odds of surviving winter. But fire can also destroy homes, crops, and habitats. For thousands of years, people have accepted the risk of fire because the expected benefits outweigh the risk.

Unexpected Effects

People cannot always predict the effects of new technology. For example, scientists developed instruments to study how atoms interact with one another. An unexpected favorable result was magnetic resonance imaging (MRI). MRI is a medical technique that looks inside the body without using harmful radiation.

In the mid-twentieth century, nontoxic chemicals made it possible to make better refrigerators for homes. An unexpected unfavorable effect was that these chemicals began destroying the protective ozone layer in the upper atmosphere.

Control of fire is one of the earliest technologies to be developed by humans.

![Active Reading] **5 Summarize** What is the difference between expected effects and unexpected effects of technology?

_____

_____

© Houghton Mifflin Harcourt Publishing Company • Image Credits: ©Gideon Mendel/Corbis

> ### Think Outside the Book
>
> **6 Classify** Use the Internet to find out how infectious diseases can spread rapidly from one continent to another. How would you classify the spread of disease as an effect of air travel?

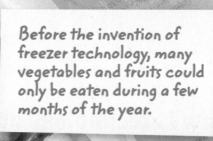

Before the invention of freezer technology, many vegetables and fruits could only be eaten during a few months of the year.

	Expected	Unexpected
Favorable	When frozen foods were developed, it was expected that frozen food would last longer than food that was not frozen. As a result, people save money because frozen vegetables do not spoil. Also, people can eat healthy foods even when they are not in season.	Surprisingly, frozen fruits and vegetables turned out to be more nutritious than fresh produce. Produce begins to lose nutrients as soon as it is picked. Food processors usually freeze fruits and vegetables soon after picking so nutrients remain in the product.
Unfavorable	An expected unfavorable effect of selling frozen foods is that local farmers and markets that provide fresh fruits and vegetables lose customers. In addition, frozen foods need more packaging than fresh foods. This adds to the cost of the food and the environmental costs of supplying it. People are willing to make these trade-offs in order to have frozen food.	When frozen foods were first developed, no one could have predicted the variety of frozen foods that would become available. Many frozen foods today contain more fat, sugar, and salt than fresh foods do. Eating too much of these substances can have unfavorable health effects.

7 Analyze Use the comparison table below to analyze the expected and unexpected effects of the development of the World Wide Web.

	Expected	Unexpected
Favorable		
Unfavorable		

Risky Business

How is technology analyzed?

There are many ways to analyze new technology. Three methods that people use are *risk-benefit analysis, life cycle analysis,* and *Pugh charts.*

Risk-Benefit Analysis

A **risk-benefit analysis** compares the risks, or unfavorable effects, to the benefits, or favorable effects, of a decision or technology. For example, x-rays are a way for doctors to look inside the body to evaluate broken bones and diagnose disease. However, as x-rays pass through the body, they can damage living cells. Medical x-rays expose patients to very small doses of radiation, so the benefits are considered greater than the risks. At one time, some shoe stores used x-rays to match shoes to customers' feet. This is no longer done because the benefit was very small compared to the risk.

Risks and Benefits of X-rays	
Risks	**Benefits**
damage to cells	quick
increased risk of cancer	painless
	saves lives

Skate parks are popular attractions. But there are definite risks involved for the skaters and the owners of the park.

8 Analyze Fill in the chart below with the risks and benefits of building a new skate park in your community.

Risks and Benefits of a New Skate Park	

Life Cycle Analysis

When analyzing technology, it is important to consider the real cost. This is done using a life cycle analysis. A **life cycle analysis** is an evaluation of the materials and energy used for the manufacture, transportation, sale, use, and disposal of a product. This analysis includes everything that the product affects, from obtaining raw materials through disposal. The costs of all of these steps are added together to find the real cost of the product. For example, a life cycle analysis of a glass bottle examines the cost of repairing environmental damage from the mining of raw materials, the cost of fuels consumed to transport materials and finished bottles, and the cost of disposal. A major reason for doing a life cycle analysis is to include environmental effects in the cost. Life cycle analyses are important to manufacturers because the analyses help engineers compare the real costs of different products and find ways to improve production.

Life Cycle of a Television

Resources

A life cycle analysis includes the cost to mine materials for television parts, for manufacturing packaging, and for repairing environmental damage.

Production

The cost of manufacturing is just one part of the overall economic effect of a television.

Consumer Use

Another part of the life cycle analysis is the cost in money and energy when people buy and use the product.

Visualize It!

9 Infer Write a title and a description for the final step in the life cycle of a television.

_____

_____

_____

_____

_____

Pugh Chart

A **Pugh chart** is a table used to compare the features of multiple items. Each row of the table shows a different product or solution. Each column of the chart lists one feature. In some Pugh charts, various options are marked as being either present or missing. Other Pugh charts rank each product as being better or worse than a standard for each feature. Another type ranks each product by feature using a numerical scale.

By looking at the table, a person can analyze and compare items. For example, a Pugh chart comparing cell phones would list different phones in the first column on the left. Then each column would be titled based on a characteristic that is important to consumers. These characteristics could include battery life, sound quality, and messaging systems. A quick look at the Pugh chart would tell you which cell phone was the best based on the qualities that you were looking for.

10 Analyze Evaluate the features of different types of containers. Place an X in each box where the quality applies to the container. Then use the chart to answer the following questions.

	Lightweight	Waterproof	Durable	Inexpensive	Transparent	Reusable
Glass jar						
Plastic bag	X					
Cardboard box	X					
Metal box						

11 Suppose that you have a collection of interesting seashells. Use the chart to help you decide which container you would use to display the collection on shelves in your room. Explain your choice.

_____

_____

_____

_____

_____

12 Why do manufacturers choose cardboard containers for products such as breakfast cereal?

_____

_____

_____

_____

_____

Building Coral Reefs

Recycling large vehicles—ships, jetliners, or railroad cars—is expensive and difficult. Scuba divers exploring wrecked ships found an unexpected solution. Aquatic organisms had moved into the sunken ships and built new coral reefs.

Potential Hazards?
Before sinking, a risk-benefit analysis is done to look for any unfavorable effects such as pollution by leftover fuel.

New Shelters
To the coral organisms, the airplane walls are like an underwater cave. As the new reef grows, many different organisms find their perfect habitat.

This airplane does not look much like a coral reef yet.

Extend

Inquiry

13 Identify How can an artificial reef be considered an unexpected favorable effect of building a plane?

14 Research Use the Internet to investigate other positive or negative effects of sinking ships or planes to build artificial reefs. What did you find?

15 Debate Some people feel that sinking ships and planes on purpose is like dumping our trash in the ocean. In your opinion, do the possible negative effects outweigh the benefits? Explain.

Visual Summary

To complete this summary, fill in the blanks with the correct word or phrase. Then, use the key below to check your answers. You can use this page to review the main concepts of the lesson.

The effects of technology can be expected favorable, expected unfavorable, unexpected favorable, and unexpected unfavorable.

16 When an effect is predicted and desired, it is an _____ effect.

Methods of Analysis

Three methods for analyzing technology are risk-benefit analysis, life cycle analysis, and Pugh charts.

17 A _____ examines every aspect of a product from obtaining raw materials through disposal or recycling.

18 A _____ uses a table to compare features of similar products.

19 An analysis that compares the favorable and unfavorable effects of a decision or technology is a _____

Answers: 16 expected favorable; 17 life cycle analysis; 18 Pugh chart; 19 risk-benefit analysis

20 Explain Why do scientists use analysis methods when developing new technology?

Lesson Review

Vocabulary

Fill in the blank with the term that best completes the following sentences.

1 A _____ happens when some benefits are lost to gain other benefits.

2 The evaluation of the materials and energy used for making, selling, using, and disposing of a product is called a _____ _____.

3 A _____ is the comparison of the favorable and unfavorable effects of a technology.

Key Concepts

4 Identify What are the four types of effects that can result from technology?

_____

_____

_____

_____

5 Analyze Which type of analysis would be most useful to someone buying a product at a store? Why?

_____

_____

_____

6 Explain How is a life cycle analysis used to make decisions about technology?

_____

_____

_____

7 Describe When do the results of a risk-benefit analysis indicate that a technology should be used?

_____

_____

_____

Critical Thinking

Use the Pugh chart below to answer the following questions about digital cameras.

+ = excellent; 0 = good; − = poor

	Zoom	Picture quality	Ease of use	Price
Camera A	−	−	+	0
Camera B	+	−	+	−
Camera C	+	0	0	+

8 Analyze Which camera received the highest overall ratings? Explain.

_____

_____

9 Infer If someone chose Camera A based on the ratings in the Pugh chart, which feature was most important to that user?

_____

_____

_____

10 Predict Imagine that a new surgical procedure has been developed to treat spinal cord injury. What are some possible risks and benefits of receiving this procedure?

_____

_____

_____

_____

11 Evaluate How has the development of social networking on the Internet had favorable and unfavorable effects?

_____

_____

_____

_____

My Notes

Systems

ESSENTIAL QUESTION

What are technological systems?

By the end of this lesson you should be able to explain how technological systems are put together, how these systems are controlled, and how systems interact.

A system is made of parts that work together to do a job. The pistons of this engine work together to convert energy from burning fuel into motion.

Lesson Labs

Quick Labs
- Model a Home Heating System
- Troubleshoot a Faulty System

S.T.E.M. Lab
- Design a Water Treatment System

 Engage Your Brain

1 Identify A slushie machine makes a refreshing drink from a combination of ingredients. Fill in the blanks with words that you think correctly complete the sentences.

To make a slushie, the operator first adds

materials such as _____

and _____

_____ to the machine.

The machine _____

_____ the

ingredients to make a smooth drink.

The valve on the bottom _____

_____ how

much drink flows into the cup.

2 Describe Write your own caption to describe what happens in the slushie machine.

_____

_____

_____

 Active Reading

3 Synthesize Compound words are built by combining two shorter words. The three vocabulary terms below are compound words. Use your knowledge of the shorter words to make a guess about the meaning of each vocabulary term.

input (in + put):

_____

_____

output (out + put):

_____

_____

feedback (feed + back):

_____

_____

Vocabulary Terms

- system
- systems theory
- input
- output
- control
- feedback

4 Apply As you learn the definition of each vocabulary term in this lesson, create your own definition or sketch to help you remember the meaning of the term.

Teamwork

What makes up a system?

The word *system* is used in many ways. A video game system combines interactive controls with amazing computer graphics and sound. Your immune system helps your body fight disease. But what is a system? A **system** is a group of interacting parts that work together to do a job. We will focus on systems that use mechanical parts, which are sometimes called *technological systems*.

Parts That Interact

Look at the parts of the bicycle on these pages. Before the parts are put together, they cannot do very much. Notice that each part fits together with the parts around it. The teeth of the gears fit perfectly into the links in the chain. The pedal and crank attach neatly to the large gears. Of course, it is no accident that the parts fit together. This bicycle was engineered so that each of the parts affect one another in a certain way. Moving one part moves other parts in a carefully designed order.

5 Apply Words are systems made up of interacting letters. When the letters are in the correct order, they interact with each other to express an idea. Unscramble the letters to spell a word from this page.

cremupot

_____

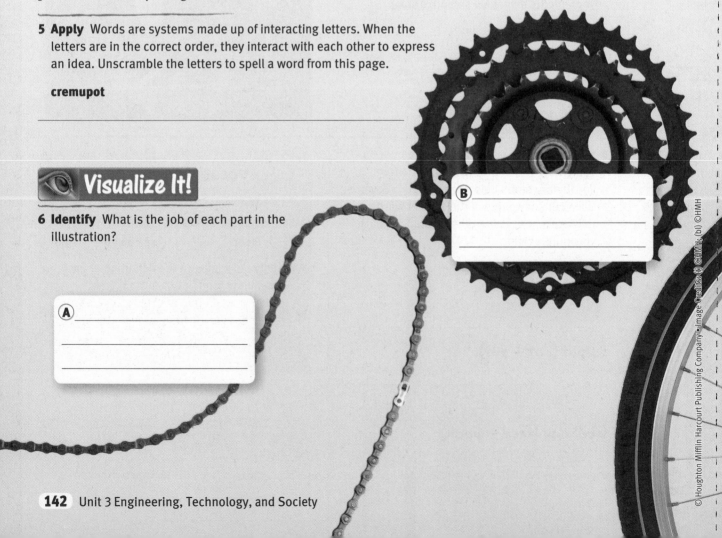

Visualize It!

6 Identify What is the job of each part in the illustration?

Ⓐ _____

Ⓑ _____

© Houghton Mifflin Harcourt Publishing Company • Image Credits: (t) ©HMH; (bl) ©HMH

Parts That Work Together

The parts of a system do more than just interact with each other. The parts of a system work together to do a job. Systems are made of parts that work together as a team. For example, a bolt and a nut are not very useful separately. But when you tighten the nut onto the bolt, the parts work as a team and can hold pieces of wood or metal together. **Systems theory** is the scientific study of systems, including the parts of systems and the ways the parts interact. According to systems theory, affecting one part of a system affects the rest of the system in predictable and unpredictable ways.

Active Reading **7 Define** In your own words, define *systems theory*.

_____

_____

Once assembled, the parts of a bicycle work together to use the force of your legs to get you rolling forward.

Ⓒ _____

_____

Ⓓ _____

_____

All Systems Go!

What do systems do?

There are many different kinds of systems and many different system functions. Some systems are designed to maintain a balance. For example, an air conditioner is designed to maintain an average air temperature by taking in warm air and blowing out cooler air. Other systems generate motion. For example, an engine converts chemical energy in fuel into kinetic energy and energy released as heat. But all systems use inputs to make outputs.

Process Inputs

Matter, energy, or information that goes into a system is called an **input**. For example, a bakery has a system that uses inputs such as flour, water, and yeast to make bread. Heat is also an input into a bread-making system. Other systems, such as computers and calculators, use energy and information as inputs.

Generate Outputs

A product of a system is its **output**. Just as there are many kinds of system inputs, there are many kinds of outputs. The output of the bakery is bread. A calculator's output is processed data. The output that you are trying to make is your intended output. Most systems also make waste, which is an unintended output. The output of one system can be the input into another system.

Visualize It!

8 Apply Fill in the blanks to label the inputs and outputs of an air-conditioning system.

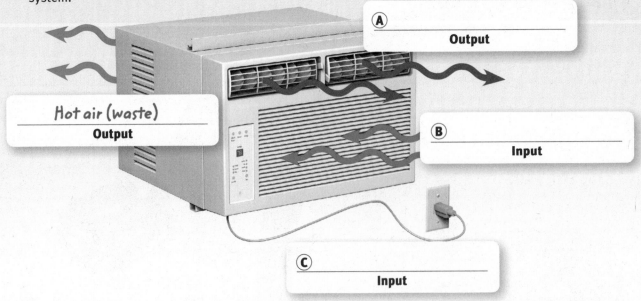

Ⓐ _____
Output

Hot air (waste)
Output

Ⓑ _____
Input

Ⓒ _____
Input

What are two kinds of systems?

Active Reading **9 Contrast** As you read, underline the difference between open and closed systems.

Two major types of technological systems are *open systems* and *closed systems.* In an open system, both matter and energy can flow into the system and out of the system. In a closed system, energy can flow into and out of the system, but matter cannot enter or leave. The photos below show an example of each kind of system.

Matter does not go in or out.

Open Systems

The open system shown here includes a pan, the water inside it, and the burner of a stove. When you turn on the burner, energy flows into the system as heat. The liquid water changes to steam. The outputs of this system are steam and excess energy.

This is an open system because matter in the form of water molecules leaves the system. Most manufacturing processes are open systems.

Closed Systems

You can change the open system into a closed system by covering the pan with a tight-fitting lid. When you turn on the burner, energy still flows as heat into the pan and the water. Energy still radiates as heat from the pan. Liquid water still changes to steam.

But the tight lid traps the steam. No matter enters or leaves the pan. As long as the lid traps the steam in the pan, the system is closed.

10 Infer Is a pencil sharpener an open or closed system? Defend your answer.

_____

_____

It's Under Control

How are systems controlled?

Most technological systems need to be regulated, which is the reason why systems have controls. A **control** is a mechanism for regulating a system so that the system works efficiently.

With Manual and Automatic Controls

A manual control regulates a technological system entirely by human actions. A simple example of a manual control is the light switch in your room. You decide whether the light should be on or off and then set the switch the way you want it. Automobiles are more complicated systems, but are also controlled manually.

Some technological systems operate without continual input from people. These systems use automatic controls. Automatic controls are first set by people. But after being set, the automatic controls regulate a system on their own. For example, traffic lights automatically control the flow of traffic, even when no one is around to operate them. The thermostat in a home automatically turns the heating system on or off, depending on temperature.

 **Visualize It!**

11 **Compare** You can water a lawn using systems that are either manually controlled or automatically controlled. List one advantage and one disadvantage of each kind of control in a lawn-watering system.

Automatic
_____
_____

Manual
_____
_____

Feedback Loop

A thermostat is a sensor that uses temperature as feedback to control a heater. If the temperature falls below a desired point, the thermostat signals the heater to turn on. When the temperature rises above the set point, it signals the heater to turn off.

OFF

If the air temperature is at or above 20 °C, the heater is turned OFF.

The thermostat is set at 20 °C.

The thermostat senses the temperature of the air.

When turned on, the heater warms the air.

Heater

If the air temperature is below 20 °C, the heater is turned ON.

ON

With Feedback

Every time a system generates an output, the system has completed a task, or a *cycle*. Sometimes information from the system cycle controls what happens in the system. When information inside a system signals the cycle to keep going, the system makes more output. When information inside the system signals that there is enough of an output, the system stops making that output.

Both kinds of signals are feedback. **Feedback** is information from one step of a cycle that affects a previous step of the cycle. Because an output from the system returns to become an input into the same system, this type of control is called a *feedback loop*.

Feedback that can stop the process of a cycle is called *negative feedback*. Negative feedback is useful as a control because it prevents a system from generating too much output. Thermostats use a negative feedback loop. Streetlights that turn off during the day when there is already plenty of light, and only turn on when there is too little light, also use negative feedback.

In some systems, increased output causes the system to make even more output. This is called *positive feedback*. A positive feedback loop is not useful as a control for a system because positive feedback never stops the cycle. These systems generate increasing output until they reach a limit. The limit may be the point at which the system runs out of inputs, or when the system goes too fast and breaks down.

© Houghton Mifflin Harcourt Publishing Company

👁 **Visualize It!**

12 Apply What happens when the temperature of the room falls to 19 °C?

Would the heater be on or off if the temperature of the room were 21 °C?

📖 **Active Reading**

13 State What can negative feedback do to a running system that positive feedback cannot do?

Systems are

How are systems studied?

The study of systems to improve how they work together and interact with each other is called *systems analysis*.

By Changing Parts

One technique used in systems analysis is to change one part of a system and watch what happens. This is an effective way to analyze how small changes can affect the whole system. For example, an automobile designer may change the shape of the hood of a car and measure how the new design affects wind resistance. Changing this part may help the car use fuel more efficiently.

Sometimes systems are so complex that analysts cannot change parts of the system. In these cases researchers often use models. Some models are physical structures that mimic a system. Computer models are also useful, especially for studying large, complicated systems such as nuclear power plants.

The **electrical system** distributes energy to all the parts of the house. Wires carry current to lights and appliances. Circuit breakers act as an automatic control to shut off the current when there is a problem.

Visualize It!

14 Predict A house is a large system made of many smaller systems that work together. Use the illustration to answer questions about how a change in one system could affect other systems in the house.

A How might installing new energy-efficient windows affect the heating and cooling system?

_____

_____

The **plumbing system** carries water to and from the house and yard. Most water systems use manual controls. The plumbing system might interact with the heating system and with the electrical system in a hot water tank.

IN THE HOUSE!

By Analyzing Interactions

Large systems are made of many smaller systems working together. Studying the way these smaller systems interact and affect the large system is another aspect of systems analysis.

You can think of a house as a big system made of many smaller systems. The electrical, plumbing, and heating systems are some you may recognize. The structure of the house, including the walls, windows, doors, and roof, is also a system.

Every part of a house is part of a smaller system that helps the large house system work. You can improve a function of the large system by improving the function of the smaller system. When people look into the benefits of upgrading parts of their home, they are doing systems analysis!

Active Reading

15 Identify What are three small systems in a house?

_____

_____

_____

B How could installing solar panels that convert sunlight to electric current affect an input to systems in the house?

_____

_____

The **heating system** and **cooling system** use a thermostat to provide feedback. When the room reaches the desired temperature, the system shuts off. Depending on the type of heating or cooling, the system may interact with the electrical and plumbing systems.

Think Outside the Book Inquiry

16 Recommend In teams, choose a system in a modern building and research how it has changed over the last 20 years. Write a report that explains how these changes have affected the way the system operates.

Visual Summary

To complete this summary, fill in the blanks in the sentences. Then, use the key below to check your answers. You can use this page to review the main concepts of the lesson.

Systems

Parts work together as a team in systems.

17 A system consists of at least two _____ that _____ together to do something that one part could not do alone.

Systems need to be regulated. A control is a mechanism for regulating a system.

19 A manual or automatic _____ is used to _____ the operation of a system.

20 An automatic control uses a _____ loop to keep the system within a desired range.

Systems take in inputs and generate outputs.

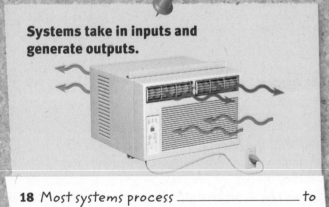

18 Most systems process _____ to generate one or more _____.

Systems and system interactions are analyzed.

21 Systems analysts study large complex systems by studying the interactions of their _____

Answers: 17 parts, work or interact; 18 inputs, outputs; 19 control, regulate; 20 feedback; 21 smaller systems

22 Apply A fire can be described as a system that combines fuel and oxygen and releases energy in the form of heat. What are two ways to affect the fire by changing its inputs?

Lesson Review

Vocabulary

Draw a line to connect the following terms with their descriptions.

1 control   **A** generated by a system

2 feedback   **B** interacting parts that work together

3 output

4 system   **C** information from inside the system

             D regulates a system

Key Concepts

5 Apply Which part of a refrigerator determines whether it is an open or closed system? How can you change the system from closed to open?

6 Explain What is the role of a control in a system that is functioning correctly?

7 Identify A flashlight is a technological system. Which part of the flashlight is the control? Is the control manual or automatic?

8 Distinguish Is a smoke alarm regulated by a manual control or an automatic control? Explain why.

9 Contrast How is a house different from a space station? How are they similar?

Critical Thinking

Use this table to answer the following questions.

10 Calculate A math formula is a system that processes inputs to generate an output. Use the formula to fill in the table below.

$(3 + x) - 2 = y$	
x	y
1	2
5	
20	

11 Apply Identify the input and output of the equation in the table.

12 Analyze What is a small system within the main equation?

13 Infer Why do engineers study the way systems interact?

14 Infer Why are negative feedback loops used more often as system controls than positive feedback loops?

My Notes

Materials and Tools

Extreme conditions call for extremely well-engineered materials. The protective clothing worn by firefighters has to be heat resistant and flame resistant. It also has to be light and flexible so firefighters can move freely and quickly.

ESSENTIAL QUESTION

How do engineers use materials and tools?

By the end of this lesson, you should be able to explain how the tools and materials of technology are chosen, tested, improved, and used.

Engage Your Brain

1 Identify Unscramble the letters below to find words that describe steel. Write your words on the blank lines.

TEMLA _____

LLYAO _____

OIDLS _____

EENSD _____

2 Hypothesize Tall buildings are supported by steel beams. What properties of steel make it safe for people to live and work in tall buildings?

_____

_____

_____

_____

Active Reading

3 Apply Use context clues to write your own definitions for the words *modify* and *physical*.

Example sentence
The experiment didn't work as planned, so the scientists decided to <u>modify</u> their procedure.

modify:

_____

_____

Example sentence
Some <u>physical</u> properties of ice are that it is hard, translucent, and cold.

physical:

_____

_____

Vocabulary Term

• materials science

4 Apply As you learn the definition of this vocabulary term, create your own definition or sketch to help you remember the meaning of the term.

From *Hammers* to *Computers*

What are the tools of technology?

Tools help us do things more easily and let us do things we could not otherwise do. There are two general types of tools: physical tools and cyber tools. Physical tools, such as hammers and bulldozers, are used to do physical work. Cyber tools, such as computers, do work in the form of electronic signals. Sometimes tools are simple, and sometimes they are complicated pieces of technology.

Physical Tools

Physical tools are helpful objects that are used to do physical work. Humans have been using physical tools for tens of thousands of years. Early physical tools were simple objects like axes, spears, and knives used for building shelter, cooking, and hunting.

Today, we still use many simple physical tools like hammers, pencils, and rulers. New materials and technology have changed some physical tools. Power saws and blenders use modern materials and electricity. Some modern tools, such as assembly line robots, combine physical work with computer technology.

Active Reading

5 Identify As you read, underline three examples of physical tools used in technology.

Visualize It!

6 Question What job does each tool make easier?

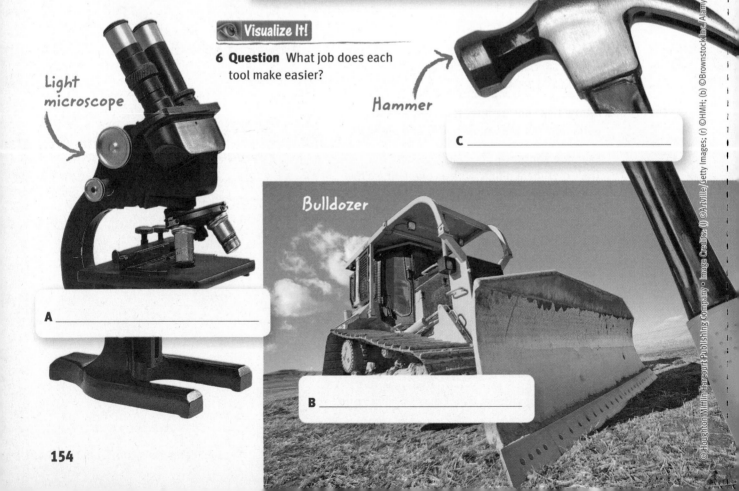

Light microscope

Hammer

Bulldozer

A _____

B _____

C _____

7 Compare What do all these cyber tools have in common?

_____

_____

_____

Computer-aided design (CAD) helps engineers design new machines, such as an aircraft.

Learning to fly a plane is safer in flight simulators than in real planes.

Predicting storm patterns using computer models helps keep people safe.

Cyber Tools

The word *cyber* means "computer." A cyber tool is a computer tool that uses programs, or *software*, to do work. Cyber tools extend our abilities by performing complex calculations at high speeds. Computer-aided design (CAD), for example, is software that is used to visualize a complex structure or design. Engineers can see how a product will look before it is built.

Cyber tools also let us try something on a computer before doing it in real life. For example, learning to fly in a real plane can be expensive and dangerous. Model cockpits that use software to simulate flying can be cheaper and safer. Computer software also models the weather so we can better predict the paths of storms.

Think Outside the Book Inquiry

8 Apply Conduct an imaginary interview with a bulldozer or other large machine about its job. Be sure to include both questions and answers.

What are some of the materials of technology?

The first materials people used were natural raw materials, such as wood, stone, and leather. Thousands of years ago, people developed the technology to change raw materials to make modified materials, such as ceramics, metal, and glass.

The modification and study of materials is the field of **materials science**. Many materials we use every day, such as plastic, polyester, and steel, were developed by materials scientists.

Materials are classified into categories based on their composition. Classifications include metals, ceramics, polymers, semiconductors, composites, and exotic materials. Simpler materials, such as glass, paper, and wood, are also still used in many technology applications.

Metals are any of the metallic elements and mixtures of those elements. Most metals are dense and strong. They can be bent into shapes and stretched into wires, and have high thermal and electrical conductivity.

Ceramics are inorganic, nonmetallic compounds. Baked clay is a simple ceramic. Ceramics tolerate heat well. Most ceramics are strong but break instead of bending, and they have low electrical conductivity.

Polymers are large molecules made up of linked smaller molecules. Many plastics are polymers made from petroleum. Most polymers have low density and low electrical conductivity.

Semiconductors are compounds that have moderate electrical conductivity but low thermal conductivity.

Composites are made of two or more types of materials that are combined. Together the two materials are much stronger than either is alone.

Exotic materials do not fit in any of the usual categories. These include things like aerogels and nanomolecules.

Disc brakes work by clamping brake pads on a disc-shaped rotor attached to the wheel. Ceramic rotors work better at high temperatures than metal rotors do.

Nonstick coatings are made of polymers.

Aerogels, which are great insulators, are formed by replacing the liquid in a gel with a gas.

Carbon Fiber Composites

Carbon fiber composites (CFCs) are a combination of a polymer coating, such as polyester or nylon, reinforced with extremely thin carbon fibers. The fibers are very strong, and the polymer bonds them together tightly. The composite they make is light, strong, and tough.

Strong and Light!
CFCs work very well when durable yet lightweight materials are required. Racing cars and fighter jets use parts made from CFCs. Many sporting goods use CFCs, too. Racquets, canoes, skis, and bicycles made of CFCs are strong and light.

An Expensive Choice
CFCs are relatively expensive, so using them requires making a trade-off. People must either be willing to pay the high price for the strongest and lightest material or switch to a less expensive material that is not quite as light or strong. For example, making the body of this car from aluminum would have cost less, but an aluminum-bodied car would be heavier.

Extend

Inquiry

10 Identify Which category of materials do CFCs belong to?

11 Research Investigate an application of carbon fiber composites and explain why CFCs are important for this application.

12 Create Illustrate three ways that carbon fiber composites could be used in your home or community. Why do you think they are not already used this way?

Decisions, Decisions...

How are materials chosen?

Materials are chosen because of their characteristics. The characteristics of a material include the material's physical and chemical properties. These properties influence the way a material functions.

By Chemical Properties

Chemical properties describe a material's ability to take part in a chemical reaction. Some materials are chosen because they are nonreactive and do not take part in chemical reactions easily. Stainless steel and some plastics are highly nonreactive. Other materials are chosen because they do react chemically. For example, ammonia is used in cleaners because it reacts with grease. After the ammonia is applied, the grease dissolves more easily in water and can be washed away.

By Physical Properties

Physical properties are the characteristics of a material that can be observed or measured without changing the material's composition. Some physical properties of materials include:

- Density
- Boiling point and melting point
- Transparency, or the ability to let light pass though
- Conductivity, or the ability to carry electric current
- Hardness

Visualize It!

13 Apply Use the table below to describe how the physical and chemical properties of each item influence the decision to use the item for the purpose shown.

Item	Chemical property	Physical property
Laminated countertop	Nonreactive with food and water	Hard, durable
Ammonia glass cleaner		Liquid at room temperature
Stainless steel sink		Hard, durable
Window	Nonreactive with water or chemical cleaners	
Plastic casing on toaster	Nonreactive with cleaners	

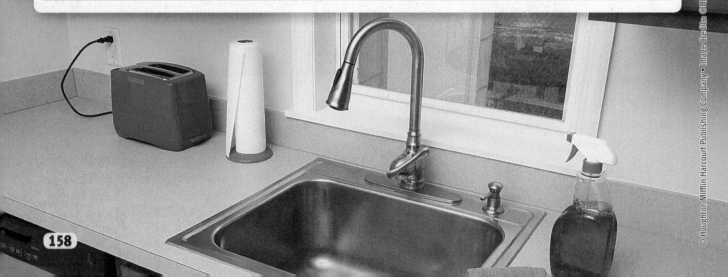

What limits a material's use?

Even though a material might be ideal for one reason, it could be a bad choice for other reasons. For example, untreated steel rusts quickly in salt water. Gold does not rust. However, gold is very expensive. Making a ship out of gold would cost a fortune! Choosing materials requires thinking about a material's availability, cost, and degree of hazard.

Sand is a common and inexpensive material used in construction and in making glass.

Availability Even though a material may be an ideal choice, it may not be available for use in technology. For example, platinum is a rare metal that is difficult to mine. Other materials, such as sand, are common and easy to obtain.

Cost When a material is scarce or difficult to make, it is usually also expensive. Even a small amount of platinum is very expensive. As a result, it is only used in small amounts as a technological material. Platinum is used when the need for it outweighs the cost.

Platinum is rare and expensive. Small amounts are used to speed up some chemical reactions.

Degree of Hazard Sometimes a material works well for its intended application but is too hazardous to be widely used. DDT is a chemical that is very good at killing insects. But it is banned in many countries because it harms other animals, too.

14 Contrast Use the Venn diagram to compare and contrast sand and platinum.

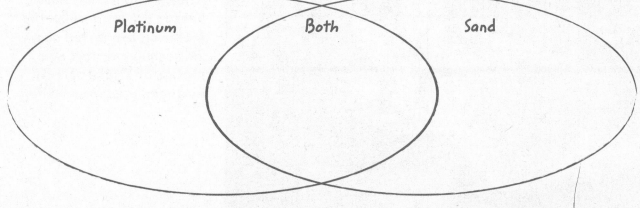

Platinum   Both   Sand

New *and* Improved

How are materials improved?

Scientists and engineers use the engineering design process when modifying materials. The design process is a series of steps that lead to a new product. After identifying and researching a problem, possible solutions are brainstormed. A solution is selected, and then testing begins.

They Are Tested

Before new materials are actually used, they must be tested. Engineers need to determine if the materials work as originally planned.

For example, a material that is supposed to withstand earthquakes better than current materials will be thoroughly tested before it is used to make a building. If the new material does not work as well as scientists thought it would, changes are made. The material gets more modifications followed by more testing.

Active Reading

15 Explain Why must materials be tested before they are used in a large production?

_____

_____

16 Design Draw a machine that would test the durability of a steel spring.

Materials used in bridges are tested for breakage before they are used. Then, after the materials have been in use for a while, the materials are tested again. This engineer is testing a section of bridge after it had been used for a while.

© Houghton Mifflin Harcourt Publishing Company • Image Credits: ©Colin Cuthbert/Photo Researchers, Inc.

They Are Modified

Materials are changed to maximize their desirable properties. For example, an alloy is a mixture of a metal with another substance. Steel is an alloy of iron and carbon. Steel keeps the conductivity of iron. But adding carbon to iron makes steel much harder than iron is by itself.

Another example of modification is the vulcanization of rubber. Natural rubber is soft and sticky. Vulcanization involves heating a mixture of natural rubber and sulfur to produce harder, more durable vulcanized rubber.

Scientific advances make new materials possible. The new materials can then lead to new technology. New technology can lead to even better new materials.

Bronze is an alloy of copper and tin that has been used for thousands of years. Bronze is stronger than either copper or tin alone. This pot is pouring molten bronze.

Natural rubber is sticky and wears down quickly. Vulcanization makes rubber hard and durable. This allows tires to withstand enormous amounts of weight and friction.

Concrete reinforced with metal bars is stronger and more stable than concrete is alone. Without reinforcement, concrete overhangs like this one would crack and break.

17 Analyze What would be an advantage of using natural rubber for the soles of shoes?

_____

_____

18 Infer What would be an advantage of using vulcanized rubber for the soles of shoes?

_____

_____

New Dog, New Tricks

How do new materials improve new technology?

The development of light bulbs dramatically changed the way people live. But developing an incandescent light bulb was difficult. Incandescent bulbs work by sending an electric current through a filament. The filament becomes hot and glows. But inventors struggled to find a material that could glow for a useful length of time. A new material was needed for this technology.

Inventor Thomas Edison and his team tried making a glowing filament for light bulbs out of 1,600 different materials. They tried materials such as platinum, coconut-shell fibers, and even human hair. None of these worked. The filament that finally worked was made of treated bamboo fibers. New materials enable new technology. Look around you and see how!

Active Reading

19 Identify As you read, underline the new material that made incandescent bulbs possible.

Thomas Edison developed practical light bulbs in the late 1800s after developing a new filament.

Battery-powered flight would have been impossible without new materials. Modern batteries and carbon fiber make this ultralight plane efficient, light, and strong.

20 Identify In each caption, underline a benefit that is made possible by each new material.

Cars are painted using electrostatic paint. The paint and the car have opposite charges, so they attract each other. Electrostatic paint pollutes far less than earlier kinds of paint.

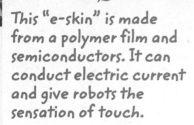

This "e-skin" is made from a polymer film and semiconductors. It can conduct electric current and give robots the sensation of touch.

Fiber-optic technology is made possible by flexible glass fibers that carry data in pulses of light. Fiber-optic cables carry much more data than copper-wire cables of similar size do.

Modern waterproof fabrics have tiny pores. The pores are too small for raindrops to fit through. But the pores do let evaporated sweat escape, so you stay dry.

Think Outside the Book Inquiry

21 Apply Research a new material not discussed on this page, and explain how it has been applied to make life better.

Visual Summary

To complete this summary, fill in the correct word or phrase.
Then, use the key below to check your answers. You can use
this page to review the main concepts of the lesson.

Materials and Tools

Physical tools do
physical work. Cyber
tools do work in the
form of electronic data.

22 A microscope is a
_____ tool,
and imaging software is a
_____ tool.

Materials are
developed, tested,
and improved by
materials scientists.

23 Steel, an alloy of iron and carbon,
is _____ than iron alone.

Types of materials
include metals,
ceramics, polymers,
semiconductors, and
composites.

24 Carbon fiber composites are
_____
and _____ Their
use is limited by _____

New materials lead to
new technologies.

25 The vulcanization of
rubber makes rubber _____
and _____

Answers: 22 physical, cyber; 23 stronger; 24 strong, light,
cost; 25 hard, durable

---

26 Synthesize What are the materials and tools you
might use to make a brochure to teach younger
students about sports safety?

Vocabulary

In your own words, define the following term.

1 materials science

_____

_____

_____

Key Concepts

2 Identify Name two physical tools you used today, and describe how you used them.

_____

_____

_____

_____

_____

3 Identify What kinds of materials have good electrical conductivity?

_____

_____

4 Relate Why is platinum used sparingly in technological applications?

_____

_____

_____

5 Infer If a material that has been used for years is modified in some way, why does it need to be retested?

_____

_____

_____

_____

6 Explain How are new materials related to new technologies?

_____

_____

_____

_____

_____

Critical Thinking

Use this table to answer the following questions.

Material	Conducts electric current?	Made from petroleum?	Was in use thousands of years ago?
A	yes	no	yes
B	no	no	yes
C	no	yes	no

7 Infer Using the data provided, fill in the blanks below with A, B, or C.

_____ CERAMIC

_____ POLYMER

_____ METAL

8 Apply Which materials from the table would be good insulators for electrical wires? Explain your answer.

_____

_____

_____

9 Solve What is an important chemical property of a plastic bottle engineered to hold ammonia?

_____

_____

_____

10 Evaluate What is a limitation of a cyber tool designed to teach people how to fly planes?

_____

_____

_____

_____

_____

My Notes

Mitchell W. Pryor

ROBOTICS ENGINEER

Do you think of robots as mostly science fiction? Can you imagine going to college to learn how to build robots? One place where you can do just that is the University of Texas at Austin (UT). Dr. Mitchell Pryor and his colleagues conduct robot research on a regular basis. Dr. Pryor's research group develops and tests new ways to use robots. They are on the cutting edge of robotics.

The group works on robots that operate both with and without human assistance. Today's robots do not look like typical robots from science fiction movies, but they do complete a wide range of tasks. In industrial settings, for example, robots are used to weld, paint, and move and assemble parts. Unlike people, the robots can perform their tasks exactly the same way every time. They also work quickly, do not get injured, can generally work for long periods of time without breaks, and do not require daily pay (although they are not cheap to make or purchase!).

Dr. Pryor, who received his Ph.D. from UT, also teaches graduate and undergraduate courses in mechanical engineering at the university. His ongoing research group gives students an opportunity for some hands-on learning, a dream for many science fiction fans!

This robot cleans areas too hazardous for humans. The robot is controlled by an operator watching a video feed.

Language Arts Connection

Robot speech must be clear, concise, and grammatically correct. Work in a group to generate acceptable robot speech for the information below. Assume that your robot is limited to eight-word statements.

- The lid on the container must be tightened before you can move the container.
- The yellow paint is finished. Red paint will be added next, after drying for 20 minutes.

JOB BOARD

Computer Scientist

What You'll Do: Computer scientists work in a wide range of jobs including Software or Website development, Systems Analyst, Systems Administrator, and Information Technology Specialist.

Where You Might Work: At a computer company, government agency, manufacturing company, software company, large office, or academic institution.

Education: At a minimum a bachelor's degree, but often an advanced degree is needed.

Other Job Requirements: You need research, critical thinking, and problem-solving skills along with knowledge of computer security management and the latest technology.

Materials Scientist

What You'll Do: Study the composition and structure of matter to build new and better products such as shoes, computer chips, vehicles, blue jeans, and baking pans.

Where You Might Work: At a manufacturing plant, environmental consulting firm, or computer company.

Education: A minimum of a bachelor's degree, but typically a master's degree or doctorate in physics or chemistry.

Other Job Requirements: Research skills, verbal and written communication skills, and the ability to solve problems.

PEOPLE IN SCIENCE NEWS

Agnes RILEY

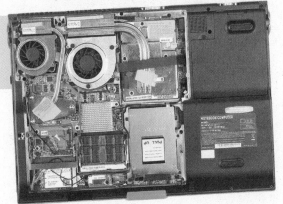

A Job for a Problem Solver

A computer is a great time-saving machine—right up until it doesn't work. If your computer isn't working right, you should try some simple steps, such as restarting it. If you are unable to solve the problem yourself, you might need to call an expert. Agnes Riley from Budapest, Hungary, is one such expert. Give her a computer that isn't working correctly, and she will take it apart, find the problem, and fix it.

Agnes learned how to fix computers by trial and error. She worked for a company in Hungary that had old computers, which needed constant repair. By experimenting, she learned to fix them.

In 1999, Agnes moved to New York City and took the exam to become a licensed computer technician. She enjoys the challenge of solving computer problems for people. If you enjoy solving problems, you might want to become a computer technician too!

Engineering and Life Science

ESSENTIAL QUESTION

How is engineering related to life science?

By the end of this lesson, you should be able to describe how organisms can be used in engineering, and how engineering can help organisms.

Studying human movement helps engineers build robots like this one.

🧠 Engage Your Brain

1 Predict Check T or F to show whether you think each sentence below about technology and life science is correct.

		Living things can inspire new technology.
☐	☐	

T F

T	F	
☐	☐	Technology is used to help people with disabilities.
☐	☐	All bacteria are harmful to humans.
☐	☐	Animals can be a product of engineering.
☐	☐	We cannot learn about engineering by observing nature.

✏️ Active Reading

3 Synthesize You can often define an unknown word if you know the meaning of its word parts. Use the word parts and sentence below to make an educated guess about the meaning of the word *biomimicry*.

Word part	Meaning
bio-	life
mimic	imitate

Example sentence
Engineers used <u>biomimicry</u> to build robots that move like spiders.

biomimicry:

_____

_____

_____

Vocabulary

4 Identify As you read, place a question mark next to any words that you do not understand. When you finish reading the lesson, go back and review the text that you marked. If the information is still confusing, consult a classmate or teacher.

Living Technology

How are organisms used as technology?

When people talk about technology, they are talking about products, processes, and systems that use science to serve a practical purpose. Technology can be a familiar, simple object like a hammer or a complex machine such as a satellite. Did you know that a living organism can also be a type of technology? *Biotechnology* is the use of living things to make products or perform tasks.

To Make Products

Active Reading **5 Identify** As you read this page, underline examples of products manufactured with the help of living organisms.

Living organisms help us make many of the products we use. For example, bakers use a microorganism, yeast, to make bread. Gas bubbles produced by the yeast give the bread a fluffy texture when it is baked. Many types of cheese get their unique flavors, odors, and textures from bacteria and fungi that cheese makers add to milk or cream. Other kinds of bacteria produce compounds that people use to make some life-saving medicines, including insulin and many antibiotics.

Visualize It!

6 Label Look at the following photographs. What two ways are microorganisms used in the making of cheese?

_____

_____

_____

_____

_____

Cheese production begins with large vats of milk to which bacteria are added to help the milk gel.

To Perform Tasks

🔍 **Active Reading** **7 Identify** As you read, underline examples of different tasks performed by organisms.

Many living organisms perform very helpful tasks. For example, people use bacteria to treat wastewater and to clean up oil spills. Leeches are used to keep blood from pooling after reattachment of a severed body part, such as a finger. Humans have trained animals to work for them for many centuries. For example, horses pull wagons and carry people from place to place. Dogs guide visually impaired people safely through busy city streets. Dogs have also been trained to search for drugs, bombs, fugitives, and hikers lost in the woods. Trained bottlenose dolphins and sea lions dive to the sea floor to retrieve lost equipment. People have even used pigeons as a form of air mail. Believe it or not, these helpful organisms are also examples of biotechnology.

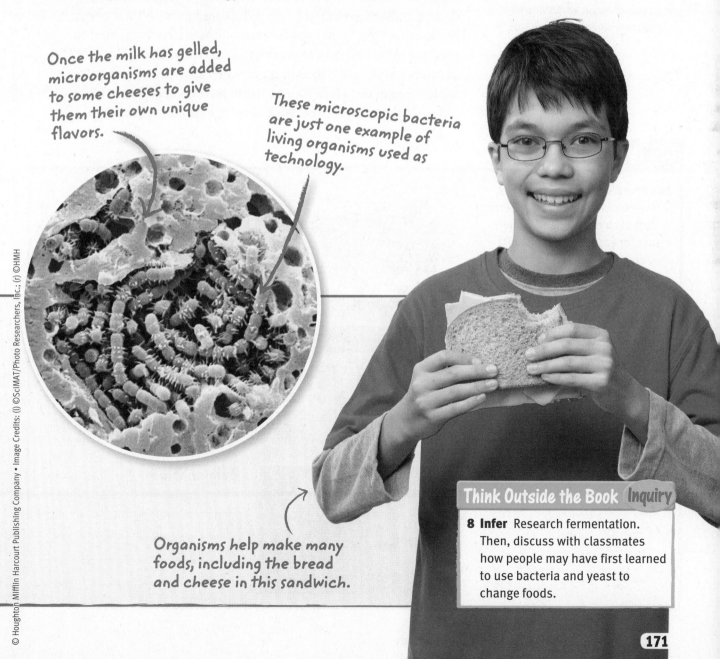

Once the milk has gelled, microorganisms are added to some cheeses to give them their own unique flavors.

These microscopic bacteria are just one example of living organisms used as technology.

Organisms help make many foods, including the bread and cheese in this sandwich.

Think Outside the Book Inquiry

8 Infer Research fermentation. Then, discuss with classmates how people may have first learned to use bacteria and yeast to change foods.

Building on Life

What technology is used to change organisms or make new organisms?

Throughout history, people have changed the traits of organisms to better meet human needs. This can be done by using naturally occurring differences among individuals or by changing an organism's DNA.

Selective Breeding

Compare two herds of cattle and you may observe many different traits. Cattle breeders use a process called *selective breeding* to emphasize traits that occur naturally in their cattle. Animals with desired traits are selected to reproduce and pass on their genes. Some cattle have been bred for meat. Others have been bred to produce milk. Still others are bred to survive in harsh climates. Farmers use selective breeding for plants as well. For example, some types of corn have been bred to have a sweet flavor. Other types are not as sweet and are grown as food for animals.

Active Reading

9 Define What does the word *selective* mean when it is used in the term *selective breeding*?

_____

_____

_____

Visualize It!

10 Compare These photos show three bulls that are very different from each other. Identify one trait for each bull and suggest a reason why that trait was selected.

Scottish Highland

_____
_____
_____
_____

Texas Longhorn

_____
_____
_____
_____

Belgian Blue

_____
_____
_____
_____

These fluorescent fish may someday help find pollution. A gene inserted into their DNA makes them glow brightly but does not make any other change.

Genetic Engineering

Traits can also be changed by modifying the DNA inside a living cell. This technology is known as *genetic engineering* or *genetic modification*. In one type of genetic modification, DNA is extracted from a donor cell. Chemicals are used to cut the DNA into small fragments. The small fragments are mixed with bacteria. Because bacteria tend to absorb DNA from their environment, some of the bacteria will take up the cut DNA. The bacteria grow and reproduce along with the inserted DNA. At this point, the bacteria will produce the protein that is coded for by the inserted DNA. That protein can be used for medical treatments. The bacteria can also be used to supply DNA for further applications.

📰 **Active Reading**

11 Sequence As you read, write the numbers 1 to 5 beside the steps that occur when scientists modify a person's DNA.

The Process of Genetic Modification

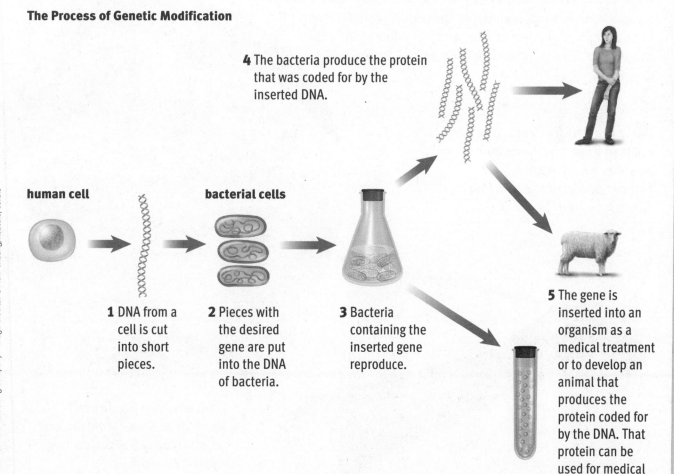

4 The bacteria produce the protein that was coded for by the inserted DNA.

human cell

bacterial cells

1 DNA from a cell is cut into short pieces.

2 Pieces with the desired gene are put into the DNA of bacteria.

3 Bacteria containing the inserted gene reproduce.

5 The gene is inserted into an organism as a medical treatment or to develop an animal that produces the protein coded for by the DNA. That protein can be used for medical treatments.

Lending a Helping Hand

What technology is used to help organisms?

One role of technology in life sciences is helping organisms, usually humans, with everyday tasks. Technology also helps organisms fight life-threatening diseases and conditions.

Assistive and Adaptive Technology

Assistive and adaptive technology plays a very important role in helping people with everyday activities. This technology includes devices such as hearing aids, wheelchairs, and titanium rods used to set broken bones. Other examples include devices that replace damaged or lost limbs, help keep hearts beating with a regular rhythm, and focus blurry vision. Some technology is so common that we seldom notice it. For example, ramps from the street to the sidewalk are a technological solution to make the use of wheelchairs, strollers, or even grocery carts easier. Other devices are less common but essential to the people who use them. For example, replacement knee and hip joints often work so well that they go unnoticed even by the person who uses them.

Active Reading

12 List What are four technological devices that assist people or help them adapt to their environments?

_____

_____

_____

_____

Early prosthetics replaced a missing limb, but the device was not really useful. The fingers could not move like those of a real hand.

This prosthetic doesn't look much like a hand, but it allowed a person to do detailed work.

© Houghton Mifflin Harcourt Publishing Company • Image Credits: (l) ©Science & Society Picture Library/Getty Images; (r) ©Lucien Aigner/Corbis

Medicines and Medical Technology

Medicines are chemical products that help an organism fight disease or regulate body functions. People have used medicines for thousands of years. Every year, scientists test thousands of chemical compounds to find new medicines. Medical technology has made many diseases easy to control or to cure. Genetic modification has added a new tool for medical research. Using specific genes to make medical compounds may help researchers find ways to design medicines that are perfectly matched to each individual patient.

Visualize It!

13 Describe What kinds of changes have allowed modern prosthetic arms to function better than those made many years ago?

_____

_____

_____

_____

Modern prosthetics combine artificial joints, for better functionality, with a more realistic appearance.

The newest prosthetics have electrodes that connect to nerves on a person's body. These devices are controlled by the user's brain.

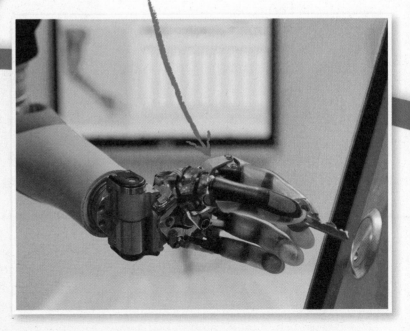

It's Natural

How can new technology be inspired by nature?

No matter what you want to do with a machine or process, there is a good chance that there is an organism that does it naturally. Do you need an aircraft that can hover and fly backwards? The hummingbird does that. How about a machine that can dig a tunnel? Moles are experts at making tunnels. Engineers often get their inspiration from nature when they want to improve a design. *Biomimicry* is the imitation of living organisms to create technological products.

By Copying Materials Made by Organisms

Just as nature has a form for just about any function, one can also find a material for just about any purpose. For example, researchers are constantly looking for ways to make a strong, yet lightweight, fiber. One of the strongest known materials is spider silk. Scientists study spider webs to find out what spider silk is made of. If researchers could synthesize natural spider silk, it would be the perfect material to manufacture strong, lightweight ropes. When barnacles attach themselves to the side of a ship, they are almost impossible to remove. Even after years of soaking in salt water and being bashed by waves, barnacles remain firmly attached to a ship. Researchers are investigating ways to make glue with the same properties as the barnacle's adhesive.

The silk made by spiders is one of the strongest materials known.

Detail of shark skin

Detail of swimsuit fabric

14 Infer Why would scientists choose shark skin as a model for a swimsuit designed for competitive swimmers?

_____

_____

_____

_____

When swimsuit designers wanted to make a surface that moves smoothly through the water, they modeled a fabric after the skin of the fast-swimming shark.

By Copying the Structure of Organisms

Engineers often use designs that mimic the shapes that are found in nature. For example, the shape of whale flippers allows whales to move water efficiently. Engineers copied this shape to build more efficient blades for wind turbines. Engineers were also inspired by nature when designing the Japanese bullet train. This train travels more than 270 km/h (168 mi/h). But when the train emerged from a tunnel, the compressed air waves created a boom that disturbed nearby residents. In order to design a quieter train, designers studied the shape of the kingfisher's beak, which cuts through water without producing waves.

Visualize It!

15 Model The photos below show how engineers copied the shape of the kingfisher beak to design the front of a fast-moving train. Look at the photo of the frog below. Use the space provided to sketch a technology that could be based on the characteristics of a frog.

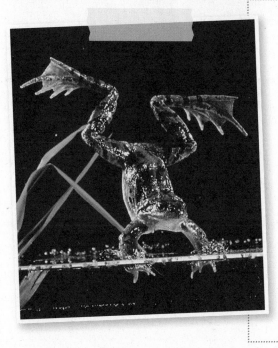

Visual Summary

To complete this summary, fill in the blanks with the correct word or phrase. Then, use the key below to check your answers. You can use this page to review the main concepts of the lesson.

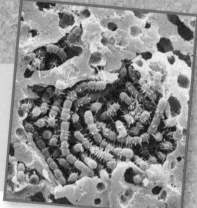

Engineering and Life Science

Organisms may be used to make products or perform tasks.

16 Using living things to perform tasks or make products is called

_____

Technology can be applied to develop new or changed organisms.

17 _____

is a process in which segments of DNA are inserted into cells in order to change the organism.

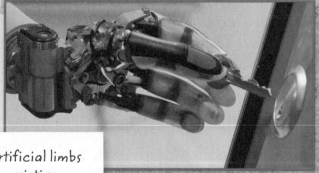

Technology helps organisms with life processes. Technology can be inspired by living things.

18 Wheelchairs, eyeglasses, and artificial limbs are all examples of adaptive or assistive

_____

Answers: 16 biotechnology; 17 genetic modification or genetic engineering; 18 technology

19 Relate How is the selective breeding process related to genetic engineering of organisms?

Lesson Review

Vocabulary

1 _____ uses natural differences in organisms to develop traits over many generations.

2 _____ introduces changes to the DNA of organisms to develop traits within a single generation.

3 _____ is the imitation of living organisms to create technological products for humans.

Key Concepts

4 List What are two ways in which living organisms can be used as part of technological applications?

_____

_____

_____

5 Explain What are some advantages to farmers of using selective breeding of crops?

_____

_____

_____

_____

6 Compare What is a benefit of genetic engineering compared to selective breeding?

_____

_____

_____

_____

7 List What are four examples of technologies used to help improve people's lives?

_____

_____

_____

_____

_____

Critical Thinking

Use this diagram to answer the following question.

8 Explain Describe the process of genetic modification shown in the diagram above.

_____

_____

_____

9 Explain Choose a medical technology and explain how it uses life sciences and engineering.

_____

_____

_____

_____

10 Predict How would a community be affected if technology such as wheelchairs and hearing aids were not available?

_____

_____

_____

_____

My Notes

Engineering and Our World

ESSENTIAL QUESTION

How are engineering and society related?

By the end of this lesson, you should be able to explain how engineering, technology, and society affect each other.

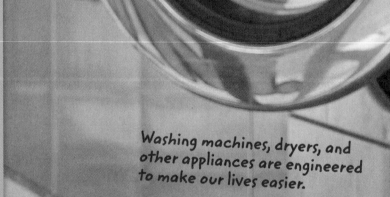

Washing machines, dryers, and other appliances are engineered to make our lives easier.

Lesson Labs

Quick Labs
• Inventor Trading Cards
• Investigate Energy Efficiency

S.T.E.M. Lab
• Investigate Digital Information

 Engage Your Brain

1 Describe Write a caption explaining what is going on in this photo.

_____

_____

2 Infer Every kind of technology has advantages and disadvantages. Think of some disadvantages to washing clothes by hand. Think of some advantages. Write your answers below.

_____

_____

_____

_____

_____

 Active Reading

3 Apply Use context clues to write your own definition for the words *technology* and *design*.

Example sentence
The tools of modern farming <u>technology</u> include chemical fertilizers, diesel-powered tractors, and automatic irrigation systems.

technology:

_____

_____

Example sentence
Landscape engineers <u>design</u> parks so that people have room to relax and play.

design:

_____

_____

Vocabulary

4 Identify As you read, place a question mark next to any words that you don't understand. When you finish reading the lesson, go back and review the text that you marked. If the information is still confusing, consult a classmate or teacher.

Got Tech?

What makes up the designed world?

Your environment is made of a designed world within a natural world. The natural world includes all the parts of the environment that were not made by people. The designed world includes all the parts of the environment that were made by people.

Big Structures and Large Machines

Look around you. What do you see? You might see houses, apartments, your school, and roads and bridges and the vehicles on them. These structures are all parts of the designed world. The designed world includes skyscrapers, cars, trains, planes, and other complex technology that require careful engineering. The highways, railroad tracks, and airports needed for transportation have also been engineered.

Other parts of the designed world are not as obvious. For example, within a city park, trees and other plants are used with engineered lights, paths, and bridges. Landscape designers use these natural and human-made things to create natural-looking spaces within cities.

 **Active Reading** **5 Identify** What is the designed world?

_____

_____

Visualize It!

6 Identify List all of the engineered objects that you can see in the photo.

_____

_____

_____

A city is a designed environment within the natural world. Architects and engineers design the buildings, roads, and parks that people use and enjoy.

Products You Use Every Day

The designed world also includes all the products you use every day. Soap, clocks, chairs, and lamps are all engineered to help you live well at home. Books, eyeglasses, and lab equipment are engineered to help you learn at school. Helmets, in-line skates, tennis rackets, and other pieces of sports equipment are designed to help you have fun safely.

Some designed products, such as hand-held games, cell phones, and computers, are complex. Other designed products, such as dinner plates and towels, are fairly simple technology. Some products are a combination of simple and complex. Shoes and waterproof clothing may be made from natural cotton cloth and materials designed by chemical engineers. All of the products you wear and use are part of a designed world.

Personal music players are engineered to store digital music and replay it through earbuds.

Books are a form of technology that people have used for centuries.

Clothing is engineered to be durable, comfortable, and attractive.

Skateboards are engineered to be durable, easy to steer, and fast.

Think Outside the Book Inquiry

7 Apply Write a script for a podcast ad for a spoon. Imagine that your audience has never seen a spoon before, so describe the spoon's design carefully!

Why is technology developed?

The designed world depends on technology. Technology includes all the inventions, processes, and tools that have been developed to meet our needs and wants.

To Meet People's Needs

Basic needs include food, water, clothing, shelter, protection, transportation, and communication. Some simple technology has been meeting people's needs for a long time. For example, people learned how to cook food over fire, use ditches to water crops, weave cloth, and use animals for work and transportation thousands of years ago.

Technology used today still meets these same needs. Modern stoves use electricity or gas to cook food. Modern farms use mechanical irrigation to water crops more efficiently and tractors to pull farm equipment. Clothes are woven using both traditional and new materials. Protective gear is made of modern plastics. Engines power cars, buses, and trains. Modern medical technology helps keep you healthy.

Visualize It!

Needs

8 Classify Identify the need that each of the items in the photos addresses.

B
_____
_____

A heart monitor

An irrigation system

A
_____
_____

C
_____
_____

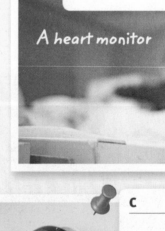
A bicycle helmet

© Houghton Mifflin Harcourt Publishing Company • Image Credits: (bl) ©Lisa Kyle Young/Photodisc/Getty Images; (tr) ©Helen Ashford/Workbook Stock/Getty Images; (br) ©Cavan Images/Taxi/Getty Images

Wants

A
_____
_____

Beads

Electronic keyboard

Video game

C
_____
_____

B
_____
_____

Visualize It!

9 Classify Identify the want that each of the items in the photos addresses.

To Meet People's Wants

Active Reading **10 Identify** As you read, underline two factors that shape people's wants.

Wants are things that people do not require to survive, but desire anyway. Wants include the desire to be more comfortable, to play, to have beautiful things, or to make music.

Inventors and engineers use technology to develop devices that meet people's wants, such as air conditioners, radios, and telephones. Plastics and other materials are used to meet the desire for play or decoration. The desire for realistic computer games has advanced the field of computer graphics.

People's technological wants often depend on their values and culture. Some cultures embrace all modern technology. Others accept only some technology. For example, some farmers choose to farm using horses instead of tractors. Additionally, wants vary from one culture to another. The definition of beautiful music, art, and fashion differs depending on whom you ask.

Inquiry

11 Justify Would you classify a cellular phone as a want or a need? Explain your answer.

_____
_____
_____
_____
_____
_____
_____
_____

Growing and Changing

Why is technology revised?

Technology is revised as society's needs and wants change. New technology often leads to new needs and wants. These new needs and wants then fuel the development of even newer technology.

12 Anticipate Before you read, write why you think technology is revised.

_____

_____

_____

_____

Needs and Wants Change

Needs and wants change when society changes. For example, years ago, most people in the United States lived on farms. When new technology made farming more efficient, fewer farmers were needed to grow food. Many people left farms and moved to cities.

The people in cities had new needs. For example, now that they were not growing food, they needed to buy and store food. Refrigerators were developed to keep food fresh. People also had more free time, and new wants. New forms of entertainment, such as movies and recorded music, were developed. All of these wants and needs drove the development of new technology and products.

Visualize It!

Computer technology was developed as society's needs changed. Computers have gotten smaller and more reliable over time. They process data faster and can share data more easily.

In the 1960s and 1970s, computers were large and processed data stored on reels of magnetic tape. Data were shared by moving the reels to another computer.

In the 1980s, engineers worked on making computers smaller. Improved hardware led to the development of personal computers.

Personal computers stored and shared information on floppy disks.

New Technology Generates New Needs

Active Reading **13 Identify** As you read, underline two examples of new technology creating new needs.

When people begin using new technology, they often develop new needs. For example, when people in cities began driving cars, they needed a way of coordinating traffic. So traffic lights were invented. One technology led to another.

Likewise, computers were developed in the 1950s to meet the need to process data. Early computers were very big machines that stored data on giant spools of magnetic tape. Even though they could process large amounts of data, they could not share that data easily. Computer scientists needed a better way to share information. As a result, engineers developed disk storage technology. As computers became smaller and more affordable, more people began using them and more information needed to be shared. Disks improved, and now one DVD can hold more data than an early computer could. Today, computers can transfer data electronically over the Internet. The Internet connects computers directly to each other and makes sharing data and images easy.

Now, computers all over the world can share data quickly over the Internet. Although the Internet was developed for scientists, people now use it for everyday activities, such as talking to friends.

14 Illustrate How do you think data storage and computer communication will change next? Draw and describe your answer.

How are society and technology related?

Society and technology affect each other. For example, when people choose to buy a technology, manufacturers continue to make and improve it. When people stop buying a technology, manufacturers no longer make it.

Society's technology choices can change in unpredictable ways. For example, in the 1940s, American society had hopes that nuclear technology could supply limitless, clean, and cheap energy. So, in the mid-1950s, engineers planned the first nuclear power plants. However, people discovered that nuclear technology has its disadvantages, too. For example, the plants are costly to build. They need expensive controls to operate safely, and they make dangerous radioactive waste. Accidents at nuclear plants in the 1980s reminded people of the risks of nuclear energy. Companies stopped building nuclear plants and built more plants that burned fossil fuels.

But fossil fuels are limited and becoming more scarce. And a new disadvantage of that technology emerged. Power plants that burn fossil fuels add greenhouse gases to the atmosphere. So the advantages of using nuclear power are being discussed again. The debate is still going on. Modern society needs energy. The values and priorities of society help us select which technology we use.

Active Reading

15 Identify As you read, underline the ways society affects which technology is developed.

16 Identify List some advantages and disadvantages of nuclear energy in the table below.

Advantages	Disadvantages

Society will choose whether nuclear power plants meet our energy needs in the future.

Going Up?

Which technology allows people to climb tall buildings with the push of a button? Elevators! The addition of elevators changed the height of buildings, the skyline of cities, and people's ability to reach the sky.

Need for Skyscrapers

In the middle 1800s, more people started moving to cities. More space was needed for homes and offices. But land in cities was limited and expensive. Building upward was less expensive than spreading out. So architects began designing taller buildings, which meant climbing more stairs to reach the upper floors.

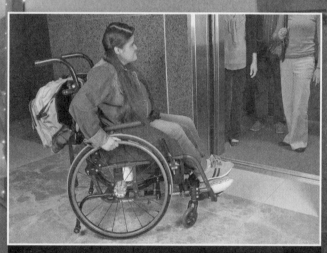

Need for Elevators

Putting elevators in buildings eliminated the need to climb stairs. Elevators make it possible for people who cannot climb stairs to move around easily in any building that has more than one floor.

Extend

Inquiry

17 Explain Why might someone put an elevator in a single-family home?

18 Relate What might be one disadvantage of elevator technology?

19 Compare Investigate and describe three types of elevator designs: hydraulic, pneumatic, and roped. Describe the advantages and drawbacks of each of the three elevator designs.

Visual Summary

To complete this summary, fill in the blanks with the correct word or phrase. Then use the key below to check your answers. You can use this page to review the main concepts of the lesson.

Engineering and Our World

The designed world includes large structures and machines and small products. Every product we use is part of the designed world.

20 Large structures in the designed world include _____

As needs and wants change, technologies are revised, too.

22 The need to process, store, and share growing amounts of information led to improved _____

Technologies are developed to meet needs and wants.

21 Clothing, shelter, food, communication, transportation are considered _____

23 Synthesize Describe how society's need to replace coal, oil, and other fossil fuels as energy sources could lead to new technology for automobiles and other motor vehicles.

Lesson Review

Vocabulary

In your own words define the following term.

1 designed world

_____

_____

Key Concepts

2 Identify What makes up the designed world?

_____

_____

3 Apply What drives companies to make batteries that cost less and last longer?

_____

_____

_____

_____

4 Explain Why does the designed world change?

_____

_____

_____

_____

5 Summarize Why did computer floppy disks develop?

_____

_____

_____

_____

6 Distinguish What is the difference between the designed world and the natural world?

_____

_____

_____

_____

_____

Critical Thinking

Use this table to answer the following question.

Solar Energy	
Advantages	**Disadvantages**
Solar cells use free solar energy.	Solar cells are expensive to make.
Solar cells reduce the need for fossil fuels.	Solar energy cannot supply all of our energy needs right now.
Solar cells do not make pollution.	Solar cells cannot generate electricity at night.

7 Predict How would switching to solar power affect a city environmentally and financially?

_____

_____

_____

_____

_____

_____

8 Analyze What parts of the designed world were developed to make air travel practical?

_____

_____

_____

9 Infer Some farmers in the United States still use horse-drawn equipment. Why might they choose to use older technology?

_____

_____

_____

_____

My Notes

Unit 3 Humans design and use systems, products, and processes to meet a variety of needs.

Lesson 1
ESSENTIAL QUESTION
What is the engineering design process?

Explain how the engineering design process develops technical solutions to meet people's needs.

Lesson 2
ESSENTIAL QUESTION
How can we evaluate technology?

Explain how scientists and engineers determine the costs, benefits, and risks of a new technology.

Lesson 3
ESSENTIAL QUESTION
What are technological systems?

Describe how technological systems are put together, how these systems are controlled, and how systems interact.

Lesson 4
ESSENTIAL QUESTION
How do engineers use materials and tools?

Explain how the tools and materials of technology are chosen, tested, improved, and used.

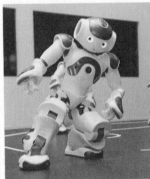

Lesson 5
ESSENTIAL QUESTION
How is engineering related to life science?

Describe how organisms can be used in engineering and how engineering can help organisms.

Lesson 6
ESSENTIAL QUESTION
How are engineering and society related?

Explain how engineering, technology, and society affect each other.

Connect ESSENTIAL QUESTIONS
Lessons 2 and 5

1 Synthesize What might be the risks and benefits of being among the first patients to receive a prototype artificial heart?

_____

_____

_____

_____

Think Outside the Book

2 Synthesize Choose one of these activities to help synthesize what you have learned in this unit.

☐ Using what you learned in lessons 2, 5, and 6, explain how plastic bags and paper bags affect our world by comparing the features of paper and plastic in a Pugh chart.

☐ Using what you learned in lessons 1, 2, 3, and 4, draw a process chart to explain how the development of artificial intelligence could affect an existing technological system, such as a home security system. Show what might be the inputs and outputs and what might go wrong.

© Houghton Mifflin Harcourt Publishing Company • Image Credits: (tl) ©Stocktrek Images/Getty Images; (tr) ©Bill Stormont/Corbis; (cl) © Josh Mitchell/Monsoon/Photolibrary/Corbis; (cr) ©Yoshikazu Tsuno/AFP/Getty Images; (bl) ©Stephen Dorey ABIPP/Alamy; (br) ©David Zaitz/Photonica/Getty Images

Unit 3 Review

Name _____

Vocabulary

Fill in each blank with the term that best completes the following sentences.

1 Applying science and mathematics to solve real-world problems is called

_____ .

  A trade-off   **C** engineering

  B risk-benefit analysis   **D** materials science

2 Testing and evaluating a(n) _____ is an important step in the design process.

  A prototype   **C** output

  B system   **D** control

3 Engineers perform a(n) _____ to compare the possible negative effects of making a decision involving technology with the possible positive effects.

  A life cycle analysis   **C** prototype

  B input   **D** risk-benefit analysis

4 To determine how a technology might affect the environment from the time it is made, sold, and used to the time it must be disposed of, engineers do a(n) _____ .

  A Pugh chart   **C** control

  B life cycle analysis   **D** trade-off

5 The information, material, energy, or any components that an engineer adds to a system are called _____ .

  A inputs

  B feedback

  C systems theory

  D outputs

Key Concepts

Read each question below, and circle the best answer.

6 Which statement best describes technology?

A the tools, machines, materials, and processes that are used for practical purposes

B the application of science and mathematics to solve problems, meeting the needs of society and improving the quality of life

C the study of the natural world

D the exploration of the nature of science

7 Krisha and many of her friends bought a new kind of cell phone that they used to make calls, text, and send pictures. Soon, they had trouble getting their phones to connect and stay connected. What was the most likely cause of the problem?

A Krisha and her friends did not know how to operate the cell phones.

B The phones were old and worn out.

C The popularity of the new phones had the unintended effect of overloading the cell phone system.

D The new phones were not designed to be used as cell phones.

8 Raoul is studying areas of the United States to find the best location for high-rise senior citizen housing.

Major Earthquakes in Northern California						
Year	1906	1911	1979	1980	1984	1989
Magnitude	7.8	6.5	5.7	5.8	6.2	6.9

To help with his decision on the best location, how could Raoul use this table listing the major earthquakes that have occurred in northern California?

A to develop a list of building materials

B to perform a life cycle analysis

C to create a model

D to perform a risk-benefit analysis

9 Which of the following is not a tool used in engineering and technology?

A computer design program   **C** suspension bridge

B electron microscope   **D** power drill

10 Technology used in developing automobiles had some unintended effects.

What unintended effect does the illustration show?

A Automobile technology led to traffic jams in urban areas.

B Technology used in developing internal combustion engines led to exhaust gases that pollute the environment.

C Automobile use led to highway accidents.

D Factories for building automobiles led to jobs and increased economic benefits.

11 Look at the image of a dam.

What class of materials did engineers choose to build the poured concrete walls of this dam?

A metals   **C** polymers

B ceramics   **D** semiconductors

12 Rosa made this chart when she was studying the properties of various materials.

Material	Time for temperature to increase by 10 degrees (hours)
plastic foam	5.10
ceramic	3.20

In what engineering design project would Rosa find this information useful?

A deciding on material for improved building insulation

B deciding on new composite materials for athletic shoes

C deciding on stronger street-paving materials

D deciding on material for a lightweight, but strong, automobile body

13 Look at the diagram of DNA.

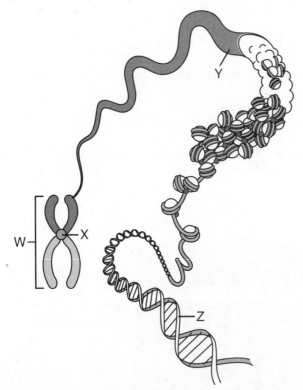

The spot labeled Z shows a place where a genetic engineer could use "chemical scissors" to cut the DNA. Why might a genetic engineer want to cut DNA?

A to create a new organism through selective breeding

B to study and learn more about what makes up DNA

C to insert a gene from a bacterium that will make a protein for use as a drug

D to create a large model of DNA

14 Iona made a list of four advances in technology that were inspired by living things. She listed one item in error. Which item should not be on Iona's list?

A cardboard boxes for shipping goods

B wings on airplanes

C a drug for treating diabetes by controlling blood sugar

D flippers scuba divers wear on their feet to help them swim

15 The social need to have living space, offices, and stores located in a downtown area led to technologies for constructing very tall buildings. Which of the following needs most likely came about because of the new building technology?

A the need for technology to develop better lighting

B the need for better street-paving materials

C the need for new communications technology

D the need for technology to develop elevators

16 Engineers built and used a prototype, based on the sketch below, to answer questions about the best design for a windmill to generate electricity.

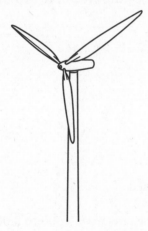

Which of these questions could not be answered by studying the prototype?

A What would the wind speed and direction be at a given location from month to month?

B What rotation speed of the blades could produce enough electricity to supply 20 homes?

C How rapidly would the windmill blades turn at different wind speeds?

D Would the blades produce high levels of sound when they turned rapidly?

Critical Thinking

Answer the following questions in the space provided.

17 A pot of boiling water on a stove is a system. What action could you take to make the pot of water an open system? What action would make it a closed system? In terms of the pot of boiling water, what is happening in the closed system that does not happen in the open system?

_____

_____

_____

18 The development of refrigeration and frozen-food technology has benefited society in different ways. Identify two ways in which refrigeration has helped people. Name two products that developed because of frozen-food technology.

_____

_____

_____

19 Kaseem included a thermostat in a diagram of his home's heating system. A thermostat is a part of the feedback system within the heating system. What type of system component is a thermostat? What does the thermostat use as feedback, and how does this feedback system cause the heating system to turn on?

_____

_____

_____

_____

Connect ESSENTIAL QUESTIONS
Lessons 1, 2, 4, and 6

Answer the following question in the space provided.

20 Charlia is creating a design for an airplane that can carry 1,500 to 3,000 people. Why would there be a need for such an airplane? What properties should the material have for the wings and body? What types of trade-off could there be in using a very expensive, new material? How could Charlia go about improving an existing material?

_____

_____

_____

_____

⟨Technology⟩ and ⟨Coding⟩

This breathtaking image of Earth was taken from the International Space Station, an international laboratory orbiting Earth. The operation of the International Space Station is controlled by 52 computers and millions of lines of computer code. Its many high-tech features include solar panels that power the laboratory and a human-like robotic astronaut.

This is Robonaut 2, a robot designed to do routine maintenance at the International Space Station.

Data Driven

What is computer science?

If you like computer technology and learning about how computers work, computer science might be for you. *Computer science* is the study of computer technology and how data is processed, stored, and accessed by computers. Computer science is an important part of many other areas, including science, math, engineering, robotics, medicine, game design, and 3D animation.

Computer technology is often described in terms of *hardware*, which are the physical components, and *software*, which are the programs or instructions that a computer runs. Computer scientists must understand how hardware and software work together. Computer scientists may develop new kinds of useful computer software. Or they may work with engineers to improve existing computer hardware.

The first electronic computer, the computer ENIAC (Electronic Numerical Integrator And Computer), was developed at the University of Pennsylvania in 1946.

The integrated circuit (IC), first developed in the 1950s, was instrumental in the development of small computer components.

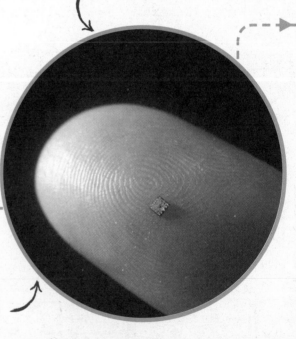

The development of the IC made it possible to reduce the overall size of computers and their components and to increase their processing speed.

How has computer technology changed over time?

Modern, digital computer technology is less than 100 years old. Yet in that short amount of time, it has advanced rapidly. The earliest digital computers could perform only a limited number of tasks and were the size of an entire room. Over the decades, engineers continued to develop smaller, faster, and more powerful computers. Today's computers can process hundreds of millions of instructions per second!

Computer scientists and engineers think about what people want or need from computer technology. The most advanced hardware is not useful if people do not know how to use it. So computer scientists and engineers work to create software that is reliable, useful, and easy to use. Today's tablet computers, cell phones, and video game consoles can be used without any special training.

Advances in digital computer technology have help make computers cheaper and easier to operate, which has allowed many more people to work and play with them.

1 Compare Are modern computers simpler or more complex than early computers? Explain.

_____

_____

_____

Computer Logic

What do computer scientists do?

Many people enjoy developing computer technology for fun. Learning how to create mobile phone games or Internet-enabled gadgets can be rewarding hobbies. For some people, that hobby may one day become a career in computer science. Working in computer science is a bit like solving a puzzle. Applying knowledge of how computers work to solve real-world problems requires collaboration, creativity, and logical, step-by-step thinking.

This is a kayak folded up.

They collaborate across many disciplines

Computers are valuable tools in math and science because they can perform complex calculations very quickly. Computers are useful to many other fields, too. For example, animators use computer technology to create realistic lighting effects in 3D animated films. Mechanics use computers to diagnose problems in car systems. For every field that relies on special software or computer technology, there is an opportunity for computer scientists and engineers to collaborate and develop solutions for those computing needs. Computer scientists must be able to define and understand the problems presented to them and to communicate and work with experts in other fields to develop the solutions.

Computational origami is a computer program used to model the ways in which different materials, including paper, can be folded. It combines computer science and the art of paper folding to create new technologies, such as this kayak.

Tracking software helps biologists study animal behavior.

satellite →

satellite data receiving center

satellite data processing center

transmitter

They help solve real-world problems

Some computer scientists carry out theoretical research. Others apply computer science concepts to develop software. Theoretical computer science and practical software development help solve real-world problems. For example, biologists need ways to safely and accurately track endangered animals. Computer science theories on artificial intelligence and pattern recognition have been applied to advanced animal-tracking technologies, such as satellite transmitters and aerial cameras. New kinds of image processing software now allow biologists to analyze the collected data in different ways.

They use logical, step-by-step thinking

Computers perform tasks given to them, and they do this very well. But in order to get the results they expect, computer scientists and programmers must write very accurate instructions. Computer science and programming requires logical thinking, deductive reasoning, and a good understanding of cause-and-effect relationships. When designing software, computer scientists must consider every possible user action and how the computer should respond to each action.

2 Explain How is computer science helping this scientist do her research?

_____

_____

_____

_____

Transmitters can be attached to animals to help track their movements.

Up to <Code>

How is computer software created?

Imagine that you are using a computer at the library to learn more about the history of electronic music. You use the library's database application to start searching for Internet resources. You also do a search to look for audio recordings. Finally, you open a word processor to take notes on the computer. Perhaps without realizing it, you've used many different pieces of software. Have you ever wondered how computer software is created?

Computer software is designed to address a need

Computer software can help us to learn more about our world. It can be useful to business. Or it can simply entertain us. Whatever its purpose, computer software should fulfill some human want or need. The first steps in creating software are precisely defining the need or want being addressed and planning how the software will work.

Computer software source code is written in a programming language

The instructions that tell a computer how to run video games, word processors, and other kinds of software are not written in a human language. They are written in a special programming language, or *code*. Javascript, C++, and Python are examples of programming languages. Programming languages—like human languages—must follow certain rules in order to be understood by the computer. A series of instructions written in a programming language is called *source code*.

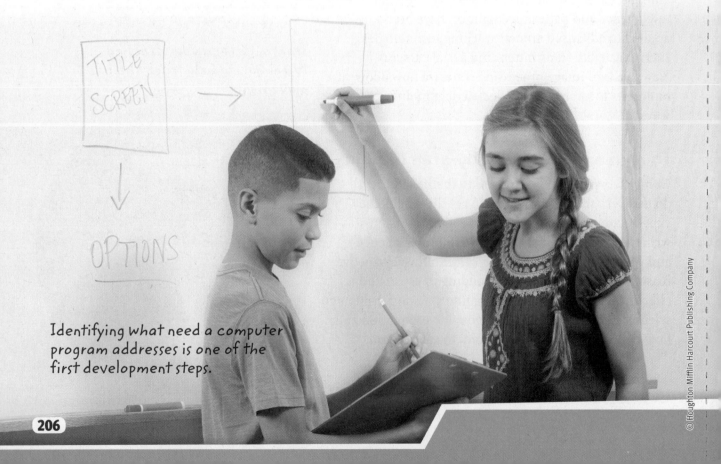

Identifying what need a computer program addresses is one of the first development steps.

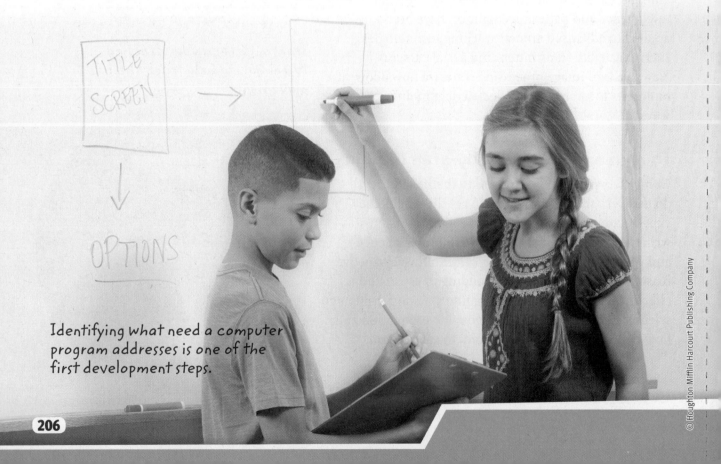

Source code is revised

Sometimes, programmers make mistakes in their code. Many programming environments have a feature that alerts the programmer to certain errors, such as spelling mistakes in commands, missing portions of code, or logical errors in the sequence of instructions. However, many mistakes go undetected, too. Some errors may cause the program to function incorrectly or not at all. When this happens, the programmer must identify the error, correct it, and test the software again.

Computer software is user tested, and revised

Once the software is created, it must be tested thoroughly to make sure it does not fail or behave in unexpected ways. It must also be tested to ensure that it meets users' needs. The creators of a piece of software might observe how people use it. Or they might ask users to provide feedback on certain features and test the software again.

3 Identify This source code contains an error. Infer where the error is located. What does this code "tell" the computer to do? Write your answers below.

_____

_____

_____

```
13
14   # Scores are not tied, so check
15   # which player wins the round
16 ▾ if player1_score > player2_score:
17       print ("Player 1 wins!")
18 ▾ else:
19       prnt ("Player 2 wins!")
20

! Syntax error, line 19
```

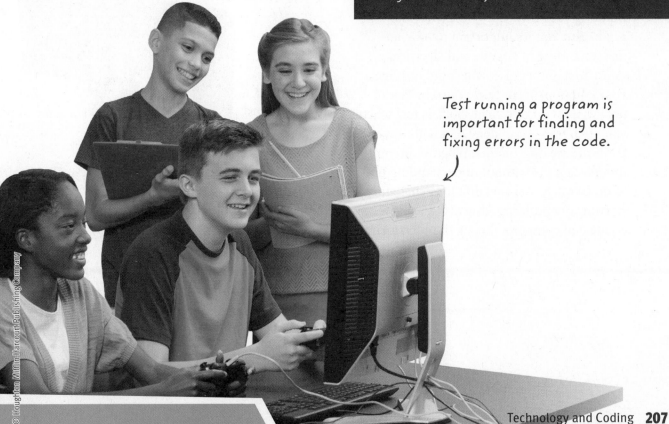

Test running a program is important for finding and fixing errors in the code.

Play it Safe

How should I work with computers?

It is easy to lose track of time when you're sitting in front of a computer or game console. It's also easy to forget that things you say or do online can be seen and shared by many different people. Here are some tips for using computers safely and responsibly.

✓ Maintain good posture

Time can pass by quickly when you are working on a computer or another device. Balance computer time with other activities, including plenty of physical activity. When you are sitting at a computer, sit upright with your shoulders relaxed. Your eyes should be level with the top of the monitor and your feet should be flat on the ground.

✓ Observe electrical safety

Building your own electronics projects can be fun, but it's important to have an understanding of circuits and electrical safety first. Otherwise, you could damage your components or hurt yourself. The potential for an electrical shock is real when you open up a computer, work with frayed cords or, use ungrounded plugs or attempt to replace parts without understanding how to do so safely. Ask an adult for help before starting any projects. Also, avoid using a connected computer during thunderstorms.

head and neck in a straight, neutral position

shoulders are relaxed

wrists are straight

feet are flat on the ground

Good posture will help you avoid the aches and injuries related to sitting in front of a computer for a long time.

✓ Handle and maintain computers properly

Be cautious when handling and transporting electronic devices. Dropping them or spilling liquids on them could cause serious damage. Keep computers away from dirt, dust, liquids, and moisture. Never use wet cleaning products unless they are specifically designed for use on electronics. Microfiber cloths can be used to clear smudges from device screens. Spilled liquids can cause circuits to short out and hardware to corrode. If a liquid spills on a device, unplug it and switch it off immediately, remove the battery and wipe up as much of the liquid inside the device as possible. Don't switch the device back on until it is completely dry.

✓ Do not post private information online

Talk to your family about rules for Internet use. Do not use the Internet to share private information such as photographs, your phone number, or your address. Do not respond to requests for personal details from people you do not know.

✓ Treat yourself and others with respect

It is important to treat others with respect when on the Internet. Don't send or post messages online that you wouldn't say to someone in person. Unfortunately, not everyone acts respectfully while online. Some people may say hurtful things to you or send you unwanted messages. Do not reply to unwanted messages. Alert a trusted adult to any forms of contact, such as messages or photos, that make you feel uncomfortable.

4 Apply Fill in the chart below with a suitable response to each scenario.

SCENARIO	YOUR RESPONSE
You receive a text message from an online store asking for your home address.	
You've been lying down in front of a laptop, and you notice that your neck is feeling a little sore.	
You need to take a laptop computer with you on your walk to school.	
You want to try assembling a robotics kit with a friend.	
Someone posts unfriendly comments directed at you.	

Career in Computing:
Game Programmer

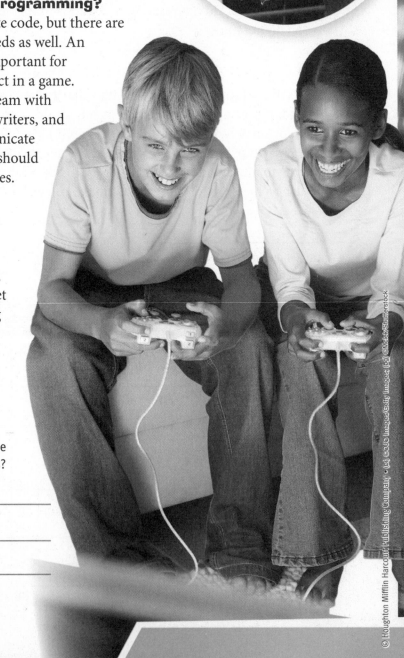

What do video game programmers do?

Creating your own universe with its own set of rules is fun. Just ask a programmer who works on video games!

What skills are needed in game programming?

A programmer should know how to write code, but there are other important skills a programmer needs as well. An understanding of physics and math is important for calculating how objects move and interact in a game. Game programmers usually work on a team with other people, such as artists, designers, writers, and musicians. They must be able to communicate effectively, and ideally, the programmer should understand the other team members' roles.

How can I get started with game development?

You don't need a big budget or years of experience to try it out. There are books, videos, and websites that can help you get started. When you're first experimenting with game development, start small. Try making a very simple game like Tic-Tac-Toe. Once you've mastered that, you can try something more complex.

5 Brainstorm Why would working on a team be important to the game development process?

_____

_____

_____

Look It Up!

References

Mineral Properties

Here are five steps to take in mineral identification:

1 Determine the color of the mineral. Is it light-colored, dark-colored, or a specific color?

2 Determine the luster of the mineral. Is it metallic or non-metallic?

3 Determine the color of any powder left by its streak.

4 Determine the hardness of your mineral. Is it soft, hard, or very hard? Using a glass plate, see if the mineral scratches it.

5 Determine whether your sample has cleavage or any special properties.

TERMS TO KNOW	DEFINITION
adamantine	a non-metallic luster like that of a diamond
cleavage	how a mineral breaks when subject to stress on a particular plane
luster	the state or quality of shining by reflecting light
streak	the color of a mineral when it is powdered
submetallic	between metallic and nonmetallic in luster
vitreous	glass-like type of luster

Silicate Minerals					
Mineral	Color	Luster	Streak	Hardness	Cleavage and Special Properties
Beryl	deep green, pink, white, bluish green, or yellow	vitreous	white	7.5–8	1 cleavage direction; some varieties fluoresce in ultraviolet light
Chlorite	green	vitreous to pearly	pale green	2–2.5	1 cleavage direction
Garnet	green, red, brown, black	vitreous	white	6.5–7.5	no cleavage
Hornblende	dark green, brown, or black	vitreous	none	5–6	2 cleavage directions
Muscovite	colorless, silvery white, or brown	vitreous or pearly	white	2–2.5	1 cleavage direction
Olivine	olive green, yellow	vitreous	white or none	6.5–7	no cleavage
Orthoclase	colorless, white, pink, or other colors	vitreous	white or none	6	2 cleavage directions
Plagioclase	colorless, white, yellow, pink, green	vitreous	white	6	2 cleavage directions
Quartz	colorless or white; any color when not pure	vitreous or waxy	white or none	7	no cleavage

Nonsilicate Minerals

Mineral	Color	Luster	Streak	Hardness	Cleavage and Special Properties
Native Elements					
Copper	copper-red	metallic	copper-red	2.5–3	no cleavage
Diamond	pale yellow or colorless	adamantine	none	10	4 cleavage directions
Graphite	black to gray	submetallic	black	1–2	1 cleavage direction
Carbonates					
Aragonite	colorless, white, or pale yellow	vitreous	white	3.5–4	2 cleavage directions; reacts with hydrochloric acid
Calcite	colorless or white to tan	vitreous	white	3	3 cleavage directions; reacts with weak acid; double refraction
Halides					
Fluorite	light green, yellow, purple, bluish green, or other colors	vitreous	none	4	4 cleavage directions; some varieties fluoresce
Halite	white	vitreous	white	2.0–2.5	3 cleavage directions
Oxides					
Hematite	reddish brown to black	metallic to earthy	dark red to red-brown	5.6–6.5	no cleavage; magnetic when heated
Magnetite	iron-black	metallic	black	5.5–6.5	no cleavage; magnetic
Sulfates					
Anhydrite	colorless, bluish, or violet	vitreous to pearly	white	3–3.5	3 cleavage directions
Gypsum	white, pink, gray, or colorless	vitreous, pearly, or silky	white	2.0	3 cleavage directions
Sulfides					
Galena	lead-gray	metallic	lead-gray to black	2.5–2.8	3 cleavage directions
Pyrite	brassy yellow	metallic	greenish, brownish, or black	6–6.5	no cleavage

References

Geologic Time Scale

Geologists developed the geologic time scale to represent the 4.6 billion years of Earth's history that have passed since Earth formed. This scale divides Earth's history into blocks of time. The boundaries between these time intervals (shown in millions of years ago or mya in the table below), represent major changes in Earth's history. Some boundaries are defined by mass extinctions, major changes in Earth's surface, and/or major changes in Earth's climate.

The four major divisions that encompass the history of life on Earth are Precambrian time, the Paleozoic era, the Mesozoic era, and the Cenozoic era. The largest divisions are eons. **Precambrian time** is made up of the first three eons, over 4 billion years of Earth's history.

The **Paleozoic era** lasted from 542 mya to 251 mya. All major plant groups, except flowering plants, appeared during this era. By the end of the era, reptiles, winged insects, and fishes had also appeared. The largest known mass extinction occurred at the end of this era.

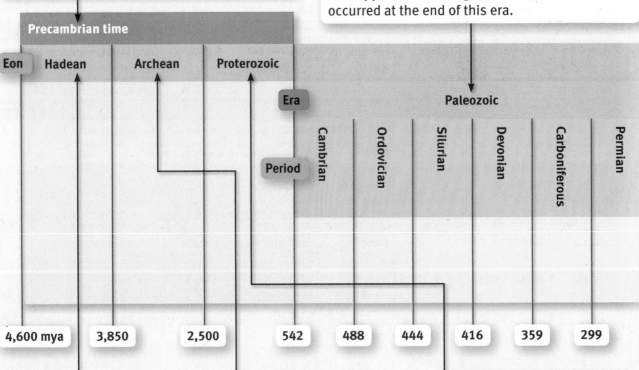

The **Hadean eon** lasted from about 4.6 billion years ago (bya) to 3.85 bya. It is described based on evidence from meteorites and rocks from the moon.

The **Archean eon** lasted from 3.85 bya to 2.5 bya. The earliest rocks from Earth that have been found and dated formed at the start of this eon.

The **Proterozoic eon** lasted from 2.5 bya to 542 mya. The first organisms, which were single-celled organisms, appeared during this eon. These organisms produced so much oxygen that they changed Earth's oceans and Earth's atmosphere.

Divisions of Time

The divisions of time shown here represent major changes in Earth's surface and when life developed and changed significantly on Earth. As new evidence is found, the boundaries of these divisions may shift. The Phanerozoic eon is divided into three eras. The beginning of each of these eras represents a change in the types of organisms that dominated Earth. And, each era is commonly characterized by the types of organisms that dominated the era. These eras are divided into periods, and periods are divided into epochs.

The **Mesozoic era** lasted from 251 mya to 65.5 mya. During this era, many kinds of dinosaurs dominated land, and giant lizards swam in the ocean. The first birds, mammals, and flowering plants also appeared during this time. About two-thirds of all land species went extinct at the end of this era.

The **Phanerozoic eon** began 542 mya. We live in this eon.

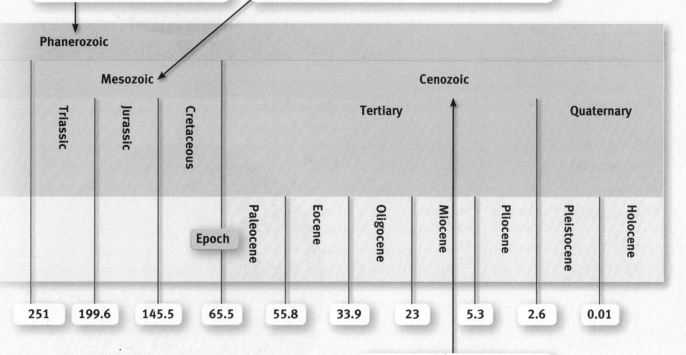

Phanerozoic

Mesozoic

Cenozoic

| Triassic | Jurassic | Cretaceous | Tertiary | | | | Quaternary | |

Epoch: Paleocene | Eocene | Oligocene | Miocene | Pliocene | Pleistocene | Holocene

251 | 199.6 | 145.5 | 65.5 | 55.8 | 33.9 | 23 | 5.3 | 2.6 | 0.01

The **Cenozoic era** began 65.5 mya and continues today. Mammals dominate this era. During the Mesozoic era, mammals were small in size but grew much larger during the Cenozoic era. Primates, including humans, appeared during this era.

Star Charts for the Northern Hemisphere

A star chart is a map of the stars in the night sky. It shows the names and positions of constellations and major stars. Star charts can be used to identify constellations and even to orient yourself using Polaris, the North Star.

Because Earth moves through space, different constellations are visible at different times of the year. The star charts on these pages show the constellations visible during each season in the Northern Hemisphere.

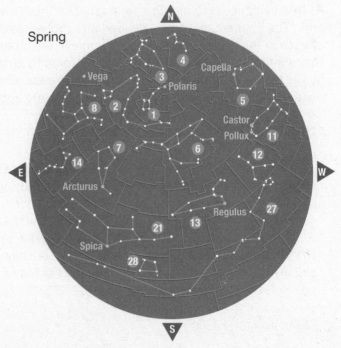

Spring

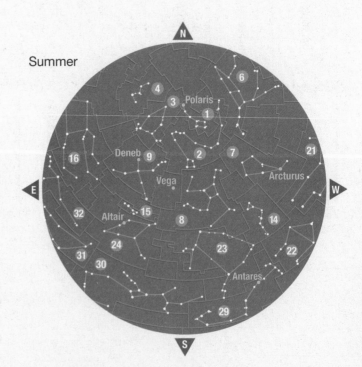

Summer

Constellations

1 Ursa Minor

2 Draco

3 Cepheus

4 Cassiopeia

5 Auriga

6 Ursa Major

7 Boötes

8 Hercules

9 Cygnus

10 Perseus

11 Gemini

12 Cancer

13 Leo

14 Serpens

15 Sagitta

16 Pegasus

17 Pisces

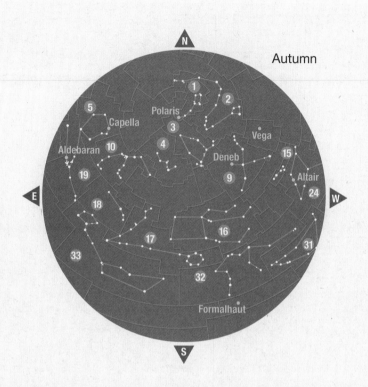

Autumn

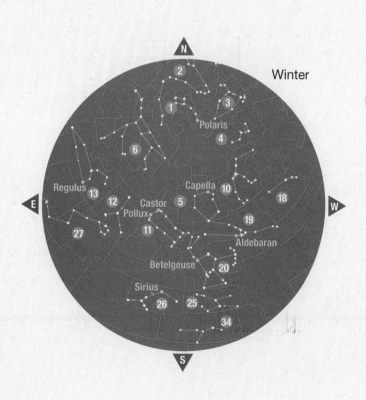

Winter

Constellations

18 Aries

19 Taurus

20 Orion

21 Virgo

22 Libra

23 Ophiuchus

24 Aquila

25 Lepus

26 Canis Major

27 Hydra

28 Corvus

29 Scorpius

30 Sagittarius

31 Capricornus

32 Aquarius

33 Cetus

34 Columba

World Map

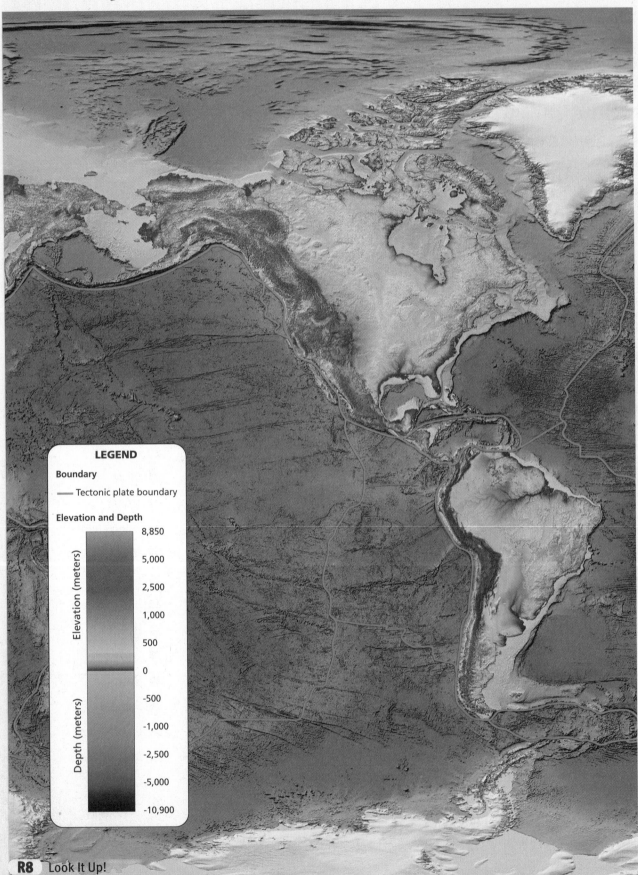

LEGEND

Boundary

—— Tectonic plate boundary

Elevation and Depth

Elevation (meters)

8,850
5,000
2,500
1,000
500
0

Depth (meters)

-500
-1,000
-2,500
-5,000
-10,900

References

Classification of Living Things

Domains and Kingdoms

All organisms belong to one of three domains: Domain Archaea, Domain Bacteria, or Domain Eukarya. Some of the groups within these domains are shown below. (Remember that genus names are italicized.)

Domain Archaea

The organisms in this domain are single-celled prokaryotes, many of which live in extreme environments.

Archaea		
Group	**Example**	**Characteristics**
Methanogens	*Methanococcus*	produce methane gas; can't live in oxygen
Thermophiles	*Sulpholobus*	require sulphur; can't live in oxygen
Halophiles	*Halococcus*	live in very salty environments; most can live in oxygen

Domain Bacteria

Organisms in this domain are single-celled prokaryotes and are found in almost every environment on Earth.

Bacteria		
Group	**Example**	**Characteristics**
Bacilli	*Escherichia*	rod shaped; some bacilli fix nitrogen; some cause disease
Cocci	*Streptococcus*	spherical shaped; some cause disease; can form spores
Spirilla	*Treponema*	spiral shaped; cause diseases such as syphilis and Lyme disease

Domain Eukarya

Organisms in this domain are single-celled or multicellular eukaryotes.

Kingdom Protista Many protists resemble fungi, plants, or animals, but are smaller and simpler in structure. Most are single celled.

Protists		
Group	**Example**	**Characteristics**
Sarcodines	*Amoeba*	radiolarians; single-celled consumers
Ciliates	*Paramecium*	single-celled consumers
Flagellates	*Trypanosoma*	single-celled parasites
Sporozoans	*Plasmodium*	single-celled parasites
Euglenas	*Euglena*	single celled; photosynthesize
Diatoms	*Pinnularia*	most are single celled; photosynthesize
Dinoflagellates	*Gymnodinium*	single celled; some photosynthesize
Algae	*Volvox*	single celled or multicellular; photosynthesize
Slime molds	*Physarum*	single celled or multicellular; consumers or decomposers
Water molds	powdery mildew	single celled or multicellular; parasites or decomposers

Kingdom Fungi Most fungi are multicellular. Their cells have thick cell walls. Fungi absorb food from their environment.

Fungi		
Group	**Examples**	**Characteristics**
Threadlike fungi	bread mold	spherical; decomposers
Sac fungi	yeast; morels	saclike; parasites and decomposers
Club fungi	mushrooms; rusts; smuts	club shaped; parasites and decomposers
Lichens	British soldier	a partnership between a fungus and an alga

Kingdom Plantae Plants are multicellular and have cell walls made of cellulose. Plants make their own food through photosynthesis. Plants are classified into divisions instead of phyla.

Plants		
Group	**Examples**	**Characteristics**
Bryophytes	mosses; liverworts	no vascular tissue; reproduce by spores
Club mosses	*Lycopodium;* ground pine	grow in wooded areas; reproduce by spores
Horsetails	rushes	grow in wetland areas; reproduce by spores
Ferns	spleenworts; sensitive fern	large leaves called fronds; reproduce by spores
Conifers	pines; spruces; firs	needlelike leaves; reproduce by seeds made in cones
Cycads	*Zamia*	slow growing; reproduce by seeds made in large cones
Gnetophytes	*Welwitschia*	only three living families; reproduce by seeds
Ginkgoes	*Ginkgo*	only one living species; reproduce by seeds
Angiosperms	all flowering plants	reproduce by seeds made in flowers; fruit

Kingdom Animalia Animals are multicellular. Their cells do not have cell walls. Most animals have specialized tissues and complex organ systems. Animals get food by eating other organisms.

Animals		
Group	**Examples**	**Characteristics**
Sponges	glass sponges	no symmetry or specialized tissues; aquatic
Cnidarians	jellyfish; coral	radial symmetry; aquatic
Flatworms	planaria; tapeworms; flukes	bilateral symmetry; organ systems
Roundworms	*Trichina;* hookworms	bilateral symmetry; organ systems
Annelids	earthworms; leeches	bilateral symmetry; organ systems
Mollusks	snails; octopuses	bilateral symmetry; organ systems
Echinoderms	sea stars; sand dollars	radial symmetry; organ systems
Arthropods	insects; spiders; lobsters	bilateral symmetry; organ systems
Chordates	fish; amphibians; reptiles; birds; mammals	bilateral symmetry; complex organ systems

References

Periodic Table of the Elements

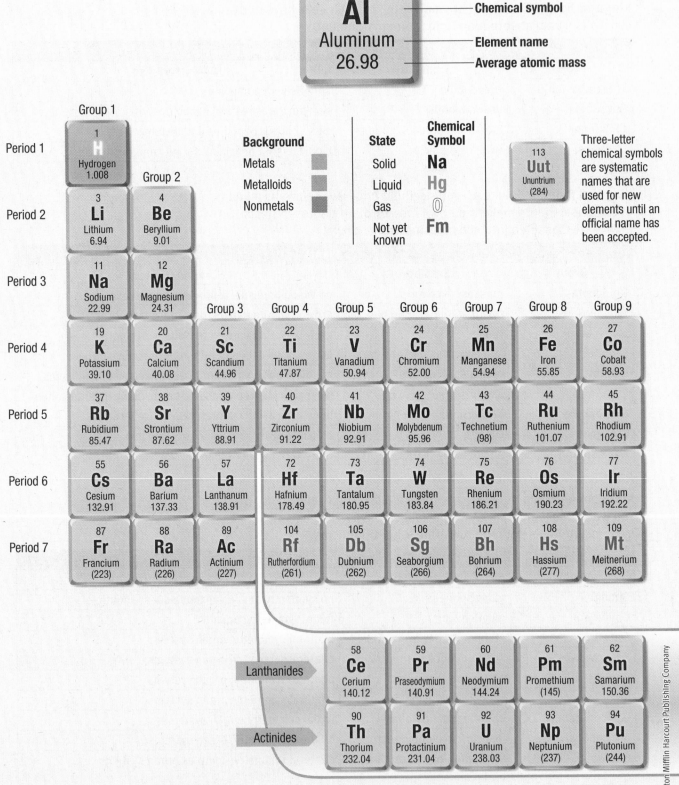

	13
	Al
	Aluminum
	26.98

- Atomic number
- Chemical symbol
- Element name
- Average atomic mass

Group 1

Period 1 — 1 **H** Hydrogen 1.008

Background
- Metals
- Metalloids
- Nonmetals

State
- Solid
- Liquid
- Gas
- Not yet known

Chemical Symbol
- **Na**
- **Hg**
- ⓞ
- **Fm**

113 **Uut** Ununtrium (284)

Three-letter chemical symbols are systematic names that are used for new elements until an official name has been accepted.

Group 2

Period 2 — 3 **Li** Lithium 6.94 | 4 **Be** Beryllium 9.01

Period 3 — 11 **Na** Sodium 22.99 | 12 **Mg** Magnesium 24.31

Group 3 | Group 4 | Group 5 | Group 6 | Group 7 | Group 8 | Group 9

Period 4 — 19 **K** Potassium 39.10 | 20 **Ca** Calcium 40.08 | 21 **Sc** Scandium 44.96 | 22 **Ti** Titanium 47.87 | 23 **V** Vanadium 50.94 | 24 **Cr** Chromium 52.00 | 25 **Mn** Manganese 54.94 | 26 **Fe** Iron 55.85 | 27 **Co** Cobalt 58.93

Period 5 — 37 **Rb** Rubidium 85.47 | 38 **Sr** Strontium 87.62 | 39 **Y** Yttrium 88.91 | 40 **Zr** Zirconium 91.22 | 41 **Nb** Niobium 92.91 | 42 **Mo** Molybdenum 95.96 | 43 **Tc** Technetium (98) | 44 **Ru** Ruthenium 101.07 | 45 **Rh** Rhodium 102.91

Period 6 — 55 **Cs** Cesium 132.91 | 56 **Ba** Barium 137.33 | 57 **La** Lanthanum 138.91 | 72 **Hf** Hafnium 178.49 | 73 **Ta** Tantalum 180.95 | 74 **W** Tungsten 183.84 | 75 **Re** Rhenium 186.21 | 76 **Os** Osmium 190.23 | 77 **Ir** Iridium 192.22

Period 7 — 87 **Fr** Francium (223) | 88 **Ra** Radium (226) | 89 **Ac** Actinium (227) | 104 **Rf** Rutherfordium (261) | 105 **Db** Dubnium (262) | 106 **Sg** Seaborgium (266) | 107 **Bh** Bohrium (264) | 108 **Hs** Hassium (277) | 109 **Mt** Meitnerium (268)

Lanthanides — 58 **Ce** Cerium 140.12 | 59 **Pr** Praseodymium 140.91 | 60 **Nd** Neodymium 144.24 | 61 **Pm** Promethium (145) | 62 **Sm** Samarium 150.36

Actinides — 90 **Th** Thorium 232.04 | 91 **Pa** Protactinium 231.04 | 92 **U** Uranium 238.03 | 93 **Np** Neptunium (237) | 94 **Pu** Plutonium (244)

The International Union of Pure and Applied Chemistry (IUPAC) has determined that, because of isotopic variance, the average atomic mass is best represented by a range of values for each of the following elements: hydrogen, lithium, boron, carbon, nitrogen, oxygen, silicon, sulfur, chlorine, and thallium. However, the values in this table are appropriate for everyday calculations.

Elements with atomic numbers of 95 and above are not known to occur naturally, even in trace amounts. They have only been synthesized in the lab. The physical and chemical properties of elements with atomic numbers 100 and above cannot be predicted with certainty. The states for elements with atomic numbers 100 and above are therefore shown as not yet known.

Group 18
2
He
Helium
4.003

Group 13	Group 14	Group 15	Group 16	Group 17
5	6	7	8	9	10
B	**C**	**N**	**O**	**F**	**Ne**
Boron	Carbon	Nitrogen	Oxygen	Fluorine	Neon
10.81	12.01	14.01	16.00	19.00	20.18
13	14	15	16	17	18
Al	**Si**	**P**	**S**	**Cl**	**Ar**
Aluminum	Silicon	Phosphorus	Sulfur	Chlorine	Argon
26.98	28.09	30.97	32.06	35.45	39.95

Group 10	Group 11	Group 12					
28	29	30	31	32	33	34	35	36
Ni	**Cu**	**Zn**	**Ga**	**Ge**	**As**	**Se**	**Br**	**Kr**
Nickel	Copper	Zinc	Gallium	Germanium	Arsenic	Selenium	Bromine	Krypton
58.69	63.55	65.38	69.72	72.63	74.92	78.96	79.90	83.80
46	47	48	49	50	51	52	53	54
Pd	**Ag**	**Cd**	**In**	**Sn**	**Sb**	**Te**	**I**	**Xe**
Palladium	Silver	Cadmium	Indium	Tin	Antimony	Tellurium	Iodine	Xenon
106.42	107.87	112.41	114.82	118.71	121.76	127.60	126.90	131.29
78	79	80	81	82	83	84	85	86
Pt	**Au**	**Hg**	**Tl**	**Pb**	**Bi**	**Po**	**At**	**Rn**
Platinum	Gold	Mercury	Thallium	Lead	Bismuth	Polonium	Astatine	Radon
195.08	196.97	200.59	204.38	207.2	208.98	(209)	(210)	(222)
110	111	112	113	114	115	116	117	118
Ds	**Rg**	**Cn**	**Uut**	**Fl**	**Uup**	**Lv**	**Uus**	**Uuo**
Darmstadtium	Roentgenium	Copernicium	Ununtrium	Flerovium	Ununpentium	Livermorium	Ununseptium	Ununoctium
(271)	(272)	(285)	(284)	(289)	(288)	(293)	(294)	(294)

63	64	65	66	67	68	69	70	71
Eu	**Gd**	**Tb**	**Dy**	**Ho**	**Er**	**Tm**	**Yb**	**Lu**
Europium	Gadolinium	Terbium	Dysprosium	Holmium	Erbium	Thulium	Ytterbium	Lutetium
151.96	157.25	158.93	162.50	164.93	167.26	168.93	173.05	174.97
95	96	97	98	99	100	101	102	103
Am	**Cm**	**Bk**	**Cf**	**Es**	**Fm**	**Md**	**No**	**Lr**
Americium	Curium	Berkelium	Californium	Einsteinium	Fermium	Mendelevium	Nobelium	Lawrencium
(243)	(247)	(247)	(251)	(252)	(257)	(258)	(259)	(262)

References

Physical Science Refresher

Atoms and Elements

Every object in the universe is made of matter. **Matter** is anything that takes up space and has mass. All matter is made of atoms. An **atom** is the smallest particle into which an element can be divided and still be the same element. An **element**, in turn, is a substance that cannot be broken down into simpler substances by chemical means. Each element consists of only one kind of atom. An element may be made of many atoms, but they are all the same kind of atom.

Atomic Structure

Atoms are made of smaller particles called **electrons**, **protons**, and **neutrons**. Electrons have a negative electric charge, protons have a positive charge, and neutrons have no electric charge. Together, protons and neutrons form the **nucleus**, or small dense center, of an atom. Because protons are positively charged and neutrons are neutral, the nucleus has a positive charge. Electrons move within an area around the nucleus called the **electron cloud**. Electrons move so quickly that scientists cannot determine their exact speeds and positions at the same time.

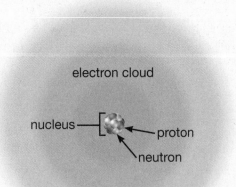

electron cloud

nucleus — proton

neutron

Atomic Number

To help distinguish one element from another, scientists use the atomic numbers of atoms. The **atomic number** is the number of protons in the nucleus of an atom. The atoms of a certain element always have the same number of protons.

When atoms have an equal number of protons and electrons, they are uncharged, or electrically neutral. The atomic number equals the number of electrons in an uncharged atom. The number of neutrons, however, can vary for a given element. Atoms of the same element that have different numbers of neutrons are called **isotopes**.

Periodic Table of the Elements

In the periodic table, each element in the table is in a separate box. And the elements are arranged from left to right in order of increasing atomic number. That is, an uncharged atom of each element has one more electron and one more proton than an uncharged atom of the element to its left. Each horizontal row of the table is called a **period**. Changes in chemical properties of elements across a period correspond to changes in the electron arrangements of their atoms.

Each vertical column of the table is known as a **group**. A group lists elements with similar physical and chemical properties. For this reason, a group is also sometimes called a family. The elements in a group have similar properties because their atoms have the same number of electrons in their outer energy level. For example, the elements helium, neon, argon, krypton, xenon, and radon all have similar properties and are known as the noble gases.

Molecules and Compounds

When two or more elements join chemically, they form a **compound**. A compound is a new substance with properties different from those of the elements that compose it. For example, water, H_2O, is a compound formed when hydrogen (H) and oxygen (O) combine. The smallest complete unit of a compound that has the properties of that compound is called a **molecule**. A chemical formula indicates the elements in a compound. It also indicates the relative number of atoms of each element in the compound. The chemical formula for water is H_2O. So, each water molecule consists of two atoms of hydrogen and one atom of oxygen. The subscript number after the symbol for an element shows how many atoms of that element are in a single molecule of the compound.

Chemical Equations

A chemical reaction occurs when a chemical change takes place. A chemical equation describes a chemical reaction using chemical formulas. The equation indicates the substances that react and the substances that are produced. For example, when carbon and oxygen combine, they can form carbon dioxide, shown in the equation below: $C + O_2 \longrightarrow CO_2$

Acids, Bases, and pH

An **ion** is an atom or group of chemically bonded atoms that has an electric charge because it has lost or gained one or more electrons. When an acid, such as hydrochloric acid, HCl, is mixed with water, it separates into ions. An **acid** is a compound that produces hydrogen ions, H^+, in water. The hydrogen ions then combine with a water molecule to form a hydronium ion, H_3O^+. A **base**, on the other hand, is a substance that produces hydroxide ions, OH^-, in water.

To determine whether a solution is acidic or basic, scientists use pH. The **pH** of a solution is a measure of the hydronium ion concentration in a solution. The pH scale ranges from 0 to 14. Acids have a pH that is less than 7. The lower the number, the more acidic the solution. The middle point, pH = 7, is neutral, neither acidic nor basic. Bases have a pH that is greater than 7. The higher the number is, the more basic the solution.

The pH of Some Common Materials

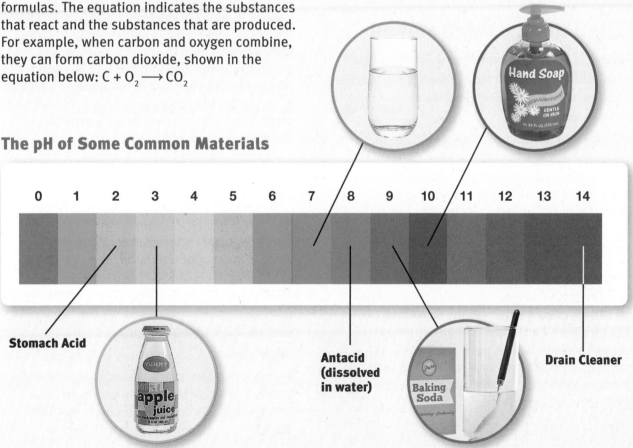

Stomach Acid

Antacid (dissolved in water)

Drain Cleaner

References

Physical Laws and Useful Equations

Law of Conservation of Mass

Mass cannot be created or destroyed during ordinary chemical or physical changes.

The total mass in a closed system is always the same no matter how many physical changes or chemical reactions occur.

Law of Conservation of Energy

Energy can be neither created nor destroyed.

The total amount of energy in a closed system is always the same. Energy can be changed from one form to another, but all of the different forms of energy in a system always add up to the same total amount of energy, no matter how many energy conversions occur.

Law of Universal Gravitation

All objects in the universe attract each other by a force called gravity. The size of the force depends on the masses of the objects and the distance between the objects.

The first part of the law explains why lifting a bowling ball is much harder than lifting a marble. Because the bowling ball has a much larger mass than the marble does, the amount of gravity between Earth and the bowling ball is greater than the amount of gravity between Earth and the marble.

The second part of the law explains why a satellite can remain in orbit around Earth. The satellite is placed at a carefully calculated distance from Earth. This distance is great enough to keep Earth's gravity from pulling the satellite down, yet small enough to keep the satellite from escaping Earth's gravity and wandering off into space.

Newton's Laws of Motion

Newton's first law of motion states that an object at rest remains at rest, and an object in motion remains in motion at constant speed and in a straight line unless acted on by an unbalanced force.

The first part of the law explains why a football will remain on a tee until it is kicked off or until a gust of wind blows it off. The second part of the law explains why a bike rider will continue moving forward after the bike comes to an abrupt stop. Gravity and the friction of the sidewalk will eventually stop the rider.

Newton's second law of motion states that the acceleration of an object depends on the mass of the object and the amount of force applied.

The first part of the law explains why the acceleration of a 4 kg bowling ball will be greater than the acceleration of a 6 kg bowling ball if the same force is applied to both balls. The second part of the law explains why the acceleration of a bowling ball will be greater if a larger force is applied to the bowling ball. The relationship of acceleration (a) to mass (m) and force (F) can be expressed mathematically by the following equation:

$$acceleration = \frac{force}{mass}, \text{ or } a = \frac{F}{m}$$

This equation is often rearranged to read $force = mass \times acceleration$, or $F = m \times a$

Newton's third law of motion states that whenever one object exerts a force on a second object, the second object exerts an equal and opposite force on the first.

This law explains that a runner is able to move forward because the ground exerts an equal and opposite force on the runner's foot after each step.

Average speed

$$\text{average speed} = \frac{\text{total distance}}{\text{total time}}$$

Example:
A bicycle messenger traveled a distance of 136 km in 8 h. What was the messenger's average speed?

$$\frac{136\ km}{8\ h} = 17\ km/h$$

The messenger's average speed was **17 km/h**.

Average acceleration

$$\text{average acceleration} = \frac{\text{final velocity} - \text{starting velocity}}{\text{time it takes to change velocity}}$$

Example:
Calculate the average acceleration of an Olympic 100 m dash sprinter who reached a velocity of 20 m/s south at the finish line. The race was in a straight line and lasted 10 s.

$$\frac{20\ m/s - 0\ m/s}{10\ s} = 2\ m/s/s$$

The sprinter's average acceleration was **2 m/s/s south**.

Pressure

Pressure is the force exerted over a given area. The SI unit for pressure is the pascal. Its symbol is Pa.

$$\text{pressure} = \frac{\text{force}}{\text{area}}$$

Net force
Forces in the Same Direction

When forces are in the same direction, add the forces together to determine the net force.

Example:
Calculate the net force on a stalled car that is being pushed by two people. One person is pushing with a force of 13 N northwest, and the other person is pushing with a force of 8 N in the same direction.

$$13\ N + 8\ N = 21\ N$$

The net force is **21 N northwest**.

Forces in Opposite Directions

When forces are in opposite directions, subtract the smaller force from the larger force to determine the net force. The net force will be in the direction of the larger force.

Example:
Calculate the net force on a rope that is being pulled on each end. One person is pulling on one end of the rope with a force of 12 N south. Another person is pulling on the opposite end of the rope with a force of 7 N north.

$$12\ N - 7\ N = 5\ N$$

The net force is **5 N south**.

Example:
Calculate the pressure of the air in a soccer ball if the air exerts a force of 10 N over an area of $0.5\ m^2$.

$$\text{pressure} = \frac{10N}{0.5\ m^2} = \frac{20N}{m^2} = 20\ Pa$$

The pressure of the air inside the soccer ball is **20 Pa**.

Reading and Study Skills

A How-To Manual for Active Reading

This book belongs to you, and you are invited to write in it. In fact, the book won't be complete until you do. Sometimes you'll answer a question or follow directions to mark up the text. Other times you'll write down your own thoughts. And when you're done reading and writing in the book, the book will be ready to help you review what you learned and prepare for tests.

Active Reading Annotations

Before you read, you'll often come upon an Active Reading prompt that asks you to underline certain words or number the steps in a process. Here's an example.

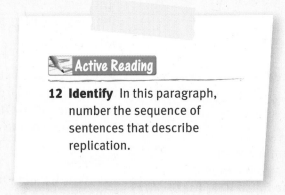

> **Active Reading**
>
> **12 Identify** In this paragraph, number the sequence of sentences that describe replication.

Marking the text this way is called **annotating**, and your marks are called **annotations**. Annotating the text can help you identify important concepts while you read.

There are other ways that you can annotate the text. You can draw an asterisk (*) by vocabulary terms, mark unfamiliar or confusing terms and information with a question mark (?), and mark main ideas with a double underline. And you can even invent your own marks to annotate the text!

Other Annotating Opportunities

Keep your pencil, pen, or highlighter nearby as you read, so you can make a note or highlight an important point at any time. Here are a few ideas to get you started.

- Notice the headings in red and blue. The blue headings are questions that point to the main idea of what you're reading. The red headings are answers to the questions in the blue ones. Together these headings outline the content of the lesson. After reading a lesson, you could write your own answers to the questions.

- Notice the bold-faced words that are highlighted in yellow. They are highlighted so that you can easily find them again on the page where they are defined. As you read or as you review, challenge yourself to write your own sentence using the bold-faced term.

- Make a note in the margin at any time. You might
  - Ask a "What if" question
  - Comment on what you read
  - Make a connection to something you read elsewhere
  - Make a logical conclusion from the text

Use your own language and abbreviations. Invent a code, such as using circles and boxes around words to remind you of their importance or relation to each other. Your annotations will help you remember your questions for class discussions, and when you go back to the lesson later, you may be able to fill in what you didn't understand the first time you read it. Like a scientist in the field or in a lab, you will be recording your questions and observations for analysis later.

Active Reading Questions

After you read, you'll often come upon Active Reading questions that ask you to think about what you've just read. You'll write your answer underneath the question. Here's an example.

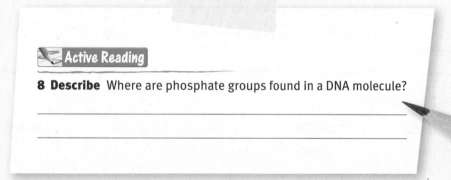

Active Reading

8 Describe Where are phosphate groups found in a DNA molecule?

_____

_____

This type of question helps you sum up what you've just read and pull out the most important ideas from the passage. In this case the question asks you to **describe** the structure of a DNA molecule that you have just read about. Other times you may be asked to do such things as **apply** a concept, **compare** two concepts, **summarize** a process, or **identify a cause-and-effect** relationship. You'll be strengthening those critical thinking skills that you'll use often in learning about science.

Reading and Study Skills

Using Graphic Organizers to Take Notes

Graphic organizers help you remember information as you read it for the first time and as you study it later. There are dozens of graphic organizers to choose from, so the first trick is to choose the one that's best suited to your purpose. Following are some graphic organizers to use for different purposes.

To remember lots of information	To relate a central idea to subordinate details	To describe a process	To make a comparison
• Arrange data in a Content Frame • Use Combination Notes to describe a concept in words and pictures	• Show relationships with a Mind Map or a Main Idea Web • Sum up relationships among many things with a Concept Map	• Use a Process Diagram to explain a procedure • Show a chain of events and results in a Cause-and-Effect Chart	• Compare two or more closely related things in a Venn Diagram

Content Frame

1 Make a four-column chart.

2 Fill the first column with categories (e.g., snail, ant, earthworm) and the first row with descriptive information (e.g., group, characteristic, appearance).

3 Fill the chart with details that belong in each row and column.

4 When you finish, you'll have a study aid that helps you compare one category to another.

Invertebrates

NAME	GROUP	CHARACTERISTICS	DRAWING
snail	mollusks	mangle	
ant	arthropods	six legs, exoskeleton	
earthworm	segmented worms	segmented body, circulatory and digestive systems	
heartworm	roundworms	digestive system	
sea star	echinoderms	spiny skin, tube feet	
jellyfish	cnidarians	stinging cells	

Combination Notes

1 Make a two-column chart.

2 Write descriptive words and definitions in the first column.

3 Draw a simple sketch that helps you remember the meaning of the term in the second column.

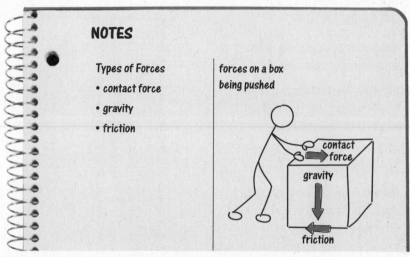

NOTES

Types of Forces
- contact force
- gravity
- friction

forces on a box being pushed

Mind Map

1 Draw an oval, and inside it write a topic to analyze.

2 Draw two or more arms extending from the oval. Each arm represents a main idea about the topic.

3 Draw lines from the arms on which to write details about each of the main ideas.

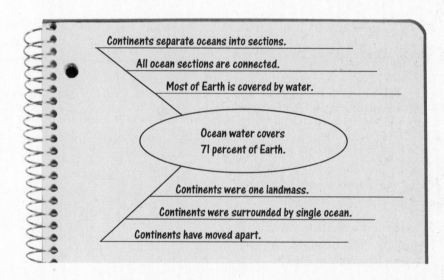

Continents separate oceans into sections.

All ocean sections are connected.

Most of Earth is covered by water.

Ocean water covers 71 percent of Earth.

Continents were one landmass.

Continents were surrounded by single ocean.

Continents have moved apart.

Main Idea Web

1 Make a box and write a concept you want to remember inside it.

2 Draw boxes around the central box, and label each one with a category of information about the concept (e.g., definition, formula, descriptive details).

3 Fill in the boxes with relevant details as you read.

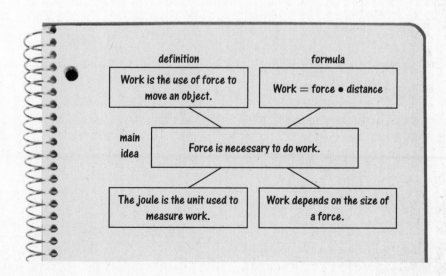

definition

Work is the use of force to move an object.

formula

Work = force • distance

main idea

Force is necessary to do work.

The joule is the unit used to measure work.

Work depends on the size of a force.

Reading and Study Skills

Concept Map

1 Draw a large oval, and inside it write a major concept.

2 Draw an arrow from the concept to a smaller oval, in which you write a related concept.

3 On the arrow, write a verb that connects the two concepts.

4 Continue in this way, adding ovals and arrows in a branching structure, until you have explained as much as you can about the main concept.

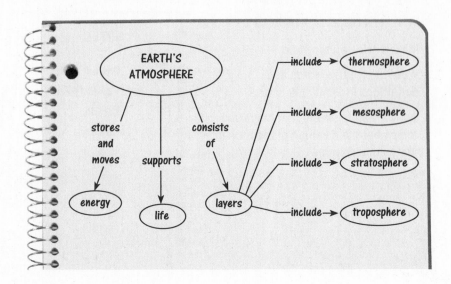

Venn Diagram

1 Draw two overlapping circles or ovals—one for each topic you are comparing—and label each one.

2 In the part of each circle that does not overlap with the other, list the characteristics that are unique to each topic.

3 In the space where the two circles overlap, list the characteristics that the two topics have in common.

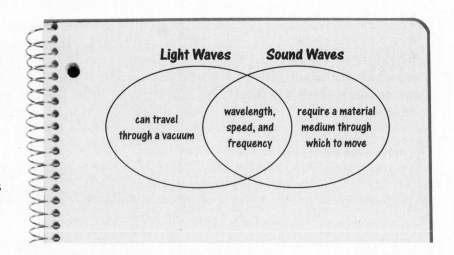

Cause-and-Effect Chart

1 Draw two boxes and connect them with an arrow.

2 In the first box, write the first event in a series (a cause).

3 In the second box, write a result of the cause (the effect).

4 Add more boxes when one event has many effects, or vice versa.

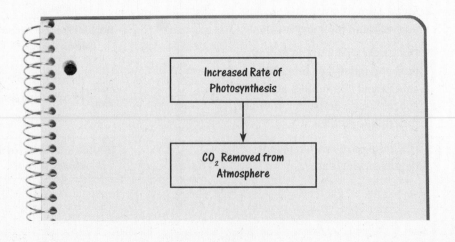

Process Diagram

A process can be a never-ending cycle. As you can see in this technology design process, engineers may backtrack and repeat steps, they may skip steps entirely, or they may repeat the entire process before a useable design is achieved.

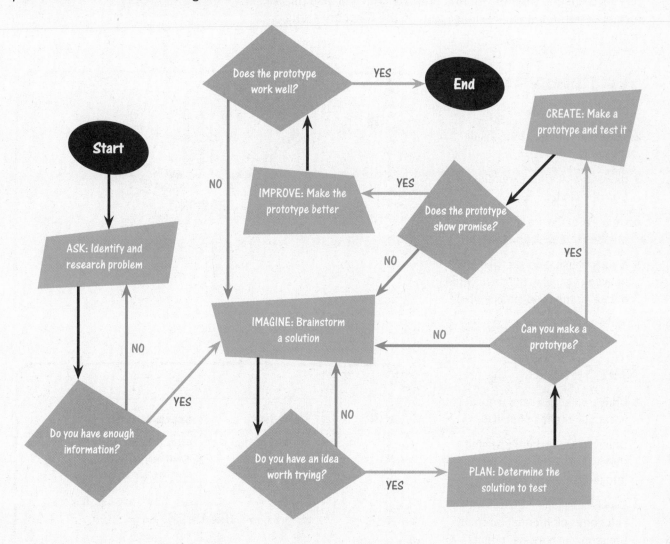

Reading and Study Skills

Using Vocabulary Strategies

Important science terms are highlighted where they are first defined in this book. One way to remember these terms is to take notes and make sketches when you come to them. Use the strategies on this page and the next for this purpose. You will also find a formal definition of each science term in the Glossary at the end of the book.

Description Wheel

1 Draw a small circle.

2 Write a vocabulary term inside the circle.

3 Draw several arms extending from the circle.

4 On the arms, write words and phrases that describe the term.

5 If you choose, add sketches that help you visualize the descriptive details or the concept as a whole.

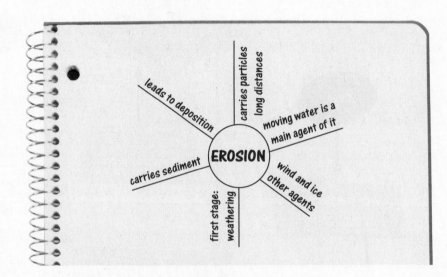

Four Square

1 Draw a small oval and write a vocabulary term inside it.

2 Draw a large rectangle around the oval, and divide the rectangle into four smaller squares.

3 Label the smaller squares with categories of information about the term, such as: definition, characteristics, examples, non-examples, appearance, and root words.

4 Fill the squares with descriptive words and drawings that will help you remember the overall meaning of the term and its essential details.

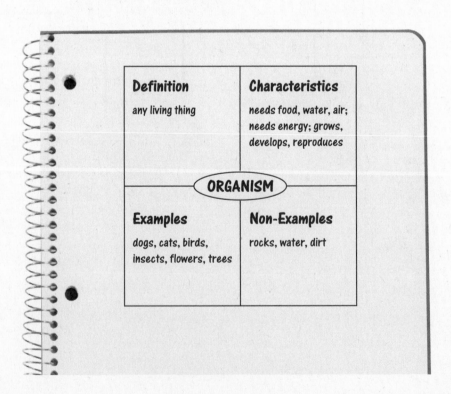

Frame Game

1 Draw a small rectangle, and write a vocabulary term inside it.

2 Draw a larger rectangle around the smaller one. Connect the corners of the larger rectangle to the corners of the smaller one, creating four spaces that frame the word.

3 In each of the four parts of the frame, draw or write details that help define the term. Consider including a definition, essential characteristics, an equation, examples, and a sentence using the term.

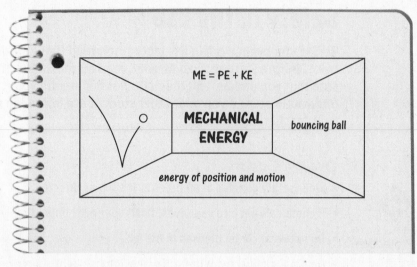

Magnet Word

1 Draw horseshoe magnet, and write a vocabulary term inside it.

2 Add lines that extend from the sides of the magnet.

3 Brainstorm words and phrases that come to mind when you think about the term.

4 On the lines, write the words and phrases that describe something essential about the term.

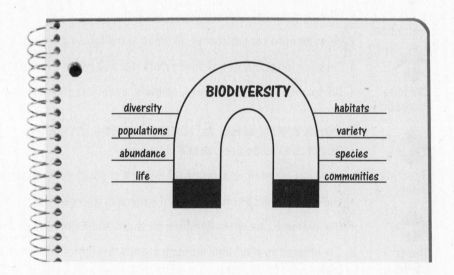

Word Triangle

1 Draw a triangle, and add lines to divide it into three parts.

2 Write a term and its definition in the bottom section of the triangle.

3 In the middle section, write a sentence in which the term is used correctly.

4 In the top section, draw a small picture to illustrate the term.

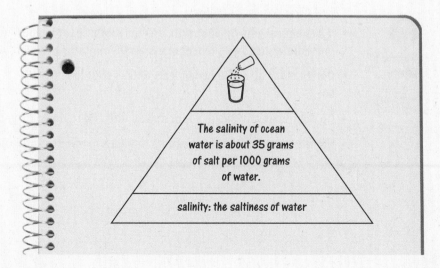

Science Skills

Safety in the Lab

Before you begin work in the laboratory, read these safety rules twice. Before starting a lab activity, read all directions and make sure that you understand them. Do not begin until your teacher has told you to start. If you or another student are injured in any way, tell your teacher immediately.

Dress Code

Eye Protection

Hand Protection

Clothing Protection

- Wear safety goggles at all times in the lab as directed.
- If chemicals get into your eyes, flush your eyes immediately.
- Do not wear contact lenses in the lab.
- Do not look directly at the sun or any intense light source or laser.
- Do not cut an object while holding the object in your hand.
- Wear appropriate protective gloves as directed.
- Wear an apron or lab coat at all times in the lab as directed.
- Tie back long hair, secure loose clothing, and remove loose jewelry.
- Do not wear open-toed shoes, sandals, or canvas shoes in the lab.

Glassware and Sharp Object Safety

Glassware Safety

Sharp Objects Safety

- Do not use chipped or cracked glassware.
- Use heat-resistant glassware for heating or storing hot materials.
- Notify your teacher immediately if a piece of glass breaks.
- Use extreme care when handling all sharp and pointed instruments.
- Cut objects on a suitable surface, always in a direction away from your body.

Chemical Safety

Chemical Safety

- If a chemical gets on your skin, on your clothing, or in your eyes, rinse it immediately (shower, faucet or eyewash fountain) and alert your teacher.
- Do not clean up spilled chemicals unless your teacher directs you to do so.
- Do not inhale any gas or vapor unless directed to do so by your teacher.
- Handle materials that emit vapors or gases in a well-ventilated area.

Electrical Safety

Electrical Safety

- Do not use equipment with frayed electrical cords or loose plugs.
- Do not use electrical equipment near water or when clothing or hands are wet.
- Hold the plug housing when you plug in or unplug equipment.

Heating and Fire Safety

Heating Safety

- Be aware of any source of flames, sparks, or heat (such as flames, heating coils, or hot plates) before working with any flammable substances.
- Know the location of lab fire extinguishers and fire-safety blankets.
- Know your school's fire-evacuation routes.
- If your clothing catches on fire, walk to the lab shower to put out the fire.
- Never leave a hot plate unattended while it is turned on or while it is cooling.
- Use tongs or appropriate insulated holders when handling heated objects.
- Allow all equipment to cool before storing it.

Wafting

Plant and Animal Safety

Plant Safety

Animal Safety

- Do not eat any part of a plant.
- Do not pick any wild plants unless your teacher instructs you to do so.
- Handle animals only as your teacher directs.
- Treat animals carefully and respectfully.
- Wash your hands thoroughly after handling any plant or animal.

Cleanup

Proper Waste Disposal

Hygienic Care

- Clean all work surfaces and protective equipment as directed by your teacher.
- Dispose of hazardous materials or sharp objects only as directed by your teacher.
- Keep your hands away from your face while you are working on any activity.
- Wash your hands thoroughly before you leave the lab or after any activity.

Science Skills

Designing, Conducting, and Reporting an Experiment

An experiment is an organized procedure to study something under specific conditions. Use the following steps of the scientific method when designing or conducting a controlled experiment.

1 Identify a Research Problem

Every day, you make observations by using your senses to gather information. Careful observations lead to good questions, and good questions can lead you to an experiment. Imagine, for example, that you pass a pond every day on your way to school, and you notice green scum beginning to form on top of it. You wonder what it is and why it seems to be growing. You list your questions, and then you do a little research to find out what is already known. A good place to start a research project is at the library. A library catalog lists all of the resources available to you at that library and often those found elsewhere. Begin your search by using:

- keywords or main topics.
- similar words, or synonyms, of your keyword.

The types of resources that will be helpful to you will depend on the kind of information you are interested in. And, some resources are more reliable for a given topic than others. Some different kinds of useful resources are:

- magazines and journals (or periodicals)—articles on a topic.
- encyclopedias—a good overview of a topic.
- books on specific subjects—details about a topic.
- newspapers—useful for current events.

The Internet can also be a great place to find information. Some of your library's reference materials may even be online. When using the Internet, however, it is especially important to make sure you are using appropriate and reliable sources. Websites of universities and government agencies are usually more accurate and reliable than websites created by individuals or businesses. Decide which sources are relevant and reliable for your topic. If in doubt, check with your teacher.

Take notes as you read through the information in these resources. You will probably come up with many questions and ideas for which you can do more research as needed. Once you feel you have enough information, think about the questions you have on the topic. Then, write down the problem that you want to investigate. Your notes might look like these.

© Houghton Mifflin Harcourt Publishing Company

Research Questions	Research Problem	Library and Internet Resources
• How do algae grow? • How do people measure algae? • What kind of fertilizer would affect the growth of algae? • Can fertilizer and algae be used safely in a lab? How?	How does fertilizer affect the algae in a pond?	Pond fertilization: initiating an algal bloom – from University of California Davis website. Blue-Green algae in Wisconsin waters-from the Department of Natural Resources of Wisconsin website.

As you gather information from reliable sources, record details about each source, including author name(s), title, date of publication, and/or web address. Make sure to also note the specific information that you use from each source. Staying organized in this way will be important when you write your report and create a bibliography or works cited list. Recording this information and staying organized will help you credit the appropriate author(s) for the information that you have gathered.

Representing someone else's ideas or work as your own, (without giving the original author credit), is known as plagiarism. Plagiarism can be intentional or unintentional. The best way to make sure that you do not commit plagiarism is to always do your own work and to always give credit to others when you use their words or ideas.

Current scientific research is built on scientific research and discoveries that have happened in the past. This means that scientists are constantly learning from each other and combining ideas to learn more about the natural world through investigation. But, a good scientist always credits the ideas and research that they have gathered from other people to those people. There are more details about crediting sources and creating a bibliography under step 9.

2 Make a Prediction

A prediction is a statement of what you expect will happen in your experiment. Before making a prediction, you need to decide in a general way what you will do in your procedure. You may state your prediction in an if-then format.

Prediction
If the amount of fertilizer in the pond water is increased, then the amount of algae will also increase.

Science Skills

3 Form a Hypothesis

Many experiments are designed to test a hypothesis. A hypothesis is a tentative explanation for an expected result. You have predicted that additional fertilizer will cause additional algae growth in pond water; your hypothesis should state the connection between fertilizer and algal growth.

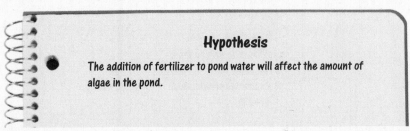

Hypothesis
The addition of fertilizer to pond water will affect the amount of algae in the pond.

4 Identify Variables to Test the Hypothesis

The next step is to design an experiment to test the hypothesis. The experimental results may or may not support the hypothesis. Either way, the information that results from the experiment may be useful for future investigations.

Experimental Group and Control Group

An experiment to determine how two factors are related has a control group and an experimental group. The two groups are the same, except that the investigator changes a single factor in the experimental group and does not change it in the control group.

Experimental Group: two containers of pond water with one drop of fertilizer solution added to each

Control Group: two containers of the same pond water sampled at the same time but with no fertilizer solution added

Variables and Constants

In a controlled experiment, a variable is any factor that can change. Constants are all of the variables that are kept the same in both the experimental group and the control group.

The independent variable is the factor that is manipulated or changed in order to test the effect of the change on another variable. The dependent variable is the factor the investigator measures to gather data about the effect.

Independent Variable	Dependent Variable	Constants
Amount of fertilizer in pond water	Growth of algae in the pond water	• Where and when the pond water is obtained • The type of container used • Light and temperature conditions where the water is stored

5 Write a Procedure

Write each step of your procedure. Start each step with a verb, or action word, and keep the steps short. Your procedure should be clear enough for someone else to use as instructions for repeating your experiment.

Procedure

1. Use the masking tape and the marker to label the containers with your initials, the date, and the identifiers "Jar 1 with Fertilizer," "Jar 2 with Fertilizer," "Jar 1 without Fertilizer," and "Jar 2 without Fertilizer."

2. Put on your gloves. Use the large container to obtain a sample of pond water.

3. Divide the water sample equally among the four smaller containers.

4. Use the eyedropper to add one drop of fertilizer solution to the two containers labeled, "Jar 1 with Fertilizer," and "Jar 2 with Fertilizer".

5. Cover the containers with clear plastic wrap. Use the scissors to punch ten holes in each of the covers.

6. Place all four containers on a window ledge. Make sure that they all receive the same amount of light.

7. Observe the containers every day for one week.

8. Use the ruler to measure the diameter of the largest clump of algae in each container, and record your measurements daily.

Science Skills

6 Experiment and Collect Data

Once you have all of your materials and your procedure has been approved, you can begin to experiment and collect data. Record both quantitative data (measurements) and qualitative data (observations), as shown below.

Algal Growth and Fertilizer

Date and Time	Experimental Group		Control Group		Observations
	Jar 1 with Fertilizer (diameter of algal clump in mm)	Jar 2 with Fertilizer (diameter of algal clump in mm)	Jar 1 without Fertilizer (diameter of algal clump in mm)	Jar 2 without Fertilizer (diameter of algal clump in mm)	
5/3 4:00 p.m.	0	0	0	0	condensation in all containers
5/4 4:00 p.m.	0	3	0	0	tiny green blobs in Jar 2 with fertilizer
5/5 4:15 p.m.	4	5	0	3	green blobs in Jars 1 and 2 with fertilizer and Jar 2 without fertilizer
5/6 4:00 p.m.	5	6	0	4	water light green in Jar 2 with fertilizer
5/7 4:00 p.m.	8	10	0	6	water light green in Jars 1 and 2 with fertilizer and Jar 2 without fertilizer
5/8 3:30 p.m.	10	18	0	6	cover off of Jar 2 with fertilizer
5/9 3:30 p.m.	14	23	0	8	drew sketches of each container

Drawings of Samples Viewed Under Microscope on 5/9 at 100x

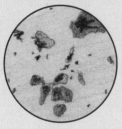
Jar 1 with Fertilizer

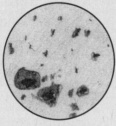
Jar 2 with Fertilizer

Jar 1 without Fertilizer

Jar 2 without Fertilizer

7 Analyze Data

After you complete your experiment, you must analyze all of the data you have gathered. Tables, statistics, and graphs are often used in this step to organize and analyze both the qualitative and quantitative data. Sometimes, your qualitative data are best used to help explain the relationships you see in your quantitative data.

Computer graphing software is useful for creating a graph from data that you have collected. Most graphing software can make line graphs, pie charts, or bar graphs from data that has been organized in a spreadsheet. Graphs are useful for understanding relationships in the data and for communicating the results of your experiment.

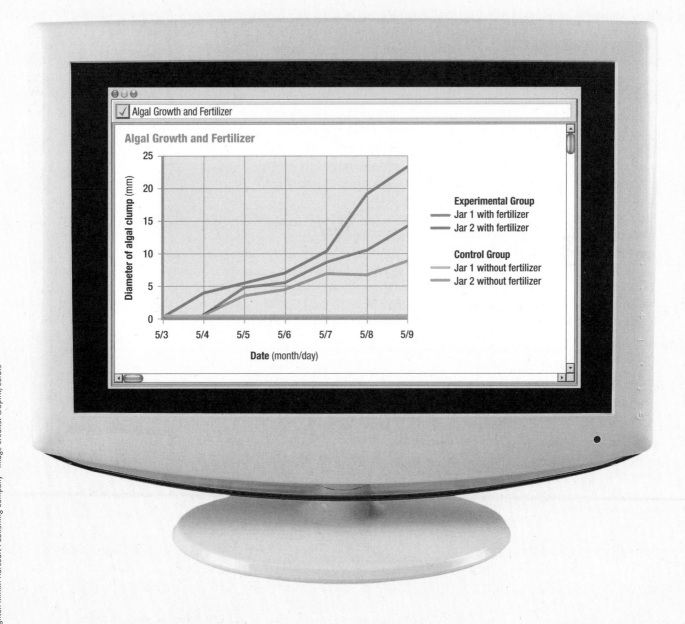

Science Skills

8 Make Conclusions

To draw conclusions from your experiment, first, write your results. Then, compare your results with your hypothesis. Do your results support your hypothesis? What have you learned?

Conclusion

More algae grew in the pond water to which fertilizer had been added than in the pond water to which fertilizer had not been added. My hypothesis was supported. I conclude that it is possible that the growth of algae in ponds can be influenced by the input of fertilizer.

9 Create a Bibliography or Works Cited List

To complete your report, you must also show all of the newspapers, magazines, journals, books, and online sources that you used at every stage of your investigation. Whenever you find useful information about your topic, you should write down the source of that information. Writing down as much information as you can about the subject can help you or someone else find the source again. You should at least record the author's name, the title, the date and where the source was published, and the pages in which the information was found. Then, organize your sources into a list, which you can title Bibliography or Works Cited.

Usually, at least three sources are included in these lists. Sources are listed alphabetically, by the authors' last names. The exact format of a bibliography can vary, depending on the style preferences of your teacher, school, or publisher. Also, books are cited differently than journals or websites. Below is an example of how different kinds of sources may be formatted in a bibliography.

BOOK: Hauschultz, Sara. *Freshwater Algae.* Brainard, Minnesota: Northwoods Publishing, 2011.

ENCYCLOPEDIA: Lasure, Sedona. "Algae is not all just pond scum." *Encyclopedia of Algae.* 2009.

JOURNAL: Johnson, Keagan. "Algae as we know it." *Sci Journal,* vol 64. (September 2010): 201-211.

WEBSITE: Dout, Bill. "Keeping algae scum out of birdbaths." *Help Keep Earth Clean.* News. January 26, 2011. <www. SaveEarth.org>.

Using a Microscope

Scientists use microscopes to see very small objects that cannot easily be seen with the eye alone. A microscope magnifies the image of an object so that small details may be observed. A microscope that you may use can magnify an object 400 times—the object will appear 400 times larger than its actual size.

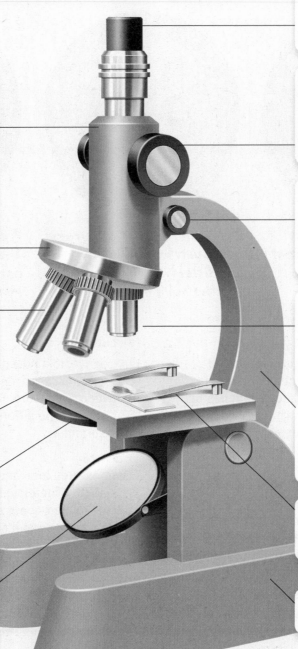

Eyepiece Objects are viewed through the eyepiece. The eyepiece contains a lens that commonly magnifies an image ten times.

Coarse Adjustment This knob is used to focus the image of an object when it is viewed through the low-power lens.

Fine Adjustment This knob is used to focus the image of an object when it is viewed through the high-power lens.

Low-Power Objective Lens This is the smallest lens on the nosepiece. It magnifies images about 10 times.

Arm The arm supports the body above the stage. Always carry a microscope by the arm and base.

Stage Clip The stage clip holds a slide in place on the stage.

Base The base supports the microscope.

Body The body separates the lens in the eyepiece from the objective lenses below.

Nosepiece The nosepiece holds the objective lenses above the stage and rotates so that all lenses may be used.

High-Power Objective Lens This is the largest lens on the nosepiece. It magnifies an image approximately 40 times.

Stage The stage supports the object being viewed.

Diaphragm The diaphragm is used to adjust the amount of light passing through the slide and into an objective lens.

Mirror or Light Source Some microscopes use light that is reflected through the stage by a mirror. Other microscopes have their own light sources.

Science Skills

Measuring Accurately

Precision and Accuracy

When you do a scientific investigation, it is important that your methods, observations, and data be both precise and accurate.

Low precision: The darts did not land in a consistent place on the dartboard.

Precision, but not accuracy: The darts landed in a consistent place, but did not hit the bull's eye.

Precision and accuracy: The darts landed consistently on the bull's eye.

Precision

In science, *precision* is the exactness and consistency of measurements. For example, measurements made with a ruler that has both centimeter and millimeter markings would be more precise than measurements made with a ruler that has only centimeter markings. Another indicator of precision is the care taken to make sure that methods and observations are as exact and consistent as possible. Every time a particular experiment is done, the same procedure should be used. Precision is necessary because experiments are repeated several times and if the procedure changes, the results might change.

Example

Suppose you are measuring temperatures over a two-week period. Your precision will be greater if you measure each temperature at the same place, at the same time of day, and with the same thermometer than if you change any of these factors from one day to the next.

Accuracy

In science, it is possible to be precise but not accurate. *Accuracy* depends on the difference between a measurement and an actual value. The smaller the difference, the more accurate the measurement.

Example

Suppose you look at a stream and estimate that it is about 1 meter wide at a particular place. You decide to check your estimate by measuring the stream with a meter stick, and you determine that the stream is 1.32 meters wide. However, because it is difficult to measure the width of a stream with a meter stick, it turns out that your measurement was not very accurate. The stream is actually 1.14 meters wide. Therefore, even though your estimate of about 1 meter was less precise than your measurement, your estimate was actually more accurate.

Graduated Cylinders

How to Measure the Volume of a Liquid with a Graduated Cylinder

- Be sure that the graduated cylinder is on a flat surface so that your measurement will be accurate.

- When reading the scale on a graduated cylinder, be sure to have your eyes at the level of the surface of the liquid.

- The surface of the liquid will be curved in the graduated cylinder. Read the volume of the liquid at the bottom of the curve, or meniscus (muh-NIHS-kuhs).

- You can use a graduated cylinder to find the volume of a solid object by measuring the increase in a liquid's level after you add the object to the cylinder.

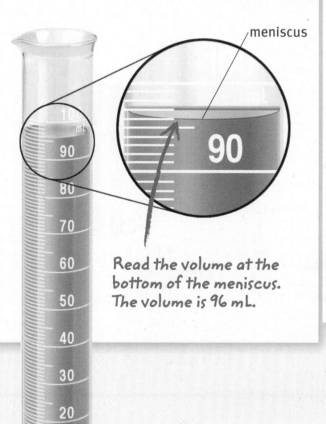

meniscus

Read the volume at the bottom of the meniscus. The volume is 96 mL.

Metric Rulers

How to Measure the Length of a Leaf with a Metric Ruler

1. Lay a ruler flat on top of the leaf so that the 1-centimeter mark lines up with one end. Make sure the ruler and the leaf do not move between the time you line them up and the time you take the measurement.

2. Look straight down on the ruler so that you can see exactly how the marks line up with the other end of the leaf.

3. Estimate the length by which the leaf extends beyond a marking. For example, the leaf below extends about halfway between the 4.2-centimeter and 4.3-centimeter marks, so the apparent measurement is about 4.25 centimeters.

4. Remember to subtract 1 centimeter from your apparent measurement, since you started at the 1-centimeter mark on the ruler and not at the end. The leaf is about 3.25 centimeters long (4.25 cm − 1 cm = 3.25 cm).

Science Skills

Triple Beam Balance

This balance has a pan and three beams with sliding masses, called riders. At one end of the beams is a pointer that indicates whether the mass on the pan is equal to the masses shown on the beams.

How to Measure the Mass of an Object

1 Make sure the balance is zeroed before measuring the mass of an object. The balance is zeroed if the pointer is at zero when nothing is on the pan and the riders are at their zero points. Use the adjustment knob at the base of the balance to zero it.

2 Place the object to be measured on the pan.

3 Move the riders one notch at a time away from the pan. Begin with the largest rider. If moving the largest rider one notch brings the pointer below zero, begin measuring the mass of the object with the next smaller rider.

4 Change the positions of the riders until they balance the mass on the pan and the pointer is at zero. Then add the readings from the three beams to determine the mass of the object.

300 g	position of largest rider
90 g	position of middle rider
+ 3 g	position of smallest rider
393 g	mass of beaker and water

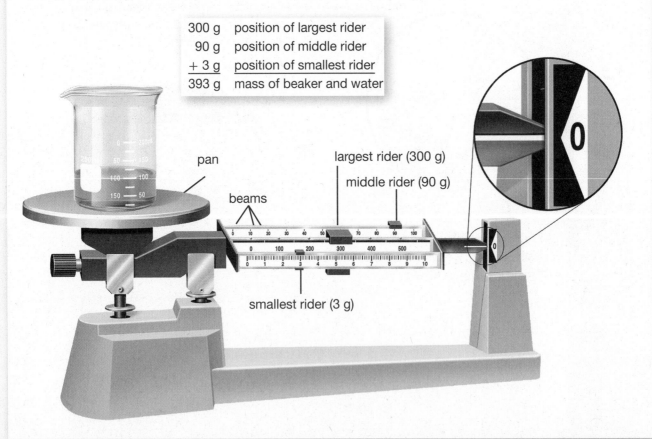

pan

beams

largest rider (300 g)

middle rider (90 g)

smallest rider (3 g)

Using the Metric System and SI Units

Scientists use International System (SI) units for measurements of distance, volume, mass, and temperature. The International System is based on powers of ten and the metric system of measurement.

Basic SI Units		
Quantity	**Name**	**Symbol**
length	meter	m
volume	liter	L
mass	gram	g
temperature	kelvin	K

SI Prefixes		
Prefix	**Symbol**	**Power of 10**
kilo-	k	1000
hecto-	h	100
deca-	da	10
deci-	d	0.1 or $\frac{1}{10}$
centi-	c	0.01 or $\frac{1}{100}$
milli-	m	0.001 or $\frac{1}{1000}$

Changing Metric Units

You can change from one unit to another in the metric system by multiplying or dividing by a power of 10.

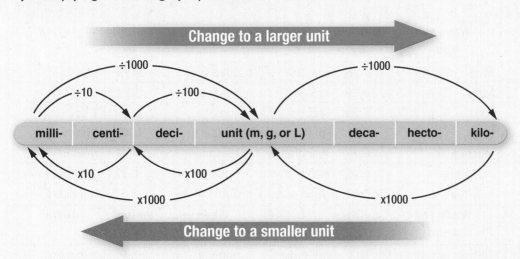

Change to a larger unit

÷1000   ÷10   ÷100   ÷1000

milli-   centi-   deci-   unit (m, g, or L)   deca-   hecto-   kilo-

x10   x100   x1000   x1000

Change to a smaller unit

Example

Change 0.64 liters to milliliters.
  1 Decide whether to multiply or divide.
  2 Select the power of 10.

Change to a smaller unit by multiplying

mL ◄——— x 1000 ——— L

0.64 x 1000 = 640.

ANSWER 0.64 L = 640 mL

Example

Change 23.6 grams to kilograms.
  1 Decide whether to multiply or divide.
  2 Select the power of 10.

Change to a larger unit by dividing

g ——— ÷ 1000 ——► kg

26.3 ÷ 1000 = 0.0263

ANSWER 23.6 g = 0.0236 kg

Science Skills

Converting Between SI and U.S. Customary Units

Use the chart below when you need to convert between SI units and U.S. customary units.

SI Unit	From SI to U.S. Customary			From U.S. Customary to SI		
Length	**When you know**	**multiply by**	**to find**	**When you know**	**multiply by**	**to find**
kilometer (km) = 1000 m	kilometers	0.62	miles	miles	1.61	kilometers
meter (m) = 100 cm	meters	3.28	feet	feet	0.3048	meters
centimeter (cm) = 10 mm	centimeters	0.39	inches	inches	2.54	centimeters
millimeter (mm) = 0.1 cm	millimeters	0.04	inches	inches	25.4	millimeters
Area	**When you know**	**multiply by**	**to find**	**When you know**	**multiply by**	**to find**
square kilometer (km²)	square kilometers	0.39	square miles	square miles	2.59	square kilometers
square meter (m²)	square meters	1.2	square yards	square yards	0.84	square meters
square centimeter (cm²)	square centimeters	0.155	square inches	square inches	6.45	square centimeters
Volume	**When you know**	**multiply by**	**to find**	**When you know**	**multiply by**	**to find**
liter (L) = 1000 mL	liters	1.06	quarts	quarts	0.95	liters
	liters	0.26	gallons	gallons	3.79	liters
	liters	4.23	cups	cups	0.24	liters
	liters	2.12	pints	pints	0.47	liters
milliliter (mL) = 0.001 L	milliliters	0.20	teaspoons	teaspoons	4.93	milliliters
	milliliters	0.07	tablespoons	tablespoons	14.79	milliliters
	milliliters	0.03	fluid ounces	fluid ounces	29.57	milliliters
Mass	**When you know**	**multiply by**	**to find**	**When you know**	**multiply by**	**to find**
kilogram (kg) = 1000 g	kilograms	2.2	pounds	pounds	0.45	kilograms
gram (g) = 1000 mg	grams	0.035	ounces	ounces	28.35	grams

Temperature Conversions

Even though the kelvin is the SI base unit of temperature, the degree Celsius will be the unit you use most often in your science studies. The formulas below show the relationships between temperatures in degrees Fahrenheit (°F), degrees Celsius (°C), and kelvins (K).

$$°C = \frac{5}{9} \ (°F - 32) \qquad °F = \frac{9}{5} \ °C + 32 \qquad K = °C + 273$$

Examples of Temperature Conversions		
Condition	**Degrees Celsius**	**Degrees Fahrenheit**
Freezing point of water	0	32
Cool day	10	50
Mild day	20	68
Warm day	30	86
Normal body temperature	37	98.6
Very hot day	40	104
Boiling point of water	100	212

Math Refresher

Performing Calculations

Science requires an understanding of many math concepts. The following pages will help you review some important math skills.

Mean

The mean is the sum of all values in a data set divided by the total number of values in the data set. The mean is also called the *average*.

Example

Find the mean of the following set of numbers: 5, 4, 7, and 8.

Step 1   Find the sum.

$$5 + 4 + 7 + 8 = 24$$

Step 2   Divide the sum by the number of numbers in your set. Because there are four numbers in this example, divide the sum by 4.

$$24 \div 4 = 6$$

Answer   The average, or mean, is 6.

Median

The median of a data set is the middle value when the values are written in numerical order. If a data set has an even number of values, the median is the mean of the two middle values.

Example

To find the median of a set of measurements, arrange the values in order from least to greatest. The median is the middle value.

13 mm   14 mm   16 mm   21 mm   23 mm

Answer   The median is 16 mm.

Mode

The mode of a data set is the value that occurs most often.

Example

To find the mode of a set of measurements, arrange the values in order from least to greatest and determine the value that occurs most often.

13 mm, 14 mm, 14 mm, 16 mm,
21 mm, 23 mm, 25 mm

Answer   The mode is 14 mm.

A data set can have more than one mode or no mode. For example, the following data set has modes of 2 mm and 4 mm:

2 mm   2 mm   3 mm   4 mm   4 mm

The data set below has no mode, because no value occurs more often than any other.

2 mm   3 mm   4 mm   5 mm

Math Refresher

Ratios

A **ratio** is a comparison between numbers, and it is usually written as a fraction.

Example
Find the ratio of thermometers to students if you have 36 thermometers and 48 students in your class.

Step 1 Write the ratio.
$$\frac{36 \text{ thermometers}}{48 \text{ students}}$$

Step 2 Simplify the fraction to its simplest form.
$$\frac{36}{48} = \frac{36 \div 12}{48 \div 12} = \frac{3}{4}$$
The ratio of thermometers to students is 3 to 4 or 3:4.

Proportions

A **proportion** is an equation that states that two ratios are equal.

$$\frac{3}{1} = \frac{12}{4}$$

To solve a proportion, you can use cross-multiplication. If you know three of the quantities in a proportion, you can use cross-multiplication to find the fourth.

Example
Imagine that you are making a scale model of the solar system for your science project. The diameter of Jupiter is 11.2 times the diameter of the Earth. If you are using a plastic-foam ball that has a diameter of 2 cm to represent the Earth, what must the diameter of the ball representing Jupiter be?

$$\frac{11.2}{1} = \frac{x}{2 \text{ cm}}$$

Step 1 Cross-multiply.
$$\frac{11.2}{1} = \frac{x}{2}$$
$$11.2 \times 2 = x \times 1$$

Step 2 Multiply.
$$22.4 = x \times 1$$
$$x = 22.4 \text{ cm}$$

You will need to use a ball that has a diameter of 22.4 cm to represent Jupiter.

Rates

A **rate** is a ratio of two values expressed in different units. A unit rate is a rate with a denominator of 1 unit.

Example
A plant grew 6 centimeters in 2 days. The plant's rate of growth was $\frac{6 \text{ cm}}{2 \text{ days}}$.
To describe the plant's growth in centimeters per day, write a unit rate.

Divide numerator and denominator by 2:
$$\frac{6 \text{ cm}}{2 \text{ days}} = \frac{6 \text{ cm} \div 2}{2 \text{ days} \div 2}$$
Simplify:
$$= \frac{3 \text{ cm}}{1 \text{ day}}$$

Answer The plant's rate of growth is 3 centimeters per day.

Percent

A **percent** is a ratio of a given number to 100. For example, 85% = 85/100. You can use percent to find part of a whole.

Example
What is 85% of 40?

Step 1 Rewrite the percent as a decimal by moving the decimal point two places to the left.

$$0.85$$

Step 2 Multiply the decimal by the number that you are calculating the percentage of.

$$0.85 \times 40 = 34$$

85% of 40 is 34.

Decimals

To **add** or **subtract decimals,** line up the digits vertically so that the decimal points line up. Then, add or subtract the columns from right to left. Carry or borrow numbers as necessary.

Example
Add the following numbers: 3.1415 and 2.96.

Step 1 Line up the digits vertically so that the decimal points line up.

$$\begin{array}{r} 3.1415 \\ + 2.96 \\ \hline \end{array}$$

Step 2 Add the columns from right to left, and carry when necessary.

$$\begin{array}{r} 3.1415 \\ + 2.96 \\ \hline 6.1015 \end{array}$$

The sum is 6.1015.

Fractions

A **fraction** is a ratio of two nonzero whole numbers.

Example
Your class has 24 plants. Your teacher instructs you to put 5 plants in a shady spot. What fraction of the plants in your class will you put in a shady spot?

Step 1 In the denominator, write the total number of parts in the whole.

$$\frac{?}{24}$$

Step 2 In the numerator, write the number of parts of the whole that are being considered.

$$\frac{5}{24}$$

So, $\frac{5}{24}$ of the plants will be in the shade.

Math Refresher

Simplifying Fractions

It is usually best to express a fraction in its simplest form. Expressing a fraction in its simplest form is called **simplifying a fraction**.

Example

Simplify the fraction $\frac{30}{45}$ to its simplest form.

Step 1   Find the largest whole number that will divide evenly into both the numerator and denominator. This number is called the greatest common factor (GCF).

Factors of the numerator 30:
1, 2, 3, 5, 6, 10, 15, 30

Factors of the denominator 45:
1, 3, 5, 9, 15, 45

Step 2   Divide both the numerator and the denominator by the GCF, which in this case is 15.

$$\frac{30}{45} = \frac{30 \div 15}{45 \div 15} = \frac{2}{3}$$

Thus, $\frac{30}{45}$ written in its simplest form is $\frac{2}{3}$.

Adding and Subtracting Fractions

To **add** or **subtract fractions** that have the same denominator, simply add or subtract the numerators.

Examples

$\frac{3}{5} + \frac{1}{5} = ?$ and $\frac{3}{4} - \frac{1}{4} = ?$

Step 1   Add or subtract the numerators.
$$\frac{3}{5} + \frac{1}{5} = \frac{4}{} \text{ and } \frac{3}{4} - \frac{1}{4} = \frac{2}{}$$

Step 2   Write in the common denominator, which remains the same.
$$\frac{3}{5} + \frac{1}{5} = \frac{4}{5} \text{ and } \frac{3}{4} - \frac{1}{4} = \frac{2}{4}$$

Step 3   If necessary, write the fraction in its simplest form.
$$\frac{4}{5} \text{ cannot be simplified, and } \frac{2}{4} = \frac{1}{2}.$$

To **add** or **subtract** fractions that have **different denominators**, first find the least common denominator (LCD).

Examples

$\frac{1}{2} + \frac{1}{6} = ?$ and $\frac{3}{4} - \frac{2}{3} = ?$

Step 1   Write the equivalent fractions that have a common denominator.
$$\frac{3}{6} + \frac{1}{6} = ? \text{ and } \frac{9}{12} - \frac{8}{12} = ?$$

Step 2   Add or subtract the fractions.
$$\frac{3}{6} + \frac{1}{6} = \frac{4}{6} \text{ and } \frac{9}{12} - \frac{8}{12} = \frac{1}{12}$$

Step 3   If necessary, write the fraction in its simplest form.
$$\frac{4}{6} = \frac{2}{3}, \text{ and } \frac{1}{12} \text{ cannot be simplifed.}$$

Multiplying Fractions

To **multiply fractions**, multiply the numerators and the denominators together, and then simplify the fraction to its simplest form.

Example

$\frac{5}{9} \times \frac{7}{10} = ?$

Step 1   Multiply the numerators and denominators.
$$\frac{5}{9} \times \frac{7}{10} = \frac{5 \times 7}{9 \times 10} = \frac{35}{90}$$

Step 2   Simplify the fraction.
$$\frac{35}{90} = \frac{35 \div 5}{90 \div 5} = \frac{7}{18}$$

Dividing Fractions

To **divide fractions,** first rewrite the divisor (the number you divide by) upside down. This number is called the reciprocal of the divisor. Then multiply and simplify if necessary.

Example

$$\frac{5}{8} \div \frac{3}{2} = ?$$

Step 1 Rewrite the divisor as its reciprocal.

$$\frac{3}{2} \rightarrow \frac{2}{3}$$

Step 2 Multiply the fractions.

$$\frac{5}{8} \times \frac{2}{3} = \frac{5 \times 2}{8 \times 3} = \frac{10}{24}$$

Step 3 Simplify the fraction.

$$\frac{10}{24} = \frac{10 \div 2}{24 \div 2} = \frac{5}{12}$$

Using Significant Figures

The **significant figures** in a decimal are the digits that are warranted by the accuracy of a measuring device.

When you perform a calculation with measurements, the number of significant figures to include in the result depends in part on the number of significant figures in the measurements. When you multiply or divide measurements, your answer should have only as many significant figures as the measurement with the fewest significant figures.

Examples

Using a balance and a graduated cylinder filled with water, you determined that a marble has a mass of 8.0 grams and a volume of 3.5 cubic centimeters. To calculate the density of the marble, divide the mass by the volume.

Write the formula for density: $\text{Density} = \frac{mass}{volume}$

Substitute measurements: $= \frac{8.0 \ g}{3.5 \ cm^3}$

Use a calculator to divide: $\approx 2.285714286 \ g/cm^3$

Answer Because the mass and the volume have two significant figures each, give the density to two significant figures. The marble has a density of 2.3 grams per cubic centimeter.

Using Scientific Notation

Scientific notation is a shorthand way to write very large or very small numbers. For example, 73,500,000,000,000,000,000,000 kg is the mass of the moon. In scientific notation, it is 7.35×10^{22} kg. A value written as a number between 1 and 10, times a power of 10, is in scientific notation.

Examples

You can convert from standard form to scientific notation.

Standard Form	Scientific Notation
720,000	7.2×10^5
5 decimal places left	Exponent is 5.
0.000291	2.91×10^{-4}
4 decimal places right	Exponent is −4.

You can convert from scientific notation to standard form.

Scientific Notation	Standard Form
4.63×10^7	46,300,000
Exponent is 7.	7 decimal places right
1.08×10^{-6}	0.00000108
Exponent is −6.	6 decimal places left

Math Refresher

Making and Interpreting Graphs

Circle Graph

A circle graph, or pie chart, shows how each group of data relates to all of the data. Each part of the circle represents a category of the data. The entire circle represents all of the data. For example, a biologist studying a hardwood forest in Wisconsin found that there were five different types of trees. The data table at right summarizes the biologist's findings.

Wisconsin Hardwood Trees	
Type of tree	**Number found**
Oak	600
Maple	750
Beech	300
Birch	1,200
Hickory	150
Total	3,000

How to Make a Circle Graph

1 To make a circle graph of these data, first find the percentage of each type of tree. Divide the number of trees of each type by the total number of trees, and multiply by 100%.

$$\frac{600 \text{ oak}}{3{,}000 \text{ trees}} \times 100\% = 20\%$$

$$\frac{750 \text{ maple}}{3{,}000 \text{ trees}} \times 100\% = 25\%$$

$$\frac{300 \text{ beech}}{3{,}000 \text{ trees}} \times 100\% = 10\%$$

$$\frac{1{,}200 \text{ birch}}{3{,}000 \text{ trees}} \times 100\% = 40\%$$

$$\frac{150 \text{ hickory}}{3{,}000 \text{ trees}} \times 100\% = 5\%$$

2 Now, determine the size of the wedges that make up the graph. Multiply each percentage by 360°. Remember that a circle contains 360°.

$20\% \times 360° = 72°$ $25\% \times 360° = 90°$

$10\% \times 360° = 36°$ $40\% \times 360° = 144°$

$5\% \times 360° = 18°$

3 Check that the sum of the percentages is 100 and the sum of the degrees is 360.

$20\% + 25\% + 10\% + 40\% + 5\% = 100\%$

$72° + 90° + 36° + 144° + 18° = 360°$

4 Use a compass to draw a circle and mark the center of the circle.

5 Then, use a protractor to draw angles of 72°, 90°, 36°, 144°, and 18° in the circle.

6 Finally, label each part of the graph, and choose an appropriate title.

A Community of Wisconsin Hardwood Trees

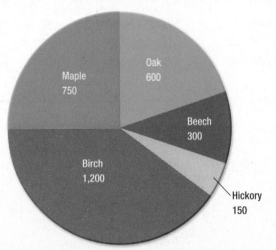

Line Graphs

Line graphs are most often used to demonstrate continuous change. For example, Mr. Smith's students analyzed the population records for their hometown, Appleton, between 1910 and 2010. Examine the data at right.

Because the year and the population change, they are the variables. The population is determined by, or dependent on, the year. Therefore, the population is called the **dependent variable,** and the year is called the **independent variable**. Each year and its population make a **data pair**. To prepare a line graph, you must first organize data pairs into a table like the one at right.

Population of Appleton, 1910–2010	
Year	**Population**
1910	1,800
1930	2,500
1950	3,200
1970	3,900
1990	4,600
2010	5,300

How to Make a Line Graph

1 Place the independent variable along the horizontal (*x*) axis. Place the dependent variable along the vertical (*y*) axis.

2 Label the *x*-axis "Year" and the *y*-axis "Population." Look at your greatest and least values for the population. For the *y*-axis, determine a scale that will provide enough space to show these values. You must use the same scale for the entire length of the axis. Next, find an appropriate scale for the *x*-axis.

3 Choose reasonable starting points for each axis.

4 Plot the data pairs as accurately as possible.

5 Choose a title that accurately represents the data.

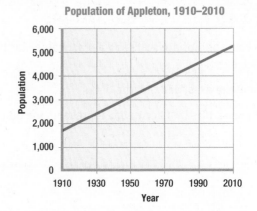

Population of Appleton, 1910–2010

How to Determine Slope

Slope is the ratio of the change in the *y*-value to the change in the x-value, or "rise over run."

1 Choose two points on the line graph. For example, the population of Appleton in 2010 was 5,300 people. Therefore, you can define point A as (2010, 5,300). In 1910, the population was 1,800 people. You can define point B as (1910, 1,800).

2 Find the change in the *y*-value.
(*y* at point A) − (*y* at point B) =
5,300 people − 1,800 people =
3,500 people

3 Find the change in the *x*-value.
(*x* at point A) − (*x* at point B) =
2010 − 1910 = 100 years

4 Calculate the slope of the graph by dividing the change in *y* by the change in *x*.

$$slope = \frac{change\ in\ y}{change\ in\ x}$$

$$slope = \frac{3,500\ people}{100\ years}$$

$$slope = 35\ people\ per\ year$$

In this example, the population in Appleton increased by a fixed amount each year. The graph of these data is a straight line. Therefore, the relationship is **linear**. When the graph of a set of data is not a straight line, the relationship is **nonlinear**.

Math Refresher

Bar Graphs

Bar graphs can be used to demonstrate change that is not continuous. These graphs can be used to indicate trends when the data cover a long period of time. A meteorologist gathered the precipitation data shown here for Summerville for April 1–15 and used a bar graph to represent the data.

Precipitation in Summerville, April 1–15			
Date	Precipitation (cm)	Date	Precipitation (cm)
April 1	0.5	April 9	0.25
April 2	1.25	April 10	0.0
April 3	0.0	April 11	1.0
April 4	0.0	April 12	0.0
April 5	0.0	April 13	0.25
April 6	0.0	April 14	0.0
April 7	0.0	April 15	6.50
April 8	1.75		

How to Make a Bar Graph

1 Use an appropriate scale and a reasonable starting point for each axis.

2 Label the axes, and plot the data.

3 Choose a title that accurately represents the data.

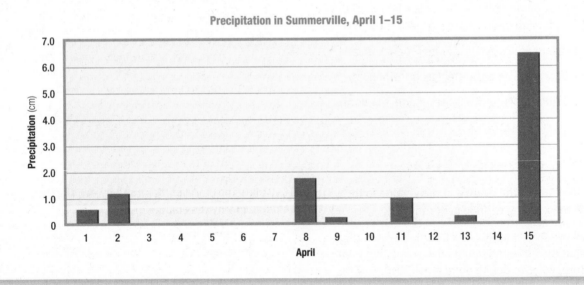

Precipitation in Summerville, April 1–15

Glossary

Pronunciation Key							
Sound	**Symbol**	**Example**	**Respelling**	**Sound**	**Symbol**	**Example**	**Respelling**
ă	a	pat	PAT	ŏ	ah	bottle	BAHT'l
ā	ay	pay	PAY	ō	oh	toe	TOH
âr	air	care	KAIR	ô	aw	caught	KAWT
ä	ah	father	FAH•ther	ôr	ohr	roar	ROHR
är	ar	argue	AR•gyoo	oi	oy	noisy	NOYZ•ee
ch	ch	chase	CHAYS	o͝o	u	book	BUK
ĕ	e	pet	PET	o͞o	oo	boot	BOOT
ĕ (at end of a syllable)	eh	settee lessee	seh•TEE leh•SEE	ou	ow	pound	POWND
ĕr	ehr	merry	MEHR•ee	s	s	center	SEN•ter
ē	ee	beach	BEECH	sh	sh	cache	CASH
g	g	gas	GAS	ŭ	uh	flood	FLUHD
ĭ	i	pit	PIT	ûr	er	bird	BERD
ĭ (at end of a syllable)	ih	guitar	gih•TAR	z	z	xylophone	ZY•luh•fohn
ī	y eye (only for a complete syllable)	pie island	PY EYE•luhnd	z	z	bags	BAGZ
				zh	zh	decision	dih•SIZH•uhn
îr	ir	hear	HIR	ə	uh	around broken focus	uh•ROWND BROH•kuhn FOH•kuhs
j	j	germ	JERM	ər	er	winner	WIN•er
k	k	kick	KIK	th	th	thin they	THIN THAY
ng	ng	thing	THING	w	w	one	WUHN
ngk	ngk	bank	BANGK	wh	hw	whether	HWETH•er

accuracy (AK·yer·uh·see) a description of how close a measurement is to the true value of the quantity measured (83)
exactitud término que describe qué tanto se aproxima una medida al valor verdadero de la cantidad medida

conceptual model (kuhn·SEP·choo·uhl MAHD·l) a verbal or graphical explanation for how a system works or is organized (100)
modelo conceptual una explicación verbal o gráfica acerca de cómo funciona o está organizado un sistema

control (kuhn·TROHL) in systems theory, a mechanism for regulating a system, process, or component of a system (146)
control según la teoría de sistemas, mecanismo que regula un sistema, proceso o componente de un sistema

data (DAY·tuh) information gathered by observation or experimentation that can be used in calculating or reasoning (19)
datos la información recopilada por medio de la observación o experimentación que puede usarse para hacer cálculos o razonar

dependent variable (dih·PEN·duhnt VAIR·ee·uh·buhl) in a scientific investigation, the factor that changes as a result of manipulation of one or more independent variables (19, 64)
variable dependiente en una investigación científica, el factor que cambia como resultado de la manipulación de una o más variables independientes

 (E)

empirical evidence (em·PIR·ih·kuhl EV·ih·duhns) the observations, measurements, and other types of data that people gather and test to support and evaluate scientific explanations (7, 36)
evidencia empírica las observaciones, mediciones y demás tipos de datos que se recopilan y examinan para apoyar y evaluar explicaciones científicas

engineering (en·juh·NIR·ing) the application of science and mathematics to real-life problems (118)
ingeniería la aplicación de las ciencias y las matemáticas para resolver problemas de la vida diaria

experiment (ek·SPEHR·uh·muhnt) an organized procedure to study something under controlled conditions (18)
experimento un procedimiento organizado que se lleva a cabo bajo condiciones controladas para estudiar algo

feedback (FEED·bak) the return of information about a system or process that may effect a change in the system or process; the information that is returned (147)
retroalimentación la información sobre un sistema o proceso que regresa y que puede producir un cambio en el sistema o proceso; la información que regresa

hypothesis (hy·PAHTH·ih·sis) a testable idea or explanation that leads to scientific investigation (18)
hipótesis una idea o explicación que conlleva a la investigación científica y que se puede probar

independent variable (in·dih·PEN·duhnt VAIR·ee·uh·buhl) in a scientific investigation, the factor that is deliberately manipulated (19, 64)
variable independiente en una investigación científica, el factor que se manipula deliberadamente

input (IN·put) information, material, or energy added to a system or process (144)
entrada información, material o energía que ingresa a un sistema o proceso

(L)

law (LAW) a descriptive statement or equation that reliably predicts events under certain conditions (34)
ley una ecuación o afirmación descriptiva que predice sucesos de manera confiable en determinadas condiciones

life cycle analysis (LYF SY·kuhl uh·NAL·ih·sis) the evaluation of the materials and energy used for the manufacture, transportation, sale, use, and disposal of a technology (135)
análisis del ciclo de vida la evaluación de los materiales y la energía usados para la fabricación, transporte, venta, uso y eliminación de una tecnología

materials science (muh·TIR·ee·uhlz SY·uhns) the study of the characteristics and uses of materials in science and technology (156)

ciencias de los materiales el estudio de las características y los usos de los materiales en las ciencias y la tecnología

mathematical model (math·uh·MAT·ih·kuhl MAHD·l) one or more equations that represent the way a system or process works (98)

modelo matemático una o más ecuaciones que representan la forma en que funciona un sistema o proceso

measurement (MEZH·uhr·muhnt) a determination of the dimensions of something using a standard unit (78)

medida una determinación de las dimensiones de algo por medio del uso de una unidad estándar

model (MAHD·l) a pattern, plan, representation, or description designed to show the structure or workings of an object, system, or concept (70, 94)

modelo un diseño, plan, representación o descripción cuyo objetivo es mostrar la estructura o funcionamiento de un objeto, sistema o concepto

observation (ahb·zer·VAY·shuhn) the process of obtaining information by using the senses (18)

observación el proceso de obtener información por medio de los sentidos

output (OWT·put) information, material, or energy resulting from a system or process (144)

salida información, material, o energía resultante de un sistema o proceso

P-Q

physical model (FIZ·ih·kuhl MAHD·l) a three-dimensional representation of an object that may be smaller or larger than the object it represents (96)

modelo físico una representación tridimensional de un objeto que puede ser más pequeña o más grande que el objeto que representa

precision (prih·SIZH·uhn) the exactness of a measurement (83)

precisión la exactitud de una medición

prototype (PROH·tuh·typ) a test model of a product (121)

prototipo prueba modelo de un producto

pseudoscience (SOO·doh·sy·uhns) a process of investigation that in one or more ways resembles science but deviates from the scientific methods (12)

pseudociencia un proceso de investigación que tiene semejanzas con la actividad científica, pero no cumple con los métodos científicos

Pugh chart (PYOO CHART) a table used to compare the features of multiple items, such as technological products or solutions (136)

tabla de Pugh una tabla que se usa para comparar las características de muchos elementos, como productos o soluciones tecnológicas

risk-benefit analysis (risk·BEN·uh·fit uh·NAL·ih·sis) the comparison of the risks and benefits of a decision or product (134)

análisis de riesgo-beneficio la comparación de los riesgos y los beneficios de una decisión o de un producto

science (SY·uhns) the knowledge obtained by observing natural events and conditions in order to discover facts and formulate laws or principles that can be verified or tested (6)

ciencia el conocimiento que se obtiene por medio de la observación natural de acontecimientos y condiciones con el fin de descubrir hechos y formular leyes o principios que puedan ser verificados o probados

scientific notation (sy·uhn·TIF·ik noh·TAY·shuhn) a method of expressing a quantity as a number multiplied by 10 to the appropriate power (82)

notación científica un método para expresar una cantidad en forma de un número multiplicado por 10 a la potencia adecuada

simulation (sim·yuh·LAY·shuhn) a method that is used to study and analyze the characteristics of an actual or theoretical system (94)

simulación un método que se usa para estudiar y analizar las características de un sistema teórico o real

system (SIS·tuhm) a set of particles or interacting components considered to be a distinct physical entity for the purpose of study (142)

sistema un conjunto de partículas o componentes que interactúan unos con otros, el cual se considera una entidad física independiente para fines de estudio

systems theory (SIS·tuhmz THEE·uh·ree) the study of systems, components of systems, and interactions of systems and system components (143)

teoría de sistemas el estudio de los sistemas, los componentes de los sistemas, y las interacciones entre los sistemas y los componentes de los sistemas

technology (tek·NAHL·uh·jee) the application of science for practical purposes; the use of tools, machines, materials, and processes to meet human needs (116)
tecnología la aplicación de la ciencia con fines prácticos; el uso de herramientas, máquinas, materiales y procesos para satisfacer las necesidades de los seres humanos

theory (THEE·uh·ree) a system of ideas that explains many related observations and is supported by a large body of evidence acquired through scientific investigation (35)
teoría un sistema de ideas que explica muchas observaciones relacionadas y que está respaldado por una gran cantidad de pruebas obtenidas mediante la investigación científica

trade-off (TRAYD·awf) the giving up of one thing in return for another, often applied to the engineering design process (119, 132)
compensación pérdida de una cosa a cambio de otra, con frecuencia aplicado al proceso de diseño en ingeniería

Index

Page numbers for definitions are printed in **boldface** type.
Page numbers for illustrations, maps, and charts are printed in *italics*.